FootprintFrance

Dordogne

chael Pauls
ana Facaros

Introducing the region

About the region

Périgord Blanc et Pourpre

Périgord Vert

Périgord Noir

Northern Lot

Lot Valley

Practicalities

Contents

About the authors

Michael & Dana

Michael Pauls and Dana Facaros met in a pre-Socratic philosophy class at university and have been travelling and writing ever since, while raising two kids who seem to have turned out all right despite having to learn lots of languages, attending school in Greece, Spain, Italy, France and Ireland. Currently re-installed in southwest France, Facaros and Pauls have written over 30 books while contributing to the *Observer*, *Sunday Times*, *Independent*, *Sunday Telegraph*, *Sunday Times Travel Magazine*, the *National Geographic Traveler*, *Wanderlust* and other publications. When not writing about travel, Michael plays the musical saw and writes about urban design and restoring the soul of American cities at recivilization.net; Dana makes and consumes Scotch bonnet hot sauce in industrial quantities, while trying hard not to become too bitter and twisted from constantly losing to her daughter at Scrabble.

Acknowledgements

The authors would first of all like to thank all the delightful people of the tourist offices across the Dordogne and Lot. We have been pestering them for years and find them unfailingly courteous and helpful. Thanks to Jackson Pauls, Bryony Coombs, Craig Pooley, Tom Jones and Laurence Porter for much help with many things; special thanks to Dani Chouet and Trish Hobbs for a Perfect Day on the Dordogne. And most assuredly, our heartfelt thanks to the legion of fine cooks in our region, in restaurants and bistros, *fermes auberges*, market stands and private domiciles, and especially Lily, without whom we would have starved in the last three months when we were too busy finishing this book to cook.

About the book

The guide is divided into four sections: Introducing the region; About the region; Around the region and Practicalities.

Introducing the region comprises: **At a glance**, which explains how the region fits together by giving the reader a snapshot of what to look out for and what makes the region distinct from other parts of the country; **Best of Dordogne & Lot** (top 20 highlights); **A year in Dordogne & Lot**, which is a month-by-month guide to pros and cons of visiting at certain times of year; and **Dordogne & Lot on screen & page**, which is a list of suggested books and films.

About the region comprises: **History**; **Art & architecture**; **Dordogne & Lot today**, which present different aspects of life in the region today; **Nature & environment** (an overview of the landscape and wildlife); **Festivals & events**; **Sleeping** (an overview of accommodation options); **Eating & drinking** (an overview of the region's cuisine, as well as advice on eating out); **Entertainment** (an overview of the region's cultural credentials, explaining what entertainment is on offer); **Shopping** (what are the region's specialities and recommendations for the best buys); and **Activities & tours**.

Around the region is then broken down into five areas, each with its own chapter. Here you'll find all the main sights and at the end of each chapter is a listings section with all the best sleeping, eating & drinking, entertainment, shopping and activities & tours options.

Sleeping price codes
€€€€ over €200 per night for a double room in high season
€€€ €100-200
€€ €60-100
€ under €60

Eating & drinking price codes
€€€€ over €40
€€€ €30-40
€€ €20-30
€ under €20

Map symbols

Symbol		Symbol	
	l'Information Information		Gare Train station
	Endroit d'intérêt Place of interest		Gare routière Bus station
	Musée/galerie Museum/gallery		Station de métro Metro station
	Théâtre Theatre		Ligne de tram Tram route
	Poste Post office		Marché Market
	Eglise/cathédrale Church/cathedral		Hôpital Hospital
	Mur de ville City wall		Pharmacie Pharmacy
	Parking		Lycée College

Picture credits

Michael Pauls pages 13, 15, 18, 19, 20, 26, 30, 47, 48, 53, 54, 63, 65, 67, 68, 69, 73, 77, 83, 87, 93, 94, 96, 99, 101, 104, 105, 109, 110, 112, 118, 120, 123, 125, 129, 134, 136, 138, 139, 140, 141, 142, 144, 155, 158, 159, 162, 163, 164, 178, 179, 185, 186, 187, 191, 192, 193, 229, 231, 232, 234, 237, 239, 240, 243, 245, 253, 256, 257, 259, 261, 262, 265, 266, 270, 271, 272, 276, 281, 282, 283.

Hemis pages 6, 49, 190: Hervé Hughes; page 10: Francis Cormon; pages 11, 15, 23, 31, 41, 71, 74, 78, 89, 90, 92, 115, 130, 132, 146, 160, 171, 173, 183: Patrick Escudero; pages 13, 80, 201, 202, 207, 211, 258: Christophe Boisvieux; page 14: Patrice Thomas; pages 16, 95, 149, 174, 177: Marc Dozier; pages 17, 254, 264, 273: Patrick Frilet; pages 22, 189: Bertrand Rieger; pages 25, 106: Philippe Roy; pages 29, 42, 45, 103, 107, 127, 128, 169: Romain Cintract; pages 32, 216: Philippe Body; pages 36, 180, 215, 268: Franck Guiziou; page 57: Camille Moirenc; pages 59, 60, 61, 194, 203, 217: Christian Guy; pages 64, 161, 199, 220, 222, 223, 255: Jean-Daniel Sudres; page 81: Sylvain Sonnet; pages 167, 181, 208, 209: Bertrand Gardel; pages 197, 213, 269: Alain Felix; page 224: Thierry Borredon; page 226: Mattieu Colin; page 235: Bruno Barbier; page 247: Jaques Sierpinski; page 251: Giovannie Bertolissio.

Shutterstock page 1: Gareth Kirdland; page 15: Duncan Gilbert; page 37: abxyz; pages 38, 196, 219, 249, 250, 274: Mark van Vuren; pages 51, 85, 114, 116, 143, 151: Elena Elisseeva; pages 82, 91: Jan van der Hoeven; page 124: rudiuk; pages 152, 153, 200: Lagui; page 166: Paul Prescott; page 227: David Hughes; page 228 : Martin Anderson.

iStock page 12: legalnursenetwork; page 48: Soundsnap; page 121: imagemonkey; page 145: Stephen Schwartz; page 148: kcline; page 157. Knud Nielsen; page 184: productionchick; page 233: digital_eye.

Tips pages 21, 117, 204, 242: Photononstop; page 58: Matt Alexander.

Alamy page 205: superclic.

Jean-Pierre Degas/Hemis Front cover.
Patrick Escudero/Hemis;
Romain Cintract/Hemis Back cover.
Paul Atkinson/Shutterstock Inside back cover.

Flock of geese, Périgord Noir.

Contents

Introducing the region

POITOU-CHARENTES
LIMOUSIN
AQUITAINE
MIDI-PYRÉNÉES
Charentes
Haute-Vienne
Corrèze
Dordogne
Gironde
Lot-et-Garonne
Lot
Cantal
Aveyron
Tarn-et-Garonne
Tarn
Cognac
Angoulême
Jonzac
Barbezieux
Nontron
St-Yrieix-la-Perche
Ussel
Tulle
Brive-la-Gaillarde
Périgueux
Bergerac
Sarlat
Mauriac
Aurillac
Blaye
Libourne
BORDEAUX
Langon
Marmande
Villeneuve-sur-Lot
Agen
Nérac
Gourdon
Cahors
Figeac
Villefranche-de-Rouergue
Decazeville
Moissac
Caussade
Brantôme
Bourdeilles
Coutras
Lascaux
Les Eyzies-de-Tayac
Rocamadour
Souillac
St-Emilion
Castillon-la Bataille
La Réole
Bazas
Fumel
Montpon-Ménestérol
Chancelade
Terrasson-Lavilledieu
LEGENDE
Route Européenne/ European Route
Autoroute/Motorway
Route Nationale/ National Road
Route Principale/ Major Road
Chemin de Fer/Railway
Limite Régionale/ Regional Boundary
Limite Départmentale/ Department Boundary

They don't have the natural grandeur of the Pyrenees or the Breton coast. There are no mountains to climb or rapids to run, and they are utterly bereft of sandy beaches and great museums of art. But over a million visitors find their way to Périgord and Quercy every year. The old folks sit out in front of their houses under the rose trellises, watching them go by in summer, and they wonder 'Why?'

Their modesty gives a clue to the answer, in this region of modest and still rather innocent charms. Right now, these two departments of France are what the whole world would like to be: a cultured, traditional, low-stress, low-pressure area that's green and lovely, with a touch of refinement and lots of good food and wine. Traffic is never a problem here. Slow tractors are, and occasionally chickens in the road.

Let's not be too modest. The area does have its share of wonderful sights: humankind's first art, on the walls of ancient caves; monuments of the early Middle Ages, untouched since the rebirth of western civilization; magnificent châteaux and gardens of noble Renaissance families with far more money and taste than was good for them.

The two departments offer these attractions with an extra helping of southwestern charm – ducks and geese and truffles and old-fashioned village inns and steep slate roofs and good strong wine. It gets intense every summer, when people from around the world descend. The days are full of art exhibitions and special tours of the châteaux. In the evenings there are village fêtes and communal picnics, dinners out on the terrace and music and fireworks. The locals and the visitors share it all with grace and laughter; you ought to come down and see.

At a glance

A whistle-stop tour of Dordogne & Lot

Château des Milandes, Périgord Noir.

The roots of our two regions run deep. Périgord (and Périgueux) take their names from the Celtic tribe that lived here, the Petrocorii. Quercy (and Cahors) get theirs from a neighbouring tribe, the Cadurcii. The French Revolution tried to sweep away the old regional identities, as it chopped the country into homogenous departments named after rivers, but in this area it proved convenient to keep most of the old boundaries. Most of Périgord became the department of the Dordogne, while Quercy was dubbed the Lot. (Both pairs of names remain in common use, which can be a little confusing, especially since part of the River Dordogne flows through the Lot department.)

Périgord is one of the biggest departments in France, and it comes in four colours: White, Purple, Green and Black.

Périgord Blanc et Pourpre

White Périgord, the area around Périgueux, is the centre of the department. Périgueux is the biggest and liveliest town in this book, and has a fascinating 2000-year history, a fine museum and just enough ruins and relics to give us a picture of what life in an important Roman provincial city was like.

For the visitor, Périgueux may seem like an oasis in the heart of Périgord Blanc, which is otherwise a hard-working farming region with plenty of corn and sunflowers and ducks, but not much else. For that, there is the area that shares this chapter – Purple Périgord, a land of sunny, vine-covered slopes around the Dordogne Valley that supplies most of the department's wine.

Bergerac is the centre of the wine trade, and the sailing barges that used to float barrels of wine down to the docks at Bordeaux now take tourists for excursion cruises on the river. Of the many small wine regions, Monbazillac is a jewel, its pampered and perfect vines draped over the hills beneath a fairytale castle. The southern reaches of Périgord Pourpre were a hotly contested frontier between English and French in the Middle Ages, and to bolster their strength both sides built and settled new towns called 'bastides': Eymet, Monpazier and many others. Efficient and modern in the 13th century, today they're lovely, quaint and full of tourists.

Périgord Vert

Rolling hills covered in chestnut and oak will be the memory you take away from this small region, with sumptuous Renaissance châteaux poking their turrets above the treetops. Green Périgord's past may be a tale of oppression and troubles, but the greedy barons who lorded it over this land for so long also gave it the gracious, aristocratic air that draws people today.

Brantôme is its centre, a delightful water-girt town in the shadow of the monumental creamy-white abbey where the younger sons of those barons enjoyed their well-endowed leisure. Drive out in any direction from here and you'll find châteaux nearly as good as those of the Loire: Bourdeilles, Mareuil, Jumilhac, Puyguilhem and best of all Hautefort, where a noble dynasty lived on a scale to rival the kings at Versailles.

Not all the attractions are down to the barons. Périgord Vert is also duck farms and trout streams, Romanesque village churches and any number of good places for country rambles and drives.

Périgord Noir

This is the Périgord that the outside world knows best: black for truffles and dark forests, the heartland of foie gras and all the other dainties granted us by the duck and the goose.

And it draws by far the biggest share of Périgord's flood of summer tourists. In August, in Sarlat and along the stretch of the Dordogne to its south, you'll be sleeping in the car and eating peanuts if you haven't made your bookings well in

The lowdown

Money matters
For two people touring and seeing the sights, count on spending *at least* €210-230 per day: €60 for a double room with breakfast in a modest Logis de France-type inn or chambre d'hôte, €40 for two three-course lunch menus (€60 and up if you choose to eat your big meal in the evening), €30 for a half-tank of petrol; €30 for admission to two sights and €50 for drinks and incidentals.

Opening hours
In rural, traditional parts of France, you can't always get things when you want them. First of all, remember that almost all shops and offices shut for lunch, between 1200 and 1400 or 1500. Get used to the tyranny of French mealtimes. Show up at the restaurant between 1200 and 1300, or 2000 and 2100, or you may well be disappointed.

Plan Sunday and Monday carefully. Monday is the most common closing day for sights, shops and restaurants. As for the sights, be careful in the late afternoon: some places won't let you in an hour or 30 minutes before the scheduled closing time. For a list of public holidays, see page 55.

Tourist information
There are over 150 tourist information offices in the towns and villages described in this book. The staff are almost always friendly, knowledgeable and efficient, usually bilingual or better, and surprisingly most offices stay open all year round, during normal business hours.

Beynac.

advance. Sarlat is a wonderfully handsome town, so well preserved that film directors use it to recreate the era of the Musketeers. On the river nearby, castles, fortified villages and châteaux crowd the banks – Beynac, Castelnaud, Les Milandes, Domme – sometimes nearly within bowshot of each other.

Périgord Noir has another river, and this one is just as popular. The Vézère Valley has a unique distinction: it is the home of humankind's earliest great art, painted or etched on the walls of Lascaux, Font-de-Gaume, Les Combarelles and the other caves, or carried off to the great museum of prehistory in Les Eyzies. For 40 km, the valley is lined not only with these, but with stalactite caves and fascinating rock fortresses that remained in use for thousands of years, some up until modern times.

Northern Lot

It's a compact region, but a choice one, with many pretty things packed into a small space. The upper Dordogne, or 'Dordogne Quercynois', has as much in common with Périgord as the rest of the Lot, such as the magnificent Renaissance palaces at Montal and Castelnau.

There are only two towns of any size: Souillac, with its Romanesque abbey church, and half-timbered St-Céré. In between there is one tiny, thoroughly charming village after another, each with a rushing stream, a church or a castle and a friendly stone-built inn to take care of your bed and board. There's a touch of great medieval art at Carennac and Martel, three first-rate caves to visit (Padirac, Presque and Lacave), and any number of exquisite corners where you can sit and dream. One of the best things to do here is just doing nothing at all.

There's plenty to do at Rocamadour, the Lot's unabashedly outrageous tourist trap. In an incredible cliff-side setting, the sincere spirituality of a 1000-year-old pilgrimage site often gets drowned out by the host of holiday attractions that has grown up around it, but seen in the right spirit it can be lot of fun.

Lot Valley

The last chapter follows the other big valley end to end: 100 km of lazy river – two or three times this if you could straighten out all the loops and kinks. Right in the middle stands Cahors, a stoutly medieval town with a surprising Italian touch in its old streets, a skyline of elegant towers, 28 secret gardens, a wonderful Saturday market and the most beautiful bridge in France, the Pont Valentré.

Head west, and you're in Quercy's big wine region, the land of dark, strong Vin de Cahors. The attractions here are small in scale: pleasant medieval villages such as Puy-l'Evêque, Luzech and Les Arques, frescoed country chapels and the cinematic Château de Bonaguil. The other side of Cahors leads you into a different world altogether: tranquil, beautiful and silent. The rosy cliffs that line the Lot and Célé Valleys provide some of the region's most dramatic scenery, and the roads on their banks aren't much wider than when they were towpaths for muleteers. Pech Merle, Quercy's own Palaeolithic cave, is here, along with the gorgeous, nearly vertical village of St-Cirq-Lapopie.

The further you go, the wilder and emptier the valleys get, though they finish with a surprise: an urbane little city graced with the towers and palaces of medieval bankers: Figeac.

Carving, Carennac.

Pont Valentré, Cahors.

Best of Dordogne & Lot

Top 20 things to see & do

❶ Roman Périgueux

Périgord was Roman for 500 years, but there is only one window into that distant past and it is right here in the *Civitas Petrocoriorum* of old Périgueux. Architect Jean Nouvel's excellent new museum stands right next to one of the very few Gallo-Roman temples to have survived. Page 88.

❷ Monbazillac

When you're ready to fall in love with wine, this may be the place to visit: a great château in the midst of the most beautiful and most pampered vineyards in Périgord. The chatêau belongs to the wine producers, who make sure you can learn everything you want to know about their very special brew. Page 104.

❸ Brantôme

The 'Venice of Périgord' is the Renaissance counterpart to the Château de Hautefort, but instead of a castle it is built around an equally aristocratic monastery. The best part is when you learn that, for all its airs and graces, the monastery is only a veneer, concealing some bizarre secrets in the cliff wall behind it. Page 123.

2 Château de Monbazillac.

❹ Château de Hautefort

As soon as it catches your eye on the horizon, you hear Baroque trumpets blaring. Hautefort is refined art and arrogant authority at once; the boldness of the architecture and the geometric perfection of the gardens capture an expansive moment of history with crystal clarity. Page 137.

❺ Sarlat

A town built for gentlemen, as they used to say. Even when it's full of tourists in shorts and bum bags, Sarlat has a way of taking us back to a more refined day. It's also the perfect base for exploring the most interesting corner of Périgord, and the best place to be initiated into the culinary cult of the duck. Page 150.

❻ Château de Castelnaud

Most of Périgord's many medieval castles either went to ruin or were converted into residential châteaux. Castelnaud survives, to tell us stories of knights of old, how they lived and how they fought. Some of the reconstructions of medieval weapons here are unique in the world. Page 164.

❼ Château des Milandes

As châteaux go, Les Milandes is a jewel, but a modest one. Here the real attraction is getting to know one of the great ladies of the last century, Josephine Baker, who came from the streets of St Louis to lead a remarkable, even inspiring life in France. Page 165.

❽ Jardins de Marqueyssac

The most ravishing of Périgord's Renaissance gardens, and perhaps the greatest, oddest topiary creation anywhere. Come anytime, but especially on a summer night when they light it up with candles. Page 166.

❾ Font-de-Gaume

Lascaux will show you only a reproduction; you have to come here to see the best of Palaeolithic art in all its mind-blowing virtuosity. Page 172.

4 Gardens of Hautefort.

5 Sarlat.

8 Jardins de Marqueyssac.

11 Lascaux II.

⑩ Roque St-Christophe

You would never imagine such an exotic thing could exist here in *la douce France* instead of in Turkish Cappadocia. It's the Invisible Castle, tunnelled on five levels through nearly 1 km of cliffs and occupied over thousands of years. If any old stones in Périgord could speak, we wish it were these. Page 174.

⑪ Lascaux II

Even if it's only a copy, there's no better place to come to grips with the fascinating and sophisticated minds that created humanity's first great art. It's all there on the walls in paintings and symbols, a way of thinking and living waiting to be deciphered. Page 176.

⑫ Souillac

Souillac has two delights, and they're next-door neighbours who couldn't have less in common: the wonderful 'dancing' Isaiah in the Romanesque abbey church, and a museum full of clockwork automata. Page 198.

⑬ Carennac

The village's current population is 373. But like so many other tiny places in this region, it is famous around the world. Carennac has one great work of art, an interesting museum, a café and a restaurant, and more charm than any village really deserves. Page 206.

⑭ Château de Montal

It's the real Renaissance, picked up on a magic carpet, transported from Italy to the Lot and made French. It's also a monument to a broken heart; the protagonists of the sad story are captured in the exquisitely sculpted roundel portraits on Montal's façade. Page 209.

⑮ Gouffre de Padirac

Lofty and solemn, the 'underground cathedral' in the cave at Padirac is one of the great sights of France. It is impossible to photograph, and difficult enough to describe. You'll really have no idea until the boatman is punting you through it down an underground river. Page 210.

⑯ Rocamadour

It's fashionable to laugh at Rocamadour and its roadside attractions, but it's even more fun to visit. In what other hallowed medieval pilgrimage site can you feed Barbary apes, or watch an Andean condor swoop over your head? Bring the kids. (Or, for a unique experience, come in January when it's nearly deserted.) Page 212.

⑰ Cahors

For the most beautiful bridge in France, the Pont Valentré; for the lovely cathedral and the Saturday market, the secret gardens and a skyline of medieval towers. It's an introspective town though, and it gives up its secrets only a little at a time. Page 228.

⑱ St-Cirq-Lapopie

Deep in the secret heartland of Quercy there's a village perched on the edge of tall cliffs that's just as visually striking as Rocamadour. This one devotes itself not to religion but to contemporary art, and it's an ideal spot from which to explore the most scenic part of the Lot Valley. Page 249.

⑲ Musée de l'Insolite

It's a single mad artist living under a cliff, expressing himself through the medium of rusty junk. His 'museum of the unusual' is there to make us laugh, while at the same time giving our contemporary culture the nice crisp punch in the nose it deserves. Page 256.

⑳ Figeac

An urban oasis in an eerily empty corner of France. In many ways Figeac is a slightly smaller version of Cahors, but this elegant city of steep slate roofs and Gothic merchants' palaces has charms of its own. Page 258.

16 Feeding the Barbary apes at Rocamadour.

Month by month

A year in Dordogne & Lot

Chateau La Grezette.

January & February

It starts with Epiphany, and a tasty cake called a *galette du roi*. Whoever gets the slice with the *fève* ('bean', but usually a tiny porcelain figurine) baked into it receives the paper crown and is king for the year.

There's not a lot to do. In this area so dependent on tourism, many places stay closed. The shops don't, and January is the month for sales. Mostly, this is a time for sitting around tables with friends and family and complaining about the state of the world.

At least the vintners are busy. One of the last labour-intensive jobs in agriculture is pruning the vines (only one shoot to the left, the most healthy one, and another to the right). Vintners worth millions will be out doing some themselves, along with their 80-year-old grandmothers.

Chances are it's still dismal outside. But the climate here is never predictable; you could get April's weather in February, or February's in April.

March & April

Some day in mid-March it begins, and it's about time. First the plum trees explode into white blossoms, then the cherries. April brings buttercups, and later bright red poppies punctuate the meadows and roadsides, while wisteria on the fronts of the old houses covers all the villages in a purple haze. Asparagus and strawberries begin to hit the markets, and the garden shops are the busiest places in town.

The people lag behind nature a little in coming back to life, but all crawl out of their caves eventually. Easter is the real beginning of spring, as the first small wave of tourists takes advantage of the school holidays. Small hotels and attractions that closed for the winter begin to open up.

May & June

Come on down: it's the best time for a visit. The weather's usually perfect, tiny wild orchids are popping up in the meadows, and in June the markets are full of cherries. The restaurants put their tables out on their terraces. Everything's open, everyone's in a good mood, and the tourist onslaught of July and August is still weeks away. The school year's almost over, and for the only time all year the teenagers simply disappear, especially the final-year students cramming for the all-important bac.

The first festivals of the year draw big crowds, like the Floralies in St-Jean-de-Côle or the Fête du Vin de Cahors in Albas. Everyone's ready to party.

July & August

'Silly Season', as the expats call it, swings into action. Bergerac's little airport heats up, while long convoys of caravans from Rotterdam and Antwerp clutter the motorways. Old gents sit on the benches in front of the Mairie and watch the Parisian girls in summer dresses go by.

It's quite mad indeed. Everything is packed all the time, and you'll be smart to hit the supermarkets at lunchtime (summer hours only!) to avoid the crush. White wine and chilled rosé, the current fad, disappear by the tanker-load. But no one complains much about the tourists; they generally behave themselves and these departments couldn't live without them. The owners of gîtes and jewellery shops and art galleries rack up half or more of their year's profits in these two summer months. Every village has its fête and there are numerous convivial *marchés nocturnes* (night markets) where you can buy local fare to eat at communal tables in the square.

September & October

The last wave of tourists consists of couples without children, young or old, who come to enjoy the post-August bargains and quiet. For the locals, meanwhile, it's the *rentrée* – back to school! Shops now are as busy as before Christmas.

Right around 15 September the air seems to change. The last fêtes are finished, the evenings are brisk, and fog and mists hang over the valleys. If it's a bad year it'll start drizzling and won't let up until December, or maybe next April. At this time the winemakers are looking at the clouds and the television every hour. Timing is crucial. When it's just right, word goes around and the big harvesters start churning down all the country roads. They'll be out all day and all night until the job's done.

In October the stripped vines turn red, and what excitement there is in rural areas is provided by the hunt. The head of the village *chasse* knows just how many excess boar and deer he has; and he does his duty. You'll sure know it on the Sunday

Beaufort Fête.

Grand Filolie Castle.

when the season starts. It's not the best time for a stroll in the woods, but plenty of people will be out at dawn anyway. They're looking for mushrooms – ceps, mostly, but also *trompettes de mort* and a few others. The old folk twitch their curtains and watch each other closely, and everyone tries to spy out some inside info on where the good mushroom spots are.

November & December

As everywhere, Christmas creeps up earlier every year. Village crews start putting up lighting displays in late November, while homeowners hang up lights of their own, or at least an effigy Santa climbing a rope up to an upstairs window – in France, Santa's a cat burglar.

November is grey and calm and usually kind, despite the drizzle. December is much the same, though by now everyone's tired of the gloom. The more rural and under-populated corners, like the eastern Lot, seem eerily empty, as if everyone's gone into hibernation along with the badgers and the hedgehogs. If there's any snow, it usually comes only once a year and stays on the ground for just a day or two; oddly enough it often happens around Christmas.

The holidays are less about presents and more about food. Two thirds of the foie gras in France, most of it produced right here, disappears in the two weeks around Christmas and New Year. Families celebrate the New Year's Eve *réveillon* with the biggest and richest dinner of the year: lots of champagne, lots of merriment – and everyone in bed before 0130.

Screen & page

Dordogne & Lot in film & literature

Films

Lacombe Lucien
Louis Malle, 1974
Though no battles were fought in the southwest, the Second World War was a profound shock to this part of France. Louis Malle's classic captures the moral ambiguity and sombre atmosphere of occupied France with clinical precision, in this story of a confused 18 year old who is rejected by the Resistance for being too young, and instead goes to work for the Gestapo. It was filmed in Figeac.

The Duellists
Ridley Scott, 1977
Scott's first film, from a story by Joseph Conrad, set in Napoleonic France. It stars Keith Carradine and Harvey Keitel as two officers locked in a bitter, endless feud, and was filmed in and around Sarlat.

Location of *The Duellists*, Sarlat.

Location of *La Fille de d'Artagnan*, Château de Biron.

La Fille de d'Artagnan (Revenge of the Musketeers)
Bertrand Tavernier, 1994
Sophie Marceau emotes all over the Château de Biron, a castle that has hosted so many costume dramas that the props they left behind have become one of its main attractions.

Ever After
Andy Tennant, 1998
You can see the Dordogne at its most romantic in this reworking of the Cinderella story, starring Drew Barrymore and Anjelica Huston; locations include the Château de Fénelon and Château de Hautefort.

Chocolat
Lasse Hallström, 2000
Based on Joanne Harris's novel about love, tolerance and sweets in a French village (see below) and partly filmed in Beynac on the Dordogne.

Jacquou le Croquant
Laurent Boutonnat, 2007
The latest film version of the story of Périgord's famous (fictional) 19th-century rebel – though it was filmed mostly in Romania.

Books

Fiction

Jacquou the Rebel (Jacquou le Croquant)
Eugène Le Roy, 1897
Set during the brief Bourbon restoration of 1815-1830, this is the story of a peasant who stands up and fights against the local noble bully. Le Roy, whose parents were servants at the Château de Hautefort, knew what he was writing about. Often adapted into films in France, his Dickensian novel is available in English only in an old translation published by Dutton in 1919, hard to find but available to download at Internet Archive (archive.org).

The Lost Upland: Stories of Southwestern France
WS Merwin, 1992
Three unusual stories by the double Pulitzer Prize-winning poet, who has a house by the Dordogne. All three deal with seeing a bit of the eternal in the countryside and the lives of its people.

Timeline
Michael Crichton, 1999
Crichton's novel is a story of time travel, in which researchers from Arizona find themselves back in the Dordogne of the 14th century, where they learn the finer points of jousting and catch the Black Death.

Chocolat
Joanne Harris, 1999
An independent-minded young woman – partially based on the author's own French grandmother – opens up a chocolate shop in a conservative village and gets some of the grumpy locals in a dither. It's chocolate versus religion, and guess which one wins.

Non-fiction

Cooking & Travelling in Southwest France
Stephanie Alexander, 2002
An exceptional book on the food, the farmers, the markets and the recipes; it covers both Quercy and Périgord. It won the 2002 award for Best Cookbook of the Year at the Salon International du Livre Gourmand in Périgueux.

The Ripening Sun: One Woman and the Creation of a Vineyard
Patricia Atkinson, 2003
Less fulsome than is usual for the expats-in-paradise genre, this tells the story of how Atkinson survived personal tragedy while learning to become a wine grower completely on her own around Bergerac. You'll learn a lot about wine.

Lunch with Madame Murat: Food of Love in a French Village
Mary Moody, 2005
An antidote, perhaps, to the plague of slushy books about trendy restaurants; the Australian Ms Moody takes an unpretentious favourite, in a Quercy village, and with affection and good humour gets to the bottom of a 100-year family story and the recipes that go with it.

Families of the Vine: Seasons Among the Winemakers of Southwest France
Michael Sanders, 2005
In the Vin de Cahors region, Sanders spent enough time with three winemaking families to learn the business inside out.

Bergerac vineyard as portrayed in *The Ripening Sun*.

About the region

Contents

Sunflowers.

History

When French historians want to tell you about their country, one point they always emphasize is its resilience – its 'amazing powers of recovery', as Andre Maurois put it – after the recurring disasters of a long and often difficult history. It's no idle boast. This country has certainly taken some hits, and its industrious people and fertile land always bounce back. Périgord and Quercy could be a microcosm for the whole. The cultured, peaceful air that hangs about them today belies a fearsome heritage of wars, invasions and troubles.

Two major calamities have marked this land more than anything else. When we show you something that has been ruined, chances are it was ruined either in the Hundred Years' War, when southwestern France's precocious medieval start turned into a nightmare of anarchy, or in the Wars of Religion, when the southwesterners inflicted most of the damage on themselves.

From Prehistory to the Romans

First Europeans

It is difficult enough to imagine people tramping through Europe during the last ice age, but in fact they go back very much further than that. *Homo erectus*, one of evolution's dead ends, was living in southwestern France around 450,000 years ago.

Because so many important discoveries of early humans have been made in the caves and *abris* (rock shelters) of Périgord, local place names are known all over the world. At Le Moustier in the Vézère Valley we got to know the Mousterian culture, chipping away at their flint tools 100,000-45,000 years ago. The Mousterians are often identified with the Neanderthals, who lasted from around 100,000-28,000 BC. They're still much in the news, as scientists debate whether or not they possessed language, or practised cannibalism, or – the most intriguing question of all – whether we are related. Neanderthals and our ancestor *Homo erectus* lived as neighbours for thousands of years, but it still isn't clear whether we intermarried or just wiped them out.

Périgord cave.

About the region

Cro-Magnon, a hamlet just down the valley from Le Moustier, gave us the first remains of some talented but quarrelsome creatures who were destined to go far in the world – us. Remains of Cro-Magnon man, the first *Homo sapiens*, date back 30,000-40,000 years. Scientists call this early culture Périgordian (or Aurignacian). And no one would quibble with calling it 'culture'. With his advanced tools, Cro-Magnon man made the first musical instruments (bone flutes), jewellery from beads and shells, bone needles to sew his socks, and the world's first great art.

These cultures were succeeded by others, differing only slightly and classified by their tools. During the Solutrian era (21,000-17,000 years ago) Cro-Magnon man might have sailed off to the Americas, according to a controversial new hypothesis. The Magdalenian era (named after the Vézère village of La Madeleine, 17,000-10,000 years ago) was the time of reindeer hunters, gradually spreading northwards as the glaciers retreated. It was the Magdalenians who created the masterpiece of Palaeolithic art in the cave at Lascaux.

The Neolithic world

The 'Neolithic Revolution', including the discovery of agriculture, the domestication of animals and the beginnings of settled community life, seems to have arrived in France around 8000-7000 BC.

Dolmen, Prayssac.

Europe's first great civilization created Stonehenge, Carnac and the other famous monuments elsewhere, but in our region they left only menhirs (standing stones with some religious significance) and dolmens (table-like constructions of large flat stones used as collective graves, sometimes covered in mounds).

Though the clues are fascinating, we can't say much for sure about the Neolithic world. It lasted an astoundingly long time – some 5000 years of cultural continuity – and it seems to have been oddly peaceful. Few weapons have been discovered, villages are generally undefended, and little evidence has turned up of social hierarchy. Some claim that it was a matriarchal world, and it certainly shared the Palaeolithic idea of a great goddess. There was no metal to make work easier, but people still apparently had plenty of leisure time for moving enormous stones and making themselves the world's first astronomers.

Gaul

The first historical people to inhabit the country were the Celts, who overran almost all of Europe north of the Alps around the sixth century BC. The Celts were a warrior society – headhunters, in fact. (The heads of their enemies captured in battle decorated their temples, which might be the origin of the little sculpted heads on corbels around the cornices of medieval churches.) At the same time they were supremely talented in poetry, and developed a fantastically vivid and complex mythology. Nevertheless, throughout their history they disdained urban life. The closest thing Celts had to a town was the *oppidum*, little more than a glorified, well-defended trading post.

The Celts divided themselves into tribes, and our region was shared by two of them, the Petrocorii in the north and the Cadurcii in the south; the latter gained notice as one of the first people in Gaul to grow their own wine grapes.

Coming of the Romans

Caesar's conquest of Gaul, beginning in 59 BC, would be one of the biggest bites Rome ever swallowed. By chance, the campaign ended at an obscure Celtic oppidum in the upper Dordogne. Uxellodunum, a site long lost and recently rediscovered near Martel (see page 205), was the Gauls' last redoubt. After its fall, organized resistance ceased, and the lands of the Petrocorii and Cadurcii were rapidly organized as parts of the new Roman province of Aquitania. Roman rule would last 500 years.

From the beginning, the Romans dragged Gaul into the economy of the wider Mediterranean world. They built roads, including an important one that passed from the Mediterranean through Cahors on its way to Lutetia (Paris). The old Celtic settlements of Périgueux and Cahors were magnified into Civitas Petrocoriorum and Divona Cadurcorum, and the Romans built imposing temples, amphitheatres, baths and aqueducts. Still, these two cities seem to have been little more than administrative centres, populated by officials and soldiers, and no other new towns were founded.

The first and second centuries found Aquitania thriving, like most of the Empire. Already though, appearances were deceiving, and the weakness of Roman Gaul would become clear after AD 256, when the barbarian Franks and Alemanni broke through the Rhine defences and ranged at will over the countryside for years. They sacked Périgueux, which declined to a shadow of its former self and never really recovered.

For the last two centuries of Roman rule, Gaul was an impoverished and troubled land. A debased currency, along with a huge tax burden to support the military and the state, slowly strangled economic life. Gradually, an increasing disparity of wealth brought much of the Empire to a condition where a few families had acquired nearly all of the land and even most of the people. Common people sold themselves into perpetual servitude just to get their names off the tax rolls – the origins of serfdom.

Roman remains, Moncaret, Périgord Pourpre.

We know relatively little about the lives of the lucky (and tax-exempt) families who owned everything, but we have almost all of their names. You'll notice dozens of villages here with names ending in -ac, or -at or -an: Bergerac, Sarlat, Mussidan. The suffix denotes a place belonging to someone. Cressensac belonged to the Crescentii, Prayssac to a family named Priscus.

While the Crescentii and the Priscii were enjoying the good life in their increasingly well-fortified villas, the chronicles drop dark hints of trouble. The *bagaudae*, guerrilla bands that controlled patches of the countryside, may have been politically motivated or just bandits, but their presence is a sure sign of a society coming apart.

The Middle Ages

Dark Age disarray

The old schoolbook account of shaggy barbarians ripping down temple colonnades and wrecking lovely Roman civilization is a bit of a fairytale. The Visigoths, Franks (again) and Vandals who passed through in the fifth century were merely helping to liquidate a bankrupt concern.

But trade and commerce had truly vanished, and there was no capital to rebuild it or authority to defend it. Life became basic and local, and the elements of urban life and high civilization withered and disappeared. As the old Roman landowning elite gradually merged with the invaders' chiefs, it was the Franks, and the Merovingian dynasty they founded, who ended up controlling most of Gaul in the sixth century. Most of our area was organized into a new Duchy of Aquitaine.

St Sauveur Church, Figeac.

The brief comet called the Carolingian Empire meant little to Aquitaine. Charlemagne's impressive state began to dissolve soon after his death in 814, leaving local dukes and barons in a state of *de facto* independence. The power vacuum invited a host of exotic troublemakers, from the Arabs to the Hungarians, and anywhere with a navigable river eventually suffered the depredations of the best-organized and most technologically advanced troublemakers Europe had ever seen: the Vikings. Beginning in the mid-ninth century, Viking raiders prodded their way up the Dordogne and Lot whenever they pleased; if there had been more to steal they would have come more often.

One exception to the general decay was Cahors. The city had had the first Christian bishop in the region, and his successors took control of it and somehow steered it through hard times. The great seventh-century Bishop Didier rebuilt the walls and aqueducts and established the episcopate as a secular power that would endure for centuries.

Occitan civilization

Economic springtime finally returned around the magic year 1000. For our region, the early medieval period was one of the best times ever. Wealth and trade made a comeback. The old Roman towns started growing again, while new ones appeared, either around a monastery or pilgrimage church (Figeac, Souillac, Sarlat) or a castle (Bergerac, Montignac).

Culture was breaking out all over. Every corner developed its own styles of architecture and art. The Occitan-speaking southern half of old Gaul became one of the most advanced and prosperous parts of Europe, with a vivid culture based on the cult of chivalry and the new poetry of the troubadours, inspired by the lyric poetry of Muslim Spain. Périgord produced some of the most famous of these, including Arnaut de Mareuil, Arnaut Daniel of Ribérac and Bertran de Born, lord of Hautefort (see page 138).

One of the first of the troubadours had been the Duke of Aquitaine himself, Guillaume IX (1071-1127). Guillaume's granddaughter, Eleanor of Aquitaine, who inherited the duchy, was the most eligible girl in Christendom. Her first marriage was to the dull and pious Louis VII of France, but the spirited Eleanor eventually managed to get a divorce from him, and in 1152 she bestowed herself and her duchy upon a very willing Henry II Plantagenet of England. The English now had their foot in the door, and Périgord, Quercy and the rest of Aquitaine wouldn't be rid of them for 300 years.

The son of Henry and Eleanor, Richard the Lionheart, spent most of his life tramping around Aquitaine besieging castles and subduing rebellious barons. (This Richard, so beloved in English legend, spent only six months of his reign in England and never even bothered to learn English. His glorious reputation is largely due to his liberality to his nobles; the common people might have written his history in less charitable terms.)

The Albigensian Crusade

After all the drama of the Angevins, fate had something even noisier in store. The heretical sect called the Cathars is generally associated with Languedoc and the lands of the Counts of Toulouse. But they were also widespread in this region. Catharism was a dualistic, Manichaean religion that looked on Creation as a fallen world, the creation not of God but of an evil demigod identified with Satan; it originated in Persia and slowly worked its way east. The Cathars' presence coincided nicely with the French king's desire to get his hands on the lands of the south. Pope Innocent III and King Philippe Auguste made a grim pact: the French would get rid of the heretics, and the Pope would sanction their land grab.

The horrific wars that would kill an estimated million people in the Occitan lands began in 1209 but didn't hit Périgord until 1214, when the Crusaders' diabolically successful leader Simon de Montfort invaded the area and had his way with Domme and Beynac. The Crusaders suffered reverses after that, but the tide turned for the last time when King Louis IX (St Louis) intervened. By the 1240s it was clear that the northerners had won.

Not long after, history played a little trick. The 1259 Treaty of Paris was meant to finally settle the quarrels between England and France, and under its terms Louis IX handed Périgord and Quercy back to the English, in return for Normandy.

Despite all the troubles, the southwest's economy was still booming. The population was rising rapidly, and lands that had been abandoned or under-populated since the end of the Roman Empire were now becoming valuable real estate again. The French and English kings were manoeuvring to gain lands and strategic position, and between 1259 and 1300 both of them founded bastides (new towns) wherever they could get control of a likely plot of ground.

The Caorsins

While all this was happening, humble Quercy, for the first and only time in its history, somehow became a real protagonist in the economic mainstream of Europe. Historians still seem thoroughly puzzled as to how it happened, but in this period a new merchant class grew up in Cahors and Figeac. The Caorsins, as they came to be called, built banking and merchant houses that conducted a lucrative trade between Italy and northern France and beyond; they're mentioned in contemporary chronicles as far afield as Norway.

Many may well have been Italians; Dante found a place for them in his *Inferno*, along with the other usurers, and French kings occasionally issued decrees against them. But a son of Cahors, Jacques Duèze, succeeded in becoming Pope John XXII in 1314. That was the height of Cahors' wealth and influence, the time when the Pont Valentré was built. It wasn't to last: only two decades later the outbreak of the longest and most destructive war in the region's history would put an end to the Caorsins and their dreams of a booming city.

The Hundred Years' War

The reckoning that was postponed by the Treaty of Paris came in 1337, with a dispute over Gascony. Probably no one guessed that the resulting war, one of so many, would be the longest and most destructive of the Middle Ages. It would be an oversimplification to think of it as merely a struggle between England and France. The titanic struggle would indeed propel the creation of those two nation states, but in 1337 no such things really existed. The Hundred Years' War was a dynastic struggle, not a national one. Its protagonists were all related, by blood or marriage.

Edward III of England had the men, the ships and the longbows, and he went on the attack. His armies in the south, directed by his son the Black Prince, moved up the Lot and Dordogne, besieging and capturing Cahors in 1362, by which time almost all the southwest was in English hands. In the 1370s, the tide began to turn slightly in France's favour. An intelligent and careful new French king, Charles V, found a general to match in Bertrand du Guesclin, who wore the English out with his delaying tactics and then struck hard and unexpectedly. He recaptured much of Quercy and Périgord, climaxing in the taking of Bergerac in 1377.

For decades after that, both sides were too exhausted, or too occupied elsewhere, to mount major efforts. But peace in the royal courts did not mean peace for the beleaguered people of the southwest. Eternal warfare had brought the region close to anarchy. The *routiers*, or 'free companies' – mercenary bands generally associated with the English cause (though their captains and men were in fact mostly French) – infested the countryside, holing up in rustic fortresses around the Lot Valley in particular, and keeping life miserable and dangerous for everyone else.

The *routier* bandits were still on the rampage when France won the final victory on the banks of the Dordogne at Castillon, near Bordeaux, in 1453. Recovery was uneven. Périgueux snapped back quickly, as you can see from the palaces around rue Limogeanne erected in the late 15th century. Cahors and Figeac never really recovered at all.

From Renaissance to Revolution

The century that followed the battle of Castillon was good to France. Instead of defending their own turf, after 1498 the kings were able to take their armies over the Alps and make life miserable for the Italians. They brought home booty, recipes and the Renaissance, just in time for the great age of château-building, when old feudal castles were transformed into sumptuous new residences *à l'italienne*.

Today, you may notice that in Quercy there are plenty of old farmhouses isolated in the countryside, while Périgord has rather fewer. The Dordogne tourist offices like to call their department 'the land of a thousand châteaux' (in truth there are nearly 1500); Quercy has relatively few. These are clues to the very different destinies of the neighbouring regions in the late Middle Ages: somehow, Quercy managed to become a land of smallholders, largely free from feudal ties, while Périgord remained completely feudal, economically and in spirit. All those châteaux were built by a nobility of unequalled arrogance, living off the sweat of a peasantry as oppressed as any in France.

The Wars of Religion

With a slightly different cast of the historical dice, France might have been as good a Protestant nation as England. The teachings of Luther and Calvin were received with enthusiasm in many quarters of France, and oddly enough more in the south than the north. In the 1550s the first Protestant churches were getting organized, and historians estimate that open dissenters made up about 10% of the population. There were plenty of zealots on both sides, and incidents multiplied with each passing year.

In 1560, 30 Protestants were massacred in Cahors, in just one of the events that drove France to the brink of civil war. The country divided itself into two armed camps, while a paralyzed monarchy, run by the hapless queen mother Catherine de' Medici, could do nothing to stop it. Open war broke out in 1562, and would continue on and off for 36 agonizing years.

The Protestants proved stronger in the southwest than anyone had expected. Like the Hundred Years' War, these wars provided an opportunity for new men of violence to make names for themselves. Among them, the most spectacular career was that of Geoffroy de Vivans of Castelnaud, called 'le Batailleur', who worked closely with the future Henri IV. Vivans swept nearly all the Catholics out of the Dordogne Valley, distinguishing himself with brutal captures of Sarlat and Belvès, and a famous night attack that won Domme for the cause.

The real power in this fight was meanwhile biding his time and consolidating his base in Gascony: Henri de Navarre, leader of the Protestant cause and just coincidentally the rightful heir to the throne of France. He brought his new army northwards and conquered the rest of the southwest, taking time off to repay Cahors for the 1560 massacre by besieging and thoroughly sacking it. Good King Henri IV brought the wars to an end by cynically converting to Catholicism to secure his rule and then issuing the 1598 Edict of Nantes, establishing religious tolerance.

Unfortunately, the kings that followed proved less tolerant. Protestants found themselves increasingly concentrated into places they controlled and felt safe in. One of these was the thriving commercial city of Bergerac.

Ruin of the southwest

Unlike the sympathetic Henri IV, who had sincerely wanted 'a chicken in the pot every Sunday' for his people, the governments of Louis XIII and Louis XIV did nothing for the peasants, while piling ever more taxes on top of the feudal duties they already owed. Other grievances weren't lacking. The increasingly centralized and despotic monarchy meant less local control, arbitrary decrees, and under Louis XIV, religious bigotry and everlasting war. The imposition of French on an Occitan-speaking country (by the decree of Villars-Cotterets in 1539) meant that people had to deal with the courts and administration in what was for most a foreign language.

In a country on its knees, with a heritage of violence and plenty of unemployed ex-soldiers, trouble was guaranteed. For the next two centuries, *jacqueries* (revolts) would break out all over France, and some of the worst occurred in Périgord and the southwest – 450 of them in fact, between 1593 and 1715. The first wave came in 1594, as the fires of the religious wars were just dying down. Scattered outbreaks were brutally put down by royal troops or local forces; at Condat in the Vézère Valley, a force of *croquants* was routed in 1595.

Croquant (literally 'cruncher') was a new word of the day. At first the peasants used the term to

Statue of Jacquou le Croquant, Domme.

describe their noble enemies, who ground money and labour out of them without pity; somehow the nobles turned it around on the peasants, though more often these liked to call themselves by the equally peculiar name of *tard-avisés* (those who 'noticed too late', as if to emphasize their reluctance to rebel against their king).

Unfortunately, the peasants lost every round. One of the biggest commotions took place in 1637, when a rebel army seized Bergerac and held it for three weeks before the king's troops came down to crunch them. Battles went on for another five years until a well-timed amnesty offered by Cardinal Richelieu quieted things. The last big eruption would not come until 1707, during the endless wars that marked the shabby end-days of Louis XIV. A spark that flared up around the Quercy villages of Cazals and Serignac, when rumours spread of a new royal tax on childbirth, resulted in a mob of 30,000 marching on the gates of Cahors.

Bust of Cardinal Richelieu.

The tinsel glories of *le Roi Soleil* tend to glare out what in reality was a disastrous reign. From Périgord and Quercy, the view is a little clearer. While their sons and their money were being carted off to feed foreign aggressions, people reverted to a state not seen since the Dark Ages. Famines are too numerous to recount. The plague passed through three times: in 1691 it took away a sixth of Périgord. Wolves, in some corners, were making a comeback.

Opulence & hard times

The dawn of the 18th century found the broken, battered southwest leading a strange double life. The impoverished countryside may have been worse off than at any time since the Dark Ages, but the favoured few could still live a rich, indolent and decorous life in the great châteaux, in the well-defended, aristocratic city of Sarlat or, more likely, at the court in Versailles. Cardinal Richelieu, who with one hand demolished so many of the castles of the quarrelsome nobility, with the other welcomed them to Paris, where he could keep an eye on them.

The result was the conversion of a grasping, useless nobility into a grasping, useless absentee nobility – one that no longer took an active role in the economic life of its lands, or invested in them, but merely sat back while its agents collected the rents. For the rest of the population, life was looking rather primeval. A lot were simply leaving. The region contributed more than its share to the colonization of French Canada, Louisiana and the Caribbean.

In the last decades of the ancien régime things finally started to improve. Despite the emigration the population suddenly jumped; the fertile land was getting back to normal. The state actually helped for once, especially by improving the roads. France built itself the best road system since the Romans, and it touched even the backwaters. Many of the roads we drive on today, such as the D820 through Cahors, were begun under Louis XV. The royal *intendants* who planned them also began the gracious custom of planting avenues of plane trees along the way, some of which survive today.

Someone else's revolution

When the French Revolution broke out in 1789, probably no one was more surprised than the Périgourdins and Quercynois. And from beginning to end, they played no great role in it. Plenty of church sculptures got smashed, though in some places the wreckers were beaten off by a loyal Catholic population. The confiscation of Church property created shady opportunities for a new class to make its fortune. In 1790, the new political division of France saw most of Périgord become the Dordogne department. Quercy was originally a single 'Department of the Lot', though later the people of southern Quercy convinced Paris to let them become a department of their own, the Tarn-et-Garonne around Montauban.

Southwesterners responded a bit more enthusiastically to Napoleon. Thousands of volunteers (and later conscripts) joined the army to see Europe, and some went a long way indeed. Joachim Murat, from the village of Labastide, ended up as King of Naples. Jean-Luc de Bessières, from Prayssac, managed the Grande Armée's occupation and retreat from Moscow.

The 19th & 20th centuries

Disappointments of modernity

The rises and falls of the various regimes that ruled France in the turbulent 19th century meant little to this neglected corner of the nation. Whatever happened generally happened here last. The first railway in the Lot, connecting Cahors with Paris and Toulouse, was not completed until 1891. But from 1850 agriculture boomed, in particular the wine business. Prosperity returned to some areas for the first time since the Middle Ages. Many villages built themselves new churches in the period 1850-1880; most of the 'traditional' farmhouses you see date from this era too, and the more prosperous farmers began to acquire their first mod cons: glass windows, and maybe a water pump of their own.

The southwest had never been a completely backward society; censuses in the Revolutionary period reported that about half the adult men could read. But comprehensive education came with the Third Republic and the *lois Ferry* of 1881-1882. Jules Ferry's reforms were a landmark for France, but they also meant the beginning of the end for the Occitan language and culture. The reformers in Paris meant to wipe it out completely: in the new schools, children were punished for speaking their own language, even at play.

The pre-1880 era of prosperity proved to be another false start. Just as the winemakers were starting to suffer competition from Algeria and elsewhere, the phylloxera epidemic of 1887 destroyed their vines. It took a long time to replant and recover, and meanwhile the rural economy suffered another dramatic collapse. It wasn't just wine; the southwest's small-scale, old-fashioned agriculture simply could not compete in the modern world. Young people fled en masse for better opportunities in the big cities or the

Cottage in Hautefort.

colonies. The southwest lost a quarter of its population between 1880 and 1940. In parts of the Lot over half the people left, and some villages nearly disappeared off the map.

The world wars

The southwest's demographic disaster was completed by the First World War. France lost a fifth of its young men in that grisly, pointless conflict, and the loss delivered the coup de grâce in turning rural areas into economic dead zones.

It also weakened the nation so much that it was able to put up little effort in the 1939 rematch. Though all the battles were fought elsewhere, the Second World War affected the southwest right from its beginning, in surprising ways. In 1939, the French government evacuated Strasbourg and other parts of Alsace, sending 100,000 people to the Dordogne and Lot. People opened their homes and their hearts to them, even though the refugees at one point amounted to a fifth of the entire population.

The Resistance thrived, especially in the empty hills between Cahors and Figeac. When the invasion of France began in June 1944, British and American agents were parachuted in to help blow up bridges and disrupt German transport and communications. The southwest was already getting a belated dose of war. The SS *Das Reich* division, made up largely of Alsatian Germans and scum dragged out of prisons, was sent on a kind of terror tour to discourage resistance. The division became infamous for its massacre of an entire village in Poitou (Oradour-sur-Glane), but on the way they also shot up several towns in the Lot, notably Frayssinet-le-Gélat.

Postwar recovery

As in many parts of France, the experience of the war and resistance gave local politics a sharp and enduring push towards the Left. Since 1945 the 'red' Lot has always been reliably socialist, though that may slowly be changing. The Lotois like to brag about their civic spirit; in national elections they usually turn out the highest percentage of voters of any department. Politics in the Dordogne are similar, and both departments are too contented ever to give more than a few votes to Le Pen and the National Front.

In their quiet way, both seem to play a role in national life out of proportion to their size – especially the Lot. To mention just a few Lotois, there was Georges Pompidou, Charles de Gaulle's successor as president, who started his political career as a local councillor in Cajarc. Gaston Monnerville, born in 1897 in Guyana, became mayor of St-Céré and the first black member of France's National Assembly. At the same time, St-Céré produced a very different character, Pierre Poujade, whose right-wing populist shopkeepers' crusade frightened the daylights out of France's *classe politique* in the 1950s. Maurice Faure went from the Mairie in Prayssac to the Ministry of Foreign Affairs, and signed the Treaty of Rome for France in 1956.

For the average Lotois and Périgourdin, the changes since the war have been truly dramatic. As late as the 1960s and 70s, they were eking out a very poor living growing tobacco and bad wine; most of the back roads remained unpaved, and today you'll still meet people who can remember when their house first got electricity and water. There's no trace of such backwardness now, and even if this region is more a playground for the global economy than a productive part of it, right now it is enjoying better times than it has known in centuries.

Art & architecture

Neither Périgord nor Quercy was ever a great centre of art, and rarely did they ever have much wealth to purchase any. Almost everything beautiful that was ever created here comes from two periods separated by over 10,000 years: the painted caves of the Palaeolithic era, and the Romanesque architecture and sculpture of the early Middle Ages.

So why do so many people say they come down here for the 'art'? It's all in the context. In truth there is no shortage of pretty things to see, on the same modest scale as everything else here. Finding the lady with the key to unlock a 14th-century chapel that has seven devils painted inside – that's the equivalent of a trip to the Louvre.

Perhaps as an act of defiance against their stormy history, people here seem to have decided long ago to reverently restore every bit of *patrimoine* (heritage) that survives, and polish up their villages and their land until they shine. Everyone has seen the 'Plus Beaux Villages de France' signs outside villages, and getting into this association requires a rather rigorous evaluation (and a commitment to keeping it *beau*). The Dordogne has more than any other department in France, and the Lot isn't far behind. Outside the villages, people give the same care to the entire countryside that others reserve for their own front gardens; it's a reflex that comes as naturally as pruning back the plane trees. The result of all this care is that the greatest work of art to be found here is the land itself.

Art of the Palaeolithic caves

Of the known 350 painted Palaeolithic caves in the world, nearly half are in France, 60 of them in Périgord. Whatever early *Homo sapiens* was up to, it didn't survive unless it was entombed in a cave. Those little shreds of evidence tourists flock to see in the Vézère Valley don't tell much, but they show us a culture that, whatever its level of technology, produced some sophisticated minds. When Picasso first saw the paintings in the Vézère he said: "We haven't learned anything new in 30,000 years."

Palaeolithic art covers a timeline between around 33,000 and 13,500 years ago; with so much time to work with, there must be many, many more caves waiting to be discovered. In fact new ones turn up all the time. Most are in places difficult of access, and traces of habitation are almost never found in them. The paintings aren't just decoration; both they and the caves must have possessed some sacred meaning. Sometimes, mysteriously, fragments of bone are found wedged into fissures in the rock near the paintings.

Palaeolithic engraving, Vézère Valley.

Palaeolithic art isn't just painting: engravings, clay modelling and relief sculpture are common as well, and there is some incredible virtuoso bone sculpture in the big museum at Les Eyzies (see page 170). But it is the paintings that capture the imagination. Careful study has revealed a lot about the techniques used. The predominant colours come from iron oxides (red) and charcoal or manganese dioxide (black); these pigments were mixed with a powdered binder (such as talc), to help them stick, and then applied with a finger or brush, or often by blowing the powder through a small tube.

There's an electric immediacy about the animals that are the paintings' main subjects: horses, mammoths, bison, reindeer. In the oldest caves (outside Périgord) depictions of big predators – such as bears, rhinos and even lions – were common, later, the artists seem to have thought more as predators themselves, and paintings of game animals begin to predominate.

Almost always, in conjunction with the animals, there are various geometric symbols: most commonly dots and bars, sometimes squiggles and a kind of latticework. No one has any good idea what these might signify. Human figures are relatively rare, and they show nothing of the life and artistic care lavished on the animals; it has been suggested that this may indicate some religious taboo. But there are quite a few representations of female genitals, and one of the most fascinating subjects, repeated in many caves, is the outline of a human hand, presumably the artist's, stencilled by blowing paint around it – almost like a signature.

The amount of ink spilled over these paintings has been considerable, and there is a wide range of interpretations and theories. Art historians emphasize the sophisticated techniques used: the working of the natural contours of the cave wall into compositions to create relief or shadow effects, or the tricks of foreshortening that would not be rediscovered by painters until the Renaissance.

Abbé Breuil, one of the first to study the paintings from an ethnological standpoint, believed they represented a kind of sympathetic magic, recreating the real-life hunt to draw the animals to their fate. Others have read lots of sex into it: springtime scenes of mating rituals that

Where to see Palaeolithic art

Most of the sights are conveniently near each other in the Vézère Valley, and you can see many in a day or two.

Musée National de Préhistoire, Les Eyzies Start here for orientation, and to see all the art and artefacts that could be moved.

Grotte de Font-de-Gaume The best art still open to the public; see it before it closes for good.

Grotte des Combarelles Almost as breathtaking as Font-de-Gaume.

Grotte de Rouffignac Mammoths are the theme here – hundreds of them.

Lascaux II A reproduction, necessarily, but still well worth seeing.

Outside the Vézère, **Pech Merle**, east of Cahors, has magnificent paintings, portraying a little bit of everything. There is also the **Grotte de Cougnac**, near Gourdon.

celebrate fertility. Some recent thinking on the subject might best be expressed by David Lewis-Williams, whose controversial but fascinating *The Mind in the Cave: Consciousness and the Origins of Art* (2002) sees the presence of the paintings as evidence for something like what we know as shamanism. He explains the paintings as an attempt to reproduce things seen in visions, perhaps in altered states of consciousness.

It's eminently plausible, but real evidence is lacking. Despite all the hard work and inspiration of scholars, we may never have more than tantalizing clues about the art and the people behind it. When you first see these paintings though, there will definitely be a spark – jumping a gap of thousands of years and making a connection, a message from someone wild and strange who was also a lot like us.

Wall art at Lascaux II.

The 10,000 years after

Neolithic Périgord and Quercy were relative backwaters, and besides the unusual sites at Prayssac in the Lot (see page 241) there are only dolmens and menhirs scattered here and there, with the greatest concentration east of Cahors. Once there were many more standing stones in Quercy, but a pious bishop of Cahors had dozens pulled down in the 18th century, because country people were still leaving offerings at them.

From the Celtic and Roman periods there are surprisingly few remains, other than the ruins and the wonderful new **Musée Gallo-Romain** in Périgueux (see page 88). Next to that museum, the **Tour de Vésone** is one of the very few surviving Gallo-Roman circular temples.

Medieval architecture & sculpture

Romanesque reawakening

It came suddenly, as springtime often does in the southwest. Before the iconic year 1000 everyone thought the world was ready to end. After it, everyone was busy building; as an English chronicler of the time put it, it seemed as if the whole world was being "covered in a white mantle of churches".

Every corner of western Europe developed its own style, or styles, of Romanesque, and this area came up with one of the earliest and most distinctive, with domed churches in the manner of St Mark's in Venice or the Holy Sepulchre in Jerusalem. No one knows exactly when Périgueux's majestic **St-Front** was built (some say as early as 984). It may well have been started before the Crusades exposed westerners to the great works of the eastern Mediterranean, so there's a possibility that unknown builders in this obscure region developed their own way of building huge, complex domes in stone.

St-Front was copied at Souillac and Cahors, though the style was too expensive for village churches. And it didn't last; Cahors got the biggest medieval domes in France, and the last. The region would have more of an influence with its bell towers. Those of St-Front and the Abbey of Brantôme are among the earliest in the country, and echoes of their style turn up across the southwest.

In the age of feudal warfare, country churches weren't just for show: they were also for defence. Their builders evolved the *clocher-mur* (steeple wall), in which the entire façade rises up above the roofline, turning the building into a kind of defensive tower. In bad times, such churches could be refuges for the entire population of a village or monastery; one of the most advanced examples is in **St-Amand-de-Coly**, north of Sarlat (see page 178).

Sculpturally, this architecture was complemented by some of the most expressive and exotic work found anywhere. It began with the School of Toulouse, and spread northwards through the great Abbey of Moissac in southern Quercy (Lot-et-Garonne). No Romanesque sculpture is more stylized and strange. Less Byzantine than is often claimed, it is something unexpected that sprang out of the Gaulish ground. In it, crisp geometrical patterns combine with sinuous curves; the obsessively perfect folds and pleats of the draperies and ribbons seem at times almost art nouveau. They combine with equally mannered figures and exaggerated poses to make some of the most unforgettable art of the Middle Ages.

Unfortunately not much survived the Protestant vandals and Classical-era remodellers of later centuries. The greatest work in this area is the famous 'dancing' Isaiah in the church at Souillac (see page 200). At Cahors, an entire Romanesque portal can be seen, in a style less wild but equally eccentric. Romanesque sculpture on the rest of the churches in the region, mostly in villages, is eclectic, reflecting no particular style or influence, though some of it is exceptional work.

Gothic interlude

Gothic, the style of Paris and the northern conquerors, arrived in the southwest in the wake of the Albigensian Crusade; as elsewhere, it swept all before it. Cahors and Figeac, the wealthiest towns in the 13th century, were the only ones with the cash to build ambitiously. Thanks to their trading connections across the Alps, both did so with a strong Italian influence. Cahors built the most beautiful of all medieval bridges, the **Pont Valentré** (see page 232), while it remodelled its cathedral in the new style, and hid its domes behind a grand Gothic version of a *clocher-mur*.

Figeac, sadly, saw most of its religious buildings damaged or destroyed in the Wars of Religion, though the interior of the great **Abbey of St-Sauveur** survives (see page 260), along with the very Tuscan palaces of the city's merchants and bankers, one of the greatest ensembles of medieval civil architecture in France. Similar palaces can be seen in Cahors, with big pointed arches on the ground floors where business was conducted, and ornate Gothic traceries around the upstairs windows where the merchants lived. One particular grace of this style, in both cities, is the top floor loggia called a *soleilho*.

Urban design is not an art usually associated with the Middle Ages, but the new towns of the southwest, the bastides (see page 97) were the first works of monumental urbanism since the Romans. Dozens of them remain essentially intact today, with their tidy grids of streets and arcaded squares – one of the most successful marriages of architecture and planning in history. Some of the best are Monpazier, Eymet, Belvès and Domme in Périgord, and Castelfranc in Quercy.

The onset of the Hundred Years' War put a rude stop to everything, and it would be much more than 100 years before France would start building again.

Age of the châteaux

The Renaissance hit France late, and the stars had to line up just right for it to find its way to this unlikely setting. By 1500, the gradual recovery of the economy after the end of the Hundred Years' War had finally put some money in the barons' purses. Madame thought it was time to recycle the stones of that draughty old castle into something a little more modern. And all this happened just as the new Renaissance styles from Italy were getting everyone excited.

Architecturally, the new châteaux had nothing to do with the southwest. With their rich sculptural decoration and fairytale steep gables and turrets, this was a metropolitan style, imported from Paris and the Loire Valley. At first, the Italian influence was strong, in the fenestration and in the style of decoration known as *grottesca* (using masks and floral arabesques, it takes its name from the grotto in Rome where parts of Nero's Domus Aurea were rediscovered in the 15th century and studied by Raphael and others). The finest example of this, particularly for its sculpture, is **Montal** in the northern Lot (see page 209).

Eventually though, the French made the original thought into something entirely their own. A Renaissance with pointed roofs was more suited to the climate and to the national sensibility, and the new style matched the ideals of the local nobility so well that it lasted into the 17th century. Some of the grandest of the châteaux were also the last to be built, such as **Hautefort** (1630) and **Jumilhac** (1655).

One important aspect of the age of châteaux is the gardens. Périgord, especially Périgord Noir, has one of the great collections of *jardins à la française*. Some, such as at Hautefort or Losse in the Vézère, remain true to their Renaissance designers' intent. Others, including the spectacular **Eyrignac** (see page 157), have been modified through the inspiration of generations of gardeners since. The 17th-century topiary fantasy of **Marqueyssac** (see page 166) is unique.

In these years, the people in the châteaux had all the money and did all the building, but occasionally a drop of Renaissance would trickle down to the common folk. All over Cahors, in villages like Puy-l'Evêque and sometimes even in minuscule hamlets, you'll see an ornately carved doorway, or a handsome 16th-century window decorated with the crisp geometric surrounds called *bâtons écotés*.

The Church did some building, often in the middle of nowhere, as with the wonderful **Collégiale de St-Martin** and its collection of tapestries at Montpezat-de-Quercy (see page 245). Many churches had to be rebuilt after the Wars of Religion (St-Jacques in Bergerac, Nôtre-Dame-du-Puy in Figeac), but the greatest urban monument of this period is Sarlat, a wealthy enclave where many elegant *hôtels particuliers* (grand private houses) were built in the 16th-18th centuries.

The 20th century

The impoverished region largely missed out on the Baroque and Neoclassical, and very little happened until the 20th century. Some important figures – such as the Surrealist André Breton in St-Cirq-Lapopie and the sculptor Ossip Zadkine in Les Arques inaugurated the phenomenon of artists installing themselves in villages instead of in Paris. Today it seems as if almost every village has a few. Some, like St-Cirq, have established themselves as art centres.

Former President Georges Pompidou gave his adopted village of **Cajarc** a museum of contemporary art (see page 253), while the eccentric Pierre Shasmoukine has built an artistic village of his own, **Gorodka**, outside Sarlat (see page 155). Nothing earth-shaking has come out of the region so far, but you'll find some talent (and some laughs) in the exhibitions and galleries that sprout up everywhere in summer.

Pierre Shasmoukine, Gorodka.

Dordogne & Lot today

France's population as a whole is over 80% urban; here it's under 50%, and that makes all the difference in the world. In the 1950s government planners were calling these departments 'underdeveloped'. Now people might call them 'lucky'. The modern industrial economy may have neglected them, but that simple fact has made them the kind of places where everyone wants to be.

Tourist economy

In other parts of France businessmen look at the stock quotes; here they may be more interested in hotel occupancy rates. Périgord gets more tourists than any department without a marine coast – nearly three million each year, making a rather astounding total of 26 million overnight stays in 2009. The Lot, a smaller department, tosses in 11 million more. If it depended on agriculture and its scattering of small industries and workshops, the region would barely make enough to scrape by; it's tourism that permits it a comfortable living.

Living off tourism changes things in many ways. It accustoms people to a different schedule, with big rushes at Easter and in summer that make the rest of the year seem like hibernation. It means a lot of local kids aiming to go to hotel and restaurant management schools. The tourists, and their cousins the retirees, helped to set off a housing boom that has only recently ground to a halt. One side effect is that the area attracts a lot of artists and creative people; in August, when there are exhibitions everywhere, you might occasionally get the impression that there are more artists than potential buyers.

No one complains much about the tourists (though everyone laughs at the Rotterdammers, with their long caravans of caravans on the motorways, heading for their Rotterdammer-run campsites). They all know how much depends on the summer season, and in fact even in August the crowds are never that much of a bother. There is very little tourist-trappery or unpleasant speculative building. Even the most crowded areas, like the Dordogne around Sarlat or the Vézère Valley, know how to retain their beauty and their dignity. Tourism operates on the locals' terms, not on those of tour operators or promoters.

Keeping them down on the farm

For the visitors who return again and again, and for those who end up buying a house and living here, the region is a rural idyll, and they hope it stays that way. For young people leaving school, the worry is how they're going to get a job that doesn't involve waiting at tables or moving to Toulouse or Bordeaux.

But both groups, strangely, have a similar vision of what they would like Périgord or Quercy to be. Everyone, socialist or conservative, hopes for a future in which the region's quality of life can be maintained. For tourism, that means encouraging the kind of quality tourism that exists now, and maintaining strict planning and land-use controls to protect the landscape. For agriculture, it means an increasing reliance on top-grade products in fields where small-scale family producers can compete: AOC wines and produce, organic foods, new crops such as saffron and Quercy melons.

For all the tourists, and all the efforts of the government, many think the work for economic development doesn't go nearly far enough. Village life is still precarious, and it can be a constant battle in some places to hold on to the foundation stones: the school, post office, train or coach service, the village shops. When these go, the younger people do too, and so does much of the sense of community.

There's one untranslatable word you hear over and over in discussions of the region's politics: *désenclavement*, which means to bring something out of isolation. That, to the planners, is the key to integrating rural enclaves like this one into the European economy. The last big hope for *désenclavement* was the opening of the A20 motorway a few years back, which finally gave the Lot a quick connection to Paris and Toulouse. It hasn't yet had quite the desired effect, and now the emphasis seems to be on regional airports. Low-cost flights to Bergerac now bring in 270,000 passengers a year, mostly on Ryanair. That has given a major boost to the tourist business, and another new airport is getting ready to open on the borders of the Lot and Corrèze, between Brive and Souillac.

Tourists in Dordogne.

Eymet.

Return of the English (& some others)

Over a century ago, the famous Château de Bonaguil was sold for 100 francs and a sack of walnuts. Thirty years ago, it was still possible to pick up a solid stone farmhouse (and the farm with it) for the equivalent of a few thousand pounds.

So the British came and picked them up. The French, who preferred well-stuccoed modern bungalows, found it amusing. In the 1980s they began calling the department 'Dordogneshire', while the Lot began to fill up too, like a sort of overflow tank. All kinds of people found their way to southwest France, from circles of very plum retirees to young families who lived like pioneers on the frontier, sleeping in tents while they fixed up that chilly old stone house.

The likes of Jean-Marie Le Pen could be heard in the 1990s complaining that the English were coming to take back what they hadn't been able to keep in the Hundred Years' War, but on the whole relations have been very good. People with children are welcomed with open arms; the kids will be assimilated fast even if their parents aren't, and even a few of them in a village can tip the balance and keep the school open. Most permanent British residents make a real effort to learn French and fit in with the community. Some go out of their way to participate in local affairs, and a few even get elected to village councils.

By 2000, reporters were filing stories from villages like Eymet, where nearly a quarter of the residents were British, though in fact anything over 10% is quite rare. With economic hard times and the slide of sterling, the invasion has all but stopped for now. House prices have fallen dramatically and some Brits have even been forced to move back. Most will weather it out. Over the last decade, they have been joined by some new arrivals: Dutch and Belgians mostly, equipped with euros and looking for a little space to plant a garden. There has been a sprinkling of Americans and Scandinavians too. Altogether it's a pretty interesting mix in this small corner of Europe.

An old new people

Who exactly are the Périgourdins and the Lotois? One of the first things you'll notice is that they're pretty short, compared to other French people. Their faces are different too. No one has yet done much detailed work with the new DNA techniques available, but it has been suggested that southwesterners in general – Gascons, Toulousains, Girondins and all the rest – are genetically the same people who have been living here since time immemorial, changing only slightly through all the comings and goings of Celts, Romans, Franks and English. They may well trace their roots back to the folk who built the dolmens in the Neolithic era, perhaps even to the artists of the Palaeolithic caves.

Up in Paris, their faces might give them away if their accent hadn't already. The rest of the French can hear a Lotois coming a mile off, and the accent is often the butt of jokes. It's more clipped than twangy, though in the mouth of a native *'vin'* can become 'vang', *'jardin'* 'jardang'. Final consonants are often pronounced (a good thing to know to avoid sounding foolish – see page 244). To a foreigner it will sound like a more straightforward kind of French – none of those slushy Parisian vowels and nasal grunts. And everyone up north knows you can tell a Lotois by his distinctive (and quite impolite) hillbilly curse: *'Putain con!'*

For a long time southwesterners have had to put up with the jokes of Parisians, who derided their old language – the language of the troubadours – as mere patois, imperfect French. But a modest revival of Occitan culture and even language is under way. Some towns and villages have put up street signs in Occitan, and a few lycées have introduced the language as a course of study. Interest is not yet as great as in the other Occitan lands, such as Languedoc and Provence, but every July Périgueux hosts a festival of Occitan poetry and culture called La Félibrée.

For such a long-settled, traditional region, the population today is much, much more diverse than you would expect. At school events where dinner is laid on it will usually be one of those two traditional southwest dishes, paella or couscous. Paella arrived with the Spanish, of course; there were already quite a few in the area when the end of the Civil War in 1939 loosed a whole wave of refugees fleeing Franco and economic misery. There are plenty of Poles too, and Italians, and especially Portuguese, who have been coming to do farm work for decades. There are Moroccans and Algerians, and a large population of *pied-noirs* – European settlers forced to leave Algeria after that country won its fight for independence in 1962. The British, Americans, Dutch and Belgians are only the latest arrivals, and they probably won't be the last.

Nature & environment

Besides foie gras and castles, this region is also famous (among ornithologists, anyhow) for buzzards. There are seven different kinds. One of them, the mournful St Martin's buzzard, is blessed with the flat face of a barn owl, making it the silliest-looking buzzard known to science. Along with these, you can look up in the afternoon and see giant kites, short-toed eagles, falcons and kestrels. On winter nights owls fly in front of your car, hoping the headlights will pick out something tasty.

The point of mentioning these is that raptors are an excellent indicator of environmental health. And this area has some of the cleanest, clearest air and water in France.

A little geology

Underneath everything lies the rock, which sets the limits and shapes the way in which people can live. Almost all of Périgord and Quercy are part of a broad belt of Cretaceous and Jurassic limestone. It's what geologists call karst topography, and it's never going to be lush farmland. The Lot, in fact, is said to have the worst soil in France. Fortunately, though, much of it is great for vines.

Karst means there will be lots of caves, and these provide the two departments with their best-known attractions: stalactite caves and those used as canvases by Palaeolithic artists. Water working on the limestone over millions of years has formed crevasses, grottoes and underground rivers. The karst soaks up rainwater like a sponge and distributes it underground, and in the places where it does this most efficiently, the soil becomes so thin and dry it isn't good for anything except raising skinny sheep. These areas are the *causses*, which cover much of eastern Quercy (see below).

On the eastern fringes of the departments, the limestone gives way to the crystalline metamorphic rocks of the volcanic Massif Central. As you drive, you'll see the change in the stone used for the village houses.

A lot of trees

Some 45% of Périgord is under trees, and for Quercy it's about the same. That's quite a bit higher than the French average of 26%. Wood and paper products are still among the most important sectors of the economy.

Throughout the region, you'll find mostly oaks and chestnut. The poor soil makes the oaks

Rock formation inside a cave.

scrubby and twisted, but the chestnuts thrive. You can pick up as many nuts as you like in the autumn; they're smaller than the ones in the market, but sweeter. There's also a lot of hornbeam and plenty of boxwood – encouraged in farming regions since the old days, when it was carved into spoons, loom spindles and toys. Groves of beech survive deep within the forested areas; they're remnants of the beech forests that covered everything at the end of the last ice age.

The forest floors are partly covered with bracken, and in autumn there are ceps and other mushrooms, if you can find them before the locals. On the eastern edges, as you get closer to the Massif Central, the mix includes more pines, Sylvester pines and even larch.

Flora & fauna

We could pack in the tourists if we told them that the departments were covered in wild orchids in May. Truth is they are, though the orchids are so small you have to look hard for them in the meadows. There are dozens of varieties, but the most common are the pink *Orchis pyramidalis* and the lovely *Ophrys apifera*, or bee orchid.

Apart from the wide variety of birds, there are no real surprises in the *dramatis personae* of the woods. They make a good home for red and roe deer, and especially for the shaggy, enormous and long-legged French boar; farmers are always complaining about these, and the *chasse* (hunt) does its best to keep them from taking over completely.

Despite the generally healthy conditions, farmers and hunters are blamed for sharp drops in the population of some species. Otters and peregrine falcons nearly disappeared, but local naturalists say both seem to be making a slow comeback. Now they are worrying about some of the small game, such as quails and partridges.

Vermin, in the heart of *la douce France*, are entirely reasonable; you'll see a few mosquitoes. There are supposed to be vipers here, but we've only heard of one sighting in 20 years.

Rivers

Like the air, the water is good here; the Dordogne and Lot are among the cleanest big rivers in France, and people enjoy a dip from one of the 'beaches' in secluded areas along their banks. Wherever there's a village quay or a good spot behind a weir, you'll find fishermen pulling out pike, pike-perch, shad, trout and smaller fish such as roach.

Some day we may be enjoying Dordogne caviar. The river always had sturgeon, but local folks never cared for the eggs – they would give them to the chickens. The fish almost disappeared, but they are now being reintroduced. There are hatcheries around Montpon-Ménestérol, and a Russian caviar man has recently retired here from the Caspian to show the locals how to do it.

The king of river life, at least in the deeper Lot, is the *silure* (wels catfish), a brute that can reach up to 5 m in length and weigh up to 400 kg. Tell the fishermen of the Lot that you don't believe they exist, and they might bring out photos of the one they caught last year. It was the fishermen who introduced them here from the Danube over a century ago for sport. Now they're a plague (and they taste awful).

As well as fish, the Lot and Dordogne are home to lots of mallards and herons, and an increasing number of imported species. These include swans, American crayfish that are driving the local ones to extinction, muskrats and fat South American coypus, which sometimes get the notion to sit in the middle of the road at three in the morning.

Farming

Agriculture lies lightly on the land here. There is no monoculture and few really large-scale operations of any kind. For a family wine estate, 15,000-20,000 vines is a good number. Some farmers clear big fields for maize (mostly to feed ducks and other animals), sunflowers and colza for oil, or wheat.

The future, though, is going to be about speciality crops, with which small-scale family farms can excel. Walnuts and strawberries abound.

Farm tools.

Farmers raise goats for Cabécou cheese, not just around Rocamadour but almost everywhere. Locally made honey turns up in all the summer farmers markets; that made from the flowers of the *causse* is especially prized. In many places, small farmers are trying to bring back old crops that once thrived here, such as saffron, or tastier but less profitable old varieties of animals such as the native Quercy sheep or the *cul-noir* (black-arse) pig of Périgord.

Causses

The word *causse* can describe any scrubby grey hillside where little grows except gnarled oaks and juniper, but it is commonly used for two big areas east of Cahors: the Causse de Gramat and Causse de Limogne. The *causses* are the empty zones of this book. They offer little or nothing to detain the visitor, and it would be a rare soul indeed who found the landscape romantic or exciting. At any time of the year except the spring, when there are plenty of wild flowers, they can be downright discouraging.

In some parts the *causse* is eerily barren, like the patches around the centre of the Causse de Gramat that the locals call 'deserts' – the sort of place where you'd expect to find a castle owned by a vampire. Here and there you'll see *cloups* (dolines) – little depressions where the rock has broken down and soil has collected. These, along with the river and stream bottoms, were the only parts of the *causses* that could be cultivated; farmers often built little walls around them to keep the sheep out.

Parks that aren't parks

There are no real natural parks or wildlife reserves in the two departments. You will, however, see signs everywhere for the Parc Naturel Régional Périgord-Limousin in Périgord Vert and the Parc Naturel Régional des Causses du Quercy east of Cahors. In fact, these are nothing but offices of the regional government, with small staffs dedicated to promoting tourism and initiating pilot projects related to sustainable development. The practice seems somewhat deceptive, little more than an exercise in public relations to convince the taxpayers they're on the job. What they produce is mostly paper for distribution in tourist offices, but at least you'll find them a source of interesting information on these two out-of-the-way areas.

Festivals & events

Long before any tourists found their way to this part of the world, people concentrated their village festivals in the summer months, when the weather was reliable and you could dance till late. It's still the party season today, and not much serious work gets done from late June to early September, when locals and visitors alike have the luxury of choosing from three or four nearby fêtes every weekend, not to mention festivals of music, theatre and cinema, Mexican bands, truffle markets, and folk dance and music from around the world.

A proper village fête will last the entire weekend and sometimes longer. The flyers that appear under your windscreen wipers on market day, and on the bulletin boards of the tourist offices, will give the full schedule. There might be a big communal dinner, and special events such as fishing or boules contests. A big village will attract some funfair rides and bumper cars, and it will probably manage two separate music nights: a *bal musette* of blazing accordions for the older folks, and a scraggly rock band, mangling the English lyrics of 80s hits, for the younger set. With luck, they'll top it all off with fireworks on Sunday night.

February

Mardi Gras

Shrove Tuesday is celebrated with parades through Périgueux, masses of confetti, music ranging from Lithuanian to sambas to country to the SNCF band, floats with half a ton of bonbons for the children and for you, and a bonfire on the *quais*. Don't forget your costume.

May

Les Floralies (second weekend)

Over 100 exhibitors cover the village of St-Jean-de-Côle in Périgord Vert with flowers and rare plants.

Fête du Vin de Cahors (Saturday near Ascension Day)

This is absolutely one of the best festivals in France. You pay €15 for a souvenir glass, then tour the *caves* of the old river port of Albas, sampling all the wine producers' best (all free) while you eat foie gras sandwiches and listen to music from all over the world. Come early – after dark it's too crowded to move.

Fête de la Fraise (Sunday late in month)

In the berry-growing village of Vergt, south of Périgueux, grown-ups dress up as strawberries to celebrate the marriage of Mademoiselle Fraise, while the world's biggest strawberry tart is baked. A day of folly.

June

Journée National des Moulins (Sunday in mid-month)

On National Windmill Day, every windmill in France is open to visitors.

La Ringueta (Pentecost Monday in even-numbered years)

In Sarlat, this is good fun – a festival of the traditional, nearly forgotten games folks used to play at festivals before there were funfairs: anything from knocking down pins to a barrel-riding rodeo. Everyone can participate, and you might win a goose.

Fête de la Musique (Saturday late in month)

It's barely 20 years old but already this fête is a French institution. Most towns all over the country will have some sort of music going on. Some villages (such as Puy-l'Evêque in the Lot) make a big party of it.

July

La Félibrée (first Sunday)

Founded in the 19th century, this festival in Périgueux promotes the revival of Occitan culture: poetry, song, theatre and traditional costumes, with lots to buy, see and eat too.

Festival des Ploucs (first week)

The 'hick festival' takes place in a different village near Bergerac each year: it's an updated version of the village fête with a touch of irony and lots of comedy and peculiar music.

Public holidays

New Year's Day
Easter Sunday
Easter Monday
1 May (Fête du Travail)
8 May (V-E Day)
Ascension Day (40 days after Easter)
Pentecost (seventh Sunday after Easter)
Pentecost Monday
14 July (Bastille Day)
15 August (Assumption)
1 November (All Saints' Day)
11 November (Armistice Day)
Christmas Day

Chemins de l'Imaginaire (second week)

Avant-garde and occasionally downright strange performances of all kinds happen in and around Terrasson-Lavilledieu's new gardens, the Jardins de l'Imaginaire.

Cahors Blues Festival (mid-month)

Music in the concert halls, and some in the streets, with plenty of talent from the US (cahorsbluesfestival.com).

Les Guitares Vertes (mid-month)

Concerts, cinema and more in Jumilhac; everything to do with the guitar, from flamenco to rock (guitaresvertes.fr).

Festival de l'Insolite (mid-month)

A bit of silliness in Puy-l'Evêque, a bit of music, and lots of Vin de Cahors.

Danses et Musiques du Monde (second half of month)

As the name says, this features music from all over: in 2009 six countries were featured, from Ireland to Chile, in Montignac.

Festival du Jazz (third weekend)

The Lot's biggest jazz event, in Souillac, always has a few big names on the bill (souillacenjazz.net).

Festival du Pays d'Ans

Two weeks of classical music and some surprises (last year, tango) in Hautefort and surrounding villages. The highlights are always the concerts held at the Château de Hautefort.

Africajarc (last week)

A remarkable celebration of music, dance, art, stories and everything else African in the village of Cajarc on the Lot (africajarc.com).

Le Grand Souk

A very switched-on four days of pop, rock, folk, jazz and the undefinable, as well as cinema, in Ribérac.

Festival des Epouvantails (weekend late in month)

Scarecrows (*épouvantails*) suddenly pop up everywhere around the village of Meyrals near St-Cyprien; there's a contest for the best, along with music, dinners and fireworks.

Festival de St-Céré (late July to August)

Two weeks of music: this will probably be your only chance to see an opera in these parts (opera-eclate.com).

L'Eté Musical en Bergerac (late July to August)

Not in Bergerac, but in the bastides around it, this is Aquitaine's biggest music and dance festival. Some concerts are held in the Château de Biron.

August

Itinérance Médiévale en Vallée du Dropt (throughout month)

A big celebration of everything medieval, held in the bastides of Eymet, Issigeac, Cadouin and other locations: music, jousts, banquets, markets and minstrelsy.

Fête de Anglars-Juillac (first week)

A boisterous village fête in Anglars-Juillac that concludes with a confetti battle (they sweep up over a tonne on Tuesday morning)

Mimos: Festival International du Mime (first week)

France's only mime festival; for four days, no place in Périgueux is safe.

Festival Mondial de Folklore (first week)

Folk music and dance in Prayssac from four different countries.

Fêtes de Puy-l'Evêque (first or second weekend)

This big village festival in Puy-l'Evêque features a world-beating fireworks show on Sunday night.

MNOP, Musiques de la Nouvelle-Orleans (second week)

A week of jazz, blues and gospel in Périgueux in honour of the Comte de Roffignac, the local boy who was New Orleans' first mayor (mnop-festival.com).

Festival International Sinfonia en Périgord (late in month)

A week of Baroque music in Périgueux.

L'Autre Festival (late in month)

A weekend in Fonroque, on a farm site near Eymet, that can include just about anything unexpected, from Turkish electro-hiphop to acrobatics workshops (lautrefestival.fr).

Rencontres Cinématographiques (last week)

A rather sophisticated international film festival that thrives in the tiny village of Gindou in the Bouriane (gindoucinema.org).

September

Grain d'Automne (September-October)

Two months of music and theatre in and around Bergerac, very welcome at a time when not much else is happening.

Pilgrimage (8th)

The Black Virgin has been carried in a torchlight procession in Rocamadour during Marian Week for over 800 years.

Journées du Patrimoine (third weekend)

Everywhere in France, this is the day when historic and cultural sights, craft workshops and many other institutions that are normally closed open their doors to the public.

Fête de la Mongolfière (last Sunday)

In Rocamadour, for everyone who likes to take photos of hot-air balloons.

November

Festival de Film (second week)

An impressive list of *avant-premières* is usually sent here to Sarlat from all over the world, even Hollywood (ville-sarlat.fr).

Turkey Festival (11th)

While the rest of France is solemnly commemorating Remembrance Day, the Périgord Vert village of Varaignes parades this year's turkeys through the streets, and then eats last year's.

December

Marché aux Truffes (December to mid-March every Tuesday)

South of Cahors in Lalbenque, this is the most famous of the truffle markets, an only-in-France ritual where baskets worth thousands are presented for the buyers. There are lots of truffle menus in the village restaurants.

Marché aux Truffes.

Sleeping

The classic accommodation in rural France is the *auberge* (inn), or hotel-restaurant. It makes sense to offer both together, just as it did in the Middle Ages, and it's convenient for you: if you find a place to stay in a rural area on the spur of the moment the restaurant in it is likely to be as good as anything else around. Not that there isn't a lot of difference in emphasis. Some places are locally popular, very good restaurants that happen to have a few rooms; others are primarily hotels, and a few might have a somewhat uninspired restaurant meant primarily for their guests.

Beyond these, there's a bit of everything. The towns have some old-line city hotels, and an increasing number of designer chambres d'hôtes (B&Bs), with comparable prices. The latter also appear in villages and in the countryside, and they can be anything from a 17th-century château to a pair of rooms in someone's modest home.

Book ahead: when you're on the road it can be hard to find a place to stay for a night if you haven't. In summer, in the main tourist areas, you don't stand a chance. If you're desperate, most of the tourist offices will lend a hand.

Many people visit the region specifically for a self-catering holiday, and there are thousands of gîtes for them – from simple apartments for two to luxurious historical conversions with all the frills, sleeping a dozen or more.

Prices

In recent years, an avalanche of costly national and EU regulations has led to the closing of many of the old mom-and-pop hotels in small towns and rural areas, and higher rates in the rest. Right now, €50 for a double room in a hotel or chambre d'hôte is the bottom limit, and you'll usually find rooms at this price only in out-of-the-way areas. Count on €60-70 or more. Most places adjust their prices according to season, but only modestly; summer rip-offs are rare. There are few single rooms, and these days they go for nearly the same price as a double.

Usually breakfast is included; if not, the average rate is €7. Many hotels with restaurants offer good value *pension* (full board) or *demi-pension* (half board) packages, even for one night, and nearly all have at least one family room. The recession has made owners more flexible, and outside high season it never hurts to ask for their best offer. With the more expensive establishments, always have a look at their websites: many offer attractive special deals for weekend, mid-week or themed breaks.

All hotel prices depend on where and when you go, whether your room has a view or a balcony, is at the back or front of the hotel, or on its plumbing, or decoration – in some places, and not only at the high end, each room has its own personality and its own price.

Hotels

One of the best things about travelling in this region is the lack of chain hotels. The cities might have one or two, but they're mostly gruesome motels for travelling salesmen, out on some suburban roundabout. In this part of France, almost everything is small scale and family run.

Hotels are still graded from one to five stars according to their amenities, but that's no more than a rough indication. There are several umbrella organizations that guarantee certain standards; two of the best known are the middle-of-the-road Logis de France (generally two to three stars) and the very posh Relais & Châteaux (four or five stars, always connected to fine restaurants). The old one-star hotels, with light timers on the stairways and toilets down the hall, have become rare.

Most hotels have checkout times between 1100 and 1200. Most websites show pictures of the rooms along with prices, so you can generally have an idea of what you're getting.

In summer, hotel-restaurants may have a half-board requirement, though these seem to be increasingly rare. Full or half board will always be on offer though, and it's often a good deal, though you might not get the pick of the menu.

Chambres d'hôtes (B&Bs)

These can be in an elegant townhouse or out on a farm. By law, the establishment will have five rooms at most. Many are part of someone's home, and they'll almost always seem a little cosier and more convivial than hotels; owners often go to great lengths to decorate the rooms with a personal touch. Some B&Bs are owned by good cooks who prepare *table d'hôte* meals; others have mini-spas, or offer courses and tours. Some also have self-catering apartments, or a mix of rooms, suites, apartments and gîtes. Not all take credit cards: be sure to ask when you book.

Self-catering gîtes

The southwest is classic gîte country, and people have been enjoying self-catering holidays here for decades. Apart from camping, this is often the cheapest way to go. There are lots of gîtes everywhere, and the choices are eclectic, from basic cottages to mansions. Almost all have a swimming pool.

Most rentals start on Saturday, and in high season they are available by the week only; however, you can also find weekend or even cheaper weekday deals, often with a minimum stay of two or three days. Many gîtes are run by British families, but don't be put off: these include some of the best, with friendly hosts who can help smooth out any difficulties.

Booking

Especially if you're coming in summer, it's important to book in advance. You can book a wide range of accommodation and holiday packages (hotels, campsites, gîtes, farm holidays, B&Bs) through official regional tourist board websites, such as enjoydordogne.co.uk and dordogne-reservations.com (T05 53 35 50 00). In the Lot, it's tourisme-lot.com.

Generally, however, it's surer and less confusing to book directly through your accommodation's own website. Be sure to print out the confirmation email, and then to re-confirm by email or phone a day or two before you arrive, letting them know your estimated time of arrival. You'll usually be asked to give a credit card number for the first night to hold the booking.

Useful websites

General
frenchentree.com Directories of hotels and self-catering in Aquitaine and Midi-Pyrénées sections.
frenchconnections.co.uk Listings of hotels, B&Bs, gîtes and campsites.
guide-du-perigord.com Good listings for every category, including farm stays.

Self-catering
chateauxcountry.com High-end property.
cheznous.com
clevacances.com
gites-de-france.com
holiday-rentals.co.uk
ownersdirect.co.uk
villanao.co.uk
vfbholidays.co.uk
vrbo.com

Farm stays
accueil-paysan.com
bienvenue-a-la-ferme.com

B&Bs
chambresdhotes.org
fleursdesoleil.fr

Camping & mobile homes
campingfrance.com
eurocamp.co.uk
keycamp.co.uk

Eating & drinking

> Gastronomy ... ranks with the other arts as a means of discovery of a nation's culture. The stomach absorbs culture as much as the mind or the eye.
>
> *Sanche de Gramont, The French (1969)*

Sanche de Gramont would be the first to agree that his observation applies not only to nations, but to regions. So what does their rich, earthy cooking say about Périgord and Quercy? That's a good point of departure for a conversation that can last through a five-course meal and beyond, but to start, no one would deny that what's put on your plate here is a cuisine of utter sincerity.

There's no foam or test tubes, no *cuisine bourgeoise* with lots of curlicues. There is nothing Grandmère wouldn't have approved. You'll learn soon enough that food here is the essence of local patriotism. Since the Middle Ages the region hasn't had much in terms of art and literature. But the intelligence and care of its farmers has made it a rich garden where all the produce is first-rate, so it's only natural that food should be a big part of the cultural identity. It's a democratic cuisine too. The duck that the truckers eat in a *routier* differs only in a degree of art from the one you get in the real-linen *restaurant gastronomique*.

A lot of people find southwestern cooking in general unfashionably heavy. It's true, and unapologetically so; this is food for people who work for a living. Despite its formidable solidity, this cuisine is winning new fans all the time. By now everyone knows about the 'French paradox': with a diet based on duck fat, garlic and red wine, southwesterners have a rate of heart disease half that of Americans, and many of them live into their nineties.

The cult of the duck

According to ancient histories, the *canard gras* first appeared in Egypt, and the inventor of *gavage* (stuffing) was none other than Imhotep, who also built the first pyramid. The fatted duck was known to the Greeks and Romans, and was a delicacy for the medieval Venetians.

Ducks grow up fast. For 10-14 weeks they wander around the farmyard, and after that they get three to four weeks of *gavage* – corn mash pumped down their beaks twice a day (animal rights campaigners who deplore the practice have probably never seen the ducks at feeding time, crowding around to make sure they get their share). After that, the duck (or goose) is ready to become a whole constellation of delicious things:

Foie gras The enlarged liver is the great delicacy of the southwest, usually served *mi-cuit* (half cooked) as a starter on little toasts, perhaps with white grapes, and a sweet white wine (Monbazillac is perfect). The liver and other parts are also made into France's best pâtés.

Magret The duck's breast, grilled for 10

Tourin.

minutes on the fatty side and just a couple on the other, is more like a steak than a bird; a little sauce with cream or mushrooms or cherries perfects it. Dried or smoked, the magret becomes heavenly charcuterie, often used in salads.

Confit The thigh of the bird is slowcooked in its own fat and preserved in a jar or tin. Just warm it up; the taste is unlike anything else. Another part of the bird subjected to the confit treatment is the *gésier* (gizzard), which is a favourite in salads.

Graisse The fat (especially from the goose, which has lots more of it) finds plenty of uses in southwestern cooking, especially for frying the potatoes that are the inevitable accompaniment to the magret or confit (see page 156).

Not much goes to waste. The *demoiselles* (carcasses) are a country delicacy too, as is *cou d'oie* (goose neck), with a stuffing of pork and foie gras.

Starters & main courses

For starters, almost every restaurant offers foie gras in some form; beyond that, dishes with smoked or marinated salmon, millefeuille tarts, coquilles St-Jacques and salads with a bit of duck are popular. In *ferme-auberges* (farm restaurants), you'll always get the traditional soup, *tourin*, which is made with an alarming amount of garlic and poured over bread. It's fantastic. At the end you're expected to *faire chabrot*: pour a bit of wine into the last of the soup and guzzle it from the bowl. If you neglect to do this in a country restaurant people will think you are Parisian, or worse.

For the main course, it's not all duck, but the other choices will usually also be meat and potatoes. *Agneau de Quercy* (lamb from the *causses* of the Lot) is justifiably famous. Chicken breasts, cooked in a tart or rolled with a stuffing to make a ballotine, are popular, though in fine restaurants you're less likely to see chicken at all than its tastier cousin the *pintade* (guinea fowl). Steaks will be there when you need a break from duck, often appearing on menus as a *tournedos* or a *pièce du boucher* or just a *pièce*, and often with a sauce involving *cèpes* or shallots. Game dishes are popular too, and many restaurants serve venison, pheasant, hare and especially stewed *marcassin* (young wild boar).

You may miss your seafood, though the markets are full of it and most restaurants will have some seafood choices. *Sandre* (zander or pike-perch) from the rivers is an excellent fish. Salmon and trout are often served, along with *brochet* (pike) and *écrevisses* (crayfish).

Black diamonds

The most famous culinary treat from this part of the world is mostly conspicuous, alas, by its absence. A little mystery still hangs over everything to do with the truffle. Once France produced over 1000 tonnes a year; now it's less than 40. Recipes in 1920s cookbooks might begin 'Slice a pound of truffles'; now we're privileged to have a smidgen grated into an omelette. No one knows for sure where the truffles went; it's possible that the big avalanche of them that washed over France a century ago was just a once-in-a-millennium thing. Today almost 90% are cultured. You can see the restaurateurs buying them at the winter truffle markets in villages like Lalbenque, south of Cahors, or Ste-Alvère, south of Périgueux. Buying a basket yourself might be a stretch (they go for up to €750 a kilo), but you can buy oak saplings impregnated with truffle spores if you want to try and grow your own.

Aperitif drink with saffron.

Cheese & dessert

People either love them or hate them, but the tidy little discs of goat cheese called Cabécou are an essential part of the southwest experience. Delicate and not too goaty, they are made everywhere, and those from around Rocamadour have AOC (*appellation d'origine contrôlée*) status, like fine wines. Another one that has been around for a long time but only now seems to be getting its hour in the spotlight is Trappe d'Echourgnac, a wonderful, nutty cheese made by nuns in the Forêt de la Double, west of Périgueux.

Local products find their way into most of the favourite desserts here. A lot of the Dordogne Valley's trillions of walnuts end up in walnut cakes and tarts. Fruits and berries – strawberries and raspberries especially – pour into local markets in abundance; along with peaches and apples, and plums from the neighbouring Lot-et-Garonne, they are made into *clafoutis*, *flognardes* (batter puddings) and crumbles. The iconic dessert, though, is the *pastis* or *tourtière*, a kind of pie made with ultra-thin pastry and flavoured with Armagnac; some are plain, some contain sliced apples or plums.

Wines & spirits

Bergerac may be one of the major wine centres of France, but stuck as it is in the shadow of its more celebrated neighbour Bordeaux, it rarely gets the attention it deserves. Some Bergerac wines – red, white and the increasingly popular rosé – are exceptional; some are just average. There are a few interesting smaller AOC denominations within the Bergerac area, most notably Pécharmant, a powerful red with lots of character, and the aristocratic white from Monbazillac.

In the Lot, it's Vin de Cahors, strong and tannic, a wine that seems made for a big duck dinner. Less known, and a little lighter and fruitier, is Côteaux du Quercy, from the *causses* south of Cahors.

Caught between Cognac to the north and Armagnac to the south, this corner of the southwest has a modest tradition of its own in spirits. The plum *eau de vie* called Vieille Prune can be quite distinguished (and correspondingly expensive); a drop of this goes down fine with your after-dinner coffee. Another is walnut liqueur, Eau de Noix. Don't drink it straight: mix a few drops with four parts Cahors wine and one part cassis to make the classic aperitif, the Fénelon. The favourite aperitif is a Kir, just a little crème de cassis in white wine (it became popular during the war, when the Germans took all the red wine); a Kir Royale uses champagne. When you get in good with the locals, people will start giving you bottles of sinister and fruity homemade ratafia, which can be made with almonds or cherry stones or just about anything.

Practical information

Eating here is a rite, and you can't escape it. The first rule is that the entire French nation and its guests sit down to eat together, at the same time. Once you get used to this, you can't imagine living any other way; it makes for a sense of community, and provides a long, civilized break in the middle of the day. But if you're travelling it can be inconvenient. Don't arrive too late: mealtimes are 1200-1300 and 2000-2100, so plan your day around them. Even in cities, restaurants that serve continuously are rare, and there are very few chances of snacks in cafés.

The secret to dining without going broke is to have your main meal in the middle of the day, as the locals do, so you can take advantage of less-expensive lunch menus, *plats du jour* and *formules*. Even most of the great gastronomic temples offer these. If you're not particular about wine, ordering a *pichet* (flagon) or bottle of the house wine, where available, can make all the difference to your bill. You can assume service is included unless the menu says otherwise.

Vegetarians beware

A few years ago, we were talking with the proprietor of one of the region's top restaurants and asked what she could do for vegetarians. "Not a problem," she replied cheerfully, "I'll just cook them some vegetables!" After some further attempts, we realized we were having an insurmountable failure to communicate.

In a part of France where even the salads are full of smoked duck breast or gizzards, a vegetarian is going to have a hard row to hoe. Keeps the riffraff out, many locals think, but slowly, glacially, things may be changing. There's a vegetarian restaurant. One. (It's in Cahors.) A few high-end establishments have come up with vegetarian menus, though purists may be dismayed to find these are usually full of fish. The purists should rent a gîte with a kitchen and hit the markets; in these, and even in the supermarkets, you can get enough good stuff to make whatever you like.

The Marché Gourmand

Also known as a *marché de nuit*, or a *marché nocturne*, this brilliant idea has been sweeping France in recent years, and these farming regions put on some of the best. Basically, a village will put out tables and chairs in the evening, and perhaps provide entertainment. Local people set up stalls with food to sell: wine, salads, soup, grilled meats, patisserie and everything else. Buy what you like (bring tableware, plates and cups if you don't like plastic), and then sit down for a deluxe picnic. You can usually cobble together a whole dinner for less than €10 a head. They're popular, so come early to make sure you get a table.

Menu reader

General
aigre-doux sweet and sour
à la jardinière with garden vegetables
à point medium-rare (steak)
au feu de bois cooked over a wood fire
au four baked
beignets fritters
bien cuit well done (steak)
bleu very rare (steak)
brochette on a spit
chaud hot
cru raw
cuit cooked
émincé thinly sliced
en croûte in a pastry crust
en papillote baked in parchment (or foil)
epicé spicy
farci stuffed
feuilleté puff pastry
fort strong
fourré stuffed
frais, fraîche fresh
frit fried
froid cold
fumé smoked
galette flaky pastry case or pancake
garni with vegetables
(au) gratin topped with breadcrumbs and grilled
haché minced
médaillon round piece
mousse foam
pané breaded
paupiette rolled thin slices
pavé slab
piquant spicy hot
saignant rare (steak)
salé salted, spicy
sucré sweet
tranche slice
vapeur steamed
velouté thick smooth sauce or soup

Drinks (boissons)
apéritif pre-dinner drink
bière/pression beer/draught beer
bouteille bottle
café coffee
café crème coffee with hot milk
eau naturel/gazeuse still/sparkling water
jus de fruit fruit juice
thé tea
tisane herbal tea
verre glass
vin blanc/rosé/rouge white/rosé/red wine

Fruit (fruits) & vegetables (légumes)
abricot apricot
ananas pineapple
artichaut artichoke
asperges asparagus
aubergine aubergine
avocat avocado
banane banana
betterave beetroot
blette chard
cassis blackcurrant
céleri (-rave) celery (celeriac)
cèpes boletus mushrooms
cerise cherry
champignons mushrooms
chanterelles wild yellow mushrooms
chou cabbage
choufleur cauliflower
ciboulette chives
citron lemon
citron vert lime
citrouille pumpkin
coco (noix de) coconut
concombre cucumber
cornichons gherkins
courgettes courgettes
cresson watercress
échalote shallot
endive chicory
épinards spinach
fenouil fennel
fèves broad beans
fraises (des bois) strawberries (wild)
framboises raspberries
groseilles redcurrants
haricots beans
haricot verts green (French) beans
laitue lettuce
lentilles lentils
maïs (épis de) sweetcorn (on the cob)
mangue mango
morilles morel mushrooms
mûre (sauvage) mulberry, blackberry

myrtilles bilberries
navet turnip
oignon onion
pamplemousse grapefruit
pastèque watermelon
pêche peach
petits pois peas
poire pear
poireaux leeks
pois chiches chickpeas
poivron sweet pepper
pomme apple
pomme de terre potato
potiron pumpkin
prune/pruneau plum/prune
radis radishes
raisins (secs) grapes (raisins)
reine-claude greengage plums
roquette rocket

Meat (viande)
agneau lamb
aiguillette thin part of a duck breast
ailerons wings
biftek beefsteak
blanc breast or white meat
bœuf beef
boudin blanc/noir sausage of white meat/ black pudding
caille quail
canard, caneton duck, duckling
capre kid
cassoulet beans baked with sausage and duck
cervelle brains
chair flesh, meat
chapon capon
charcuterie mixed cold meats, salami, etc
cheval horsemeat
civet meat (usually game) stewed in wine and blood sauce
cœur heart
confit meat cooked and preserved in its own fat
côte, côtelette chop, cutlet
cuisse thigh or leg
dinde, dindon turkey
entrecôte ribsteak
épaule shoulder
faux-filet sirloin
foie liver
gésier gizzard
gibier game
gigot leg of lamb
graisse/gras fat
grillade grilled meat
jambon ham
jarret knuckle
lapin rabbit
lardons diced bacon
lièvre hare
magret breast of duck
marcassin young boar
noix de veau (agneau) topside of veal (lamb)
oie goose
os bone
petit salé salt pork
pièce (de boucher) steak
pieds trotters
pintade guinea fowl
porc pork
pot au feu meat and vegetables cooked in stock
poulet chicken
poussin young chicken
queue de bœuf oxtail
ris (de veau) sweetbreads (veal)
rognons kidneys

rôti roast
sanglier wild boar
saucisse sausage
saucisson dry sausage
selle (d'agneau) saddle (of lamb)
tournedos thick round slices of beef fillet
travers de porc spare ribs
veau veal
venaison venison

Fish, seafood & shellfish (poissons, fruits de mer & coquillages)
anchois anchovies
anguille eel
bar sea bass
barbue brill
brandade salt cod with mashed potates and olive oil
bulot whelk
cabillaud cod
calmar squid
colin hake
congre conger eel
coques cockles
coquillages shellfish
coquilles St-Jacques scallops
crabe crab
crevettes prawns
darne transverse slice of fish
daurade sea bream
écrevisse crayfish
espadon swordfish
flétan halibut
gambas giant prawns
homard Atlantic lobster
huîtres oysters
langouste spiny lobster
langoustines Dublin Bay prawns
limande lemon sole
lotte monkfish
loup sea bass
merlan whiting
morue salt cod
moules mussels
palourdes clams
poulpe octopus
praires small clams
raie skate
rascasse scorpion fish
rouget red mullet
St-Pierre John Dory
sar silver bream
saumon salmon
seiche cuttlefish
telline tiny clam
thon tuna
truite trout

Desserts
bavarois mousse or custard in a mould
chantilly sweet whipped cream
charlotte sponge fingers and custard cream dessert
clafoutis batter fruit cake
coulis thick fruit sauce
coupe ice cream: a scoop or in a cup
crème anglaise custard
crème caramel custard with caramel sauce
gâteau cake
glace ice cream
parfait frozen mousse
profiteroles choux pastry balls, often filled with chocolate or ice cream
sablé shortbread
savarin a filled yeast cake, shaped like a ring

Other
addition bill
ail garlic
aïoli garlic mayonnaise
amandes almonds
amuse-gueule appetizer
aneth dill

beurre butter
bouquet garni mixed herbs
brebis (fromage de) sheep's cheese
cacahouètes peanuts
cannelle cinnamon
chèvre goat's cheese
crème fraîche light sour cream
confiture jam
crudités raw vegetable platter
escargots snails
frites chips
fromage cheese
genièvre juniper
gingembre ginger
huile (d'olive) oil (olive)
lait milk
marrons chestnuts
menthe mint
miel honey
moutarde mustard
noisette hazelnut
noix walnut
nouilles noodles
œufs eggs
oseille sorrel
pain bread
pâte pastry, crust
pâtes pasta
persil parsley
pignons pinenuts
piment chilli
poivre pepper
potage thick vegetable soup
riz rice
sarrasin buckwheat
sel salt
sucre sugar
truffes truffles
vinaigre vinegar
yaourt yoghurt

Useful phrases
I'd like to reserve a table *Je voudrais réserver une table*
For two people at 8pm *Pour deux personnes, à vingt heures*
What do you recommend? *Qu'est-ce que vous me conseillez?*
I'd like the set menu please *Je vais prendre le menu / la formule s'il vous plait*
Does it come with salad? *Est-ce que c'est servi avec de la salade?*
I'd like something to drink *Je voudrais quelque chose à boire*
I'm a vegetarian *Je suis végétarien / végétarienne*
I don't eat… *Je ne mange pas de…*
Where are the toilets? *Où sont les toilettes?*
The bill, please *L'addition, s'il vous plait*

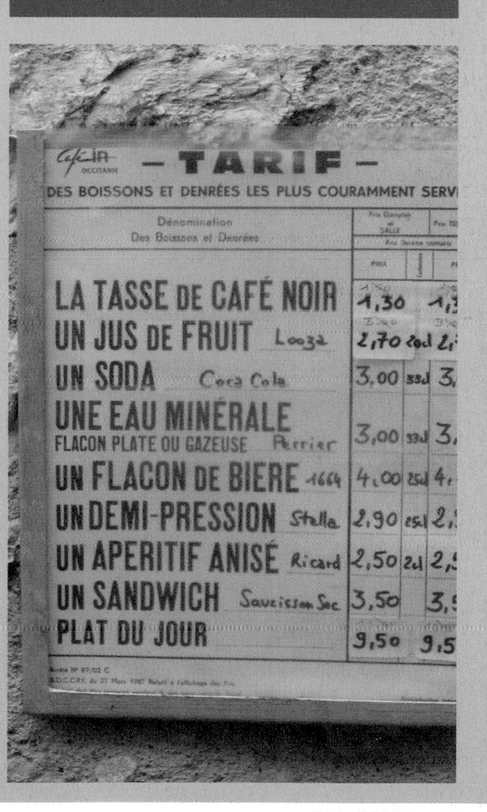

Entertainment

Keep in mind that it's *rural* here; for most people 'entertainment' means lotto night, and the chance of winning half a sheep. What entertainment there is, like everything else, is largely dependent on tourism. So residents and visitors alike have grown accustomed to a feast-or-famine schedule of events. From about mid-June to mid-September life is a permanent party; the rest of the year it's just work.

Bars & clubs

Don't expect many of these; Périgueux and Bergerac are the two places you're most likely to find somewhere to go after dark. A night out will usually mean a polite bar with some music, though there are some surprises, like genuine music hall entertainments in Bergerac and dinner theatre in Périgueux. Many bars have an occasional music night, especially in summer, but they aren't always good at advertising them; the tourist offices usually know what's on.

Even in some of the larger villages, there are discos designed primarily for teenagers. You can drop yours off in the knowledge that nothing too scary is likely to happen to them.

Fêtes & festivals

In summer, especially in the intense months of July and August, village fêtes provide all the fun anyone needs. The event is not necessarily proportional to the size of the village; some places take great pride in putting on a good show for their neighbours and the visitors.

Beyond these, music is everywhere: blues in Cahors, jazz in Souillac, Baroque music in Périgueux, traditional dance in Montignac, guitars at the Château de Jumilhac. Some of the performances are first-rate. With all the people who come down in summer, there are opportunities for some big-city sophistication in the meadows, as at Gindou in the Lot, where a village of 323 people puts on an international film festival.

Children

The crumbsnatchers, at least, will always have something to do. Many of the cultural sights, such as Castelnaud with its medieval weaponry, and the gardens of Marqueyssac, offer special activities for kids. Quercyland, the water park and funfair near Souillac, is just one of several such facilities in the region. If they're five or older (three in some places), they can try the popular new sport of swinging from the trees at a *parc aventure* (see page 180). By all means take the kids to Rocamadour, where they can meet the birds at the Rocher des Aigles and the monkeys at the Forêt des Singes, among the many other attractions.

The best show in the Lot

He's elusive, but if you can find him don't miss it; Tony Bram's (the French think adding a gratuitous apostrophe to anything is way cool) is a fine trumpeter who runs a French version of a Vegas stage show, with elaborate sets, video and lighting, tons of dry ice and sequins, and a score of musicians, singers and dancers who change costumes so fast you'll think there are 100 of them. At least once each summer he'll bring his tour back home to the Lot, popping up with little warning somewhere in a village square (maybe Luzech or Gigouzac) or a cow field. The professionalism and energy are utterly amazing, and once the themed show is over (2009's was dedicated to Marilyn Monroe) they play dance music all night long. Check out the site: tony-brams.com. Tony also sells used pool tables.

Jazz at Château de Marqueyssac.

Shopping

What shopping?

Maybe the tourist offices could make it a selling point in these cost-conscious times. Down in the southwest, you can usually just keep your hand in your pocket.

Don't expect a lot of designer labels. The region hasn't any big cities at all, and opportunities for retail therapy are severely limited. Frankly, a lot of people down here get their clothes at the seed-and-feed store, or in the supermarket. There are exceptions, of course. French women still prefer to buy their fancy duds at small shops, not big chain outlets or department stores, and you will find some rather smart articles even in village shops. Prices, unfortunately, will usually be more than what you'd pay at home.

Occasionally you'll come across a village with a modest collection of sophisticated boutiques; they look a little out of place, and you wonder how they get by. Monpazier is one of these; another is Aubeterre-sur-Dronne on the Dordogne's eastern border. They make their living mostly from the tourist trade in summer.

Antiques, junk and everything in between are a thriving business here. Tourist offices have lists of all the antique dealers in the area, most of which occupy barns out in the country. In summer there will be a show somewhere nearby every weekend; learn the difference between a *brocante* (real antiques) and a *vide-grenier* (literally 'empty-the-attic' – a boot sale).

Food

What visitors mostly buy is food. So many of the delights of Périgourdine and Lotoise cuisine are eminently portable; when you take home some *confits de canard* to cook at home no one will believe they came out of a tin. A town of any size will have at least one temple of gastronomy; those little tins of foie gras, rillettes and pâtés, confits and such are all good, not to mention the walnut oil, wines and liqueurs.

Wine estates almost always have some sort of cartons to pack up bottles for you, and those that sell wine *en vrac* (in bulk) will supply you with an 11- or 22-litre container (known as a *cubi*) so you can carry home a good stock at a bargain price. Many people buy it this way and bottle it themselves.

Artists & artisans

In summer, you would think that half the potters and glass blowers in the world had set up shop in the region. Artists and craftspeople from all over France and beyond live here because they like it, and they find a summer market for their creations that keeps them alive. The beautiful things they make will be your best option for a memorable souvenir or gift. Along with art galleries, they tend to congregate around the tourist sights, with small shops that generally open in season only. In some big towns, such as Montignac and Bergerac, or at

some tourist sights (Cadouin, St-Jean-de-Côle) you'll find a co-op or commission shop with a wide range, where clothing, jewellery, paintings, sculptures, ceramics and everything else is on display.

Markets

If you're staying in a gîte for a week or more, you'll be hitting the village markets to give the restaurants (and your wallet) the odd night off. The produce and selection are great, and prices are comparable with the supermarkets; some items will be much cheaper, some much more expensive, and as has been true in this fallen world since the beginning of time, you'll have to keep an eye on the fishmongers. There is usually a choice of ready-made delicacies to take home for lunch: roast chickens and quails, paella, Alsatian *choucroute* (sauerkraut and meats) and Vietnamese *nems* are always popular. The markets aren't just about food; in summer, especially, you can expect to find some local artists and artisans, African peddlers, clothes stands, garden supplies and more.

Beyond simple matters of provisioning, the market is the event of the week in a village, and everyone who isn't working will come out for the sights and smells and colours, and to meet friends. See the listings for the best village markets. Each takes place on a fixed day, which probably hasn't changed since the Middle Ages, when the village got the original royal charter to hold it. Almost all are held in the mornings only, and many vendors start packing up hurriedly at noon. Big markets have everything you could dream of and more: the Saturday morning market in Cahors has won prizes as the best in France (Jamie Oliver just popped up there, filming a new show).

In summer, scores of villages hold special farmers markets on a different day. These are generally small, but most of the stalls will feature home-grown produce. Towns and some villages also have a *foire foraine* once a month, usually coinciding with the regular market day; this is an extra-large market selling lots of bargain clothes and household goods – everything from cooking pots to cowbells.

Activities & tours

There's little here to encourage the more extreme sports; no mountains to climb or slopes to ski, but you will find any number of gentler reasons to get out in the green countryside. A lot of people head straight for the water; the most popular pastime is paddling a canoe.

Canoes & kayaks

Large firms and small start bringing their boats out of the sheds in May, or even at the Easter break if the weather permits. With most of these, you can just paddle about or go on an excursion: the owner will drive you to a spot upstream so you can let the current help you get home, on trips lasting from an hour to a whole day or more, along the most scenic parts of the Dordogne, Lot and Vézère. Many of the larger firms that rent canoes are really all-purpose activity centres, and they can arrange outings involving spelunking, rock-climbing, canyoning or other sports.

The Lot is the deepest of the rivers, and right now it is on the eve of a big Renaissance in river touring. For years, the department's Conseil Général has been working to restore old locks and add new ones; they aren't quite finished yet, but eventually the entire length will be open, and already new facilities are appearing. You can rent cruise boats and even houseboats at Douelle and around St-Cirq-Lapopie.

Cycling

Both departments are making an effort to make the roads bike-friendly, especially in the river valleys where there is some flat land. The three big valleys – Dordogne, Lot and Vézère – can be packed with bikes (mostly Dutch!) on summer weekends.

Look for green-and-white signs indicating bike routes, and the new green chequerboards that mark them at crossings and roundabouts. Many of the same firms that rent canoes and kayaks also offer bicycles, mostly mountain bikes. Otherwise

Cycling near Cathédrale St-Front.

it's a case of hiring from small village shops: ask at the tourist offices. Most people bring their own; it's worth remembering that most SNCF trains still take bikes.

Sport

Golfers coming to the Dordogne need to plan ahead. Despite the number of Brits in the area, the sport has been slow to catch on. There are good 18-hole courses at Souillac, Siorac-en-Périgord and Périgueux, and two lavish golf resort-hotels built around châteaux near Bergerac.

A village of any size should have some tennis courts. If there is no one present the key will usually be at the tourist office or the Mairie; in summer you may have to book in advance. The village may also have a swimming pool; these become very crowded with other peoples' children in summer, and they'll be a good place to drop off yours. Even better than the pool is the *plan d'eau*, a small lake for swimming. Some of these have cafés, and some even have lifeguards. In summer they often host special dinners or entertainments.

More exotic sports are not entirely lacking. Young folk (and older ones, if you're game) can swing around the trees at a *parc aventure* (see page 180), and there are hang-gliding schools at Douelle, in the Lot Valley, and Floirac, near Martel.

As for spectator sports, winter and spring are rugby season, and the village matches can have a lot of atmosphere. Horse racing has its fans too, and some villages such as Villeréal (Lot-et-Garonne) and St-Cyprien on the Dordogne put on a summer schedule of straight and harness races.

Alternative excursions

There are a few ways of getting around we haven't mentioned yet. In some places, gentlemen equipped with a horse and a light carriage called a *calèche* are available to take you for rides in the country. On the Dordogne, at Beynac, La Roque-Gageac and Bergerac, you can go for a pleasant hour's cruise in a *gabarre*, a recreated version of the old-time barges that once carried the river trade.

Train buffs never sleep, and though the old Quercyrail east of Cahors may be temporarily closed while they look for money to fix the track, the Train du Haut Quercy has old steam and diesel trains rolling again for summer trips at Martel (see page 223). The SNCF operates the Autorail Espérance for wine-oriented tours up the Dordogne Valley.

One means of transport that is definitely making a comeback is that great French invention, the *montgolfière* (hot-air balloon). There are firms waiting to take you up, up and away in the Dordogne Valley around Beynac and Domme, over the Château de Hautefort, and in the Lot at Montcuq, usually for about €200 per person.

And for something completely different, you can wander around the hills of the eastern Lot accompanied by a donkey (hikingwithdonkey.com).

Cultural & gastronomic activities

When you want to learn a little more about the sights that interest you, the local tourist offices are the places to start. Many of them offer interesting tours, which are inexpensive or even free. There are night tours, tours with experts on local history and culture, and some that take you into places not normally open to visitors. Périgueux's tourist office is especially creative in this respect.

In both departments, cookery and wine appreciation classes are very popular, and are offered by some specialist firms as well as many local operators of gîtes and hotels (there are long lists of these at dordogne.angloinfo.com). In addition you'll find painting and other art workshops, courses on medicinal plants or how to make Stone Age tools in the old haunts of Cro-Magnon man, or any number of other subjects. Farm visits are popular, where you can learn about ducks or sheep and help out with the chores. A lot of these activities in the Dordogne can be arranged through a firm called **Peritrek** (T05 53 31 17 62, peritrek.com).

Walking in Dordogne & Lot

Everyone here likes to walk. The country lanes can get busy on Sunday afternoons when people go out for their postprandial promenades. And plenty of summer visitors enjoy hiking the Grandes Randonnées (long-distance footpaths), such as the famous cross-France GR36 that passes along the hills over both the Lot and Dordogne, or the GR64 that runs from Rocamadour to Les Eyzies.

The Grandes Randonnées are wonderful, but there are other ways of walking than just following a path to a destination. Exploring the countryside can be a truly rewarding way of really getting to know the culture, people and history of a place.

The two most renowned French historians of our time, Fernand Braudel and Emmanuel Le Roy Ladurie, spent much of their careers working out the concept of 'microhistory' – seeing how the little things of everyday life sometimes explain just as much about the past as the macrohistory of memorable dates, great men and battles. That's an idea that suits this modest corner of France just fine. People here can be passionate about the minutiae of their traditional life. If you're lucky, and if you can understand him, just when you've come upon something really puzzling in the woods some old gentleman with a beret and walking stick might come along and explain it all to you.

The first thing you'll need, for a place that catches your fancy, is the relevant IGN 1:25000 scale Série Bleue map, which you can get at almost any newsstand or bookshop. The map in itself has a lot to say; it contains enough detail to make something of rural life come alive, in the pattern of cleared fields around villages and hamlets that may not have changed much for centuries.

And it shows all the good places to go for a hike. In much of this area, inhabited for so many millennia, it's hard to poke around in the woods for 10 minutes without running into something interesting. Look for forested spots among the hills where there's a lot of level ground, preferably far from a paved road. These neglected corners are the best bets for finding ruins, Neolithic monuments, tombs or the mysterious stone constructions of all kinds that turn up everywhere.

Occasionally the map can give you clues to a place's history. A village that has roadside crosses on all the routes leading into it may have been a *sauveterre*, where the Church had the power to ban feudal warfare in the Middle Ages; the crosses (replacing older ones) marked the sanctuary's limits. Learning some key words in Occitan can help. When you see the common place name Peyrelevade ('lifted stone'), for example, you'll know there was a dolmen around somewhere, though it might be gone now.

Like anything worthwhile, it takes time. Getting acquainted with the deepest secrets of an ancient land can't be done overnight. It takes some reading too (if you read French, the series of books on the departments of France called the *Encyclopédie Bonneton* makes a perfect introduction). Even if you're only staying for a week or two, you might as well get started – because nobody comes down here just once.

Exterior furniture

To the French, these structures are the *petit patrimoine*, just as important to the landscape as churches and castles. To start learning the countryside, get to know these common features:

Croix de chemin A roadside cross: some of these replaced menhirs from the Neolithic era; some showed the limits of someone's authority in medieval times. They are everywhere, especially in Quercy.

Gariotte This, in a way, is the real symbol of the region: a circular, dry stone hut with a corbelled dome, built as a shelter for hunters and shepherds. There are thousands of these hobbit-houses about; in some corners they're called *bories*, *cazelles* or any number of other names. They come in handy when it rains on your picnic.

Lavoir A wash-house with a tiled roof on the edge of a village. No peasant women have come down to do their laundry in them for 30 years, but they are scrupulously maintained. You never know.

Mai Following an ancient Périgord custom, a tall cut sapling, decorated and garlanded with the national colours, is installed in front of a house to celebrate a victorious candidate or a newborn, newlyweds, or maybe a successful rugby side.

Moulin à vent The region used to have hundreds of windmills; now only the cylindrical towers remain. Some working models can be seen south of Cahors.

Pigeonnier Often grandiose half-timbered or stone buildings (see page 245), these local landmarks recall a day when pigeon poo meant serious money.

Travail de bestiaux An odd wooden frame in the middle of a village, with odder bits of mechanism attached, was once used for shoeing livestock. Like the *lavoirs*, they're ready to use if they're ever needed.

Croix de chemin.

Périgord Blanc et Pourpre

Doorway in Périgueux.

Contents

Introduction

Périgord Blanc (like Quercy Blanc, southwest of Cahors) gets its name from the white, slightly chalky-looking local stone. You won't see a lot of it under the carpet of fields and forests that covers the area, but this is the stone that glistens so attractively in the rain in Périgueux, Périgord's capital.

Périgueux is very much the main attraction, a thriving city big enough to be full of interest yet small enough to be intimate and fun. It has a wealth of history and not one but two old centres, one medieval and the other Roman. The rest of White Périgord is good, honest farming country without much to detain visitors, but further south there's a pleasant stretch of the Dordogne Valley, and beyond that lie the surprisingly charming medieval planned towns known as 'bastides'.

It wasn't a tourist board or a committee of businessmen that decided to divide Périgord into Green, White and Black, but a custom that grew up over centuries. Unfortunately, like a careless child, Périgord neglected to colour in one small corner. That corner was Bergerac, with its vine-covered hinterlands, so it was only natural to call that Périgord Pourpre – Purple Périgord.

Périgueux rooftops.

What to see in...

...one day
It would take a whole day at least to do **Périgueux** justice. To fans of history the **Gallo-Roman Museum**, the **Vesunna Tower** and the other sights in the Cité may be a revelation. Save some time for a visit to **St-Front** and a tour around the little squares and museums of the centre.

...a weekend or more
After a day in the big city, you can relax by the river in the truly laid-back stretch of the Dordogne around **Limeuil** and **Trémolat**. Take out a canoe or go for a swim. After that, head to **Monbazillac** to visit a château and have a glass of wine. Then a tour of the bastides is in order – **Eymet**, **Villereal** and **Montpazier** – finishing up at the wonderful **Château de Biron**.

Périgueux

In French, someone from Périgueux is called a Pétrocorien, a reminder of the Celtic Petrocorii who built a settlement here around the sacred spring Vesunna; when the Romans took over they founded a new city of that name on the opposite bank of the River Isle.

If you're the type who needs a little urban buzz in your life from time to time, Périgueux, the Dordogne's capital, is the only place in this book where you're going to find it. Just don't expect Broadway; even when you include the suburbs, the population is only 65,000. But its jealously preserved historic core is attractive and alive: rather intense in the daytime and pleasant for a stroll and a drink in the evening. Périgueux also has a lot to show from over 2000 years of history, including the most Roman remains of any place in southwest France.

Périgueux cathedral.

Puy St-Front

Today, while the old Roman Cité has become a quiet residential area, 'le Puy' is the lively heart of the city. Gathered around the tremendous cathedral, the restored buildings of the city centre glisten anew, and its convivial little squares are full of café and restaurant tables in the warm months.

Cathédrale St-Front

Place de la Clautre.
Daily 0900-1200 and 1430-1900, closed during Mass.
Map: Périgueux D3, p84.

This rambling, slightly sooty hulk, looming up from the river to dominate the centre of Périgueux, has an air of strangeness and immense antiquity. Périgueux's cathedral gets written up in every history of architecture, partly for the medieval building itself and partly because it was the victim of a sensational crime – history's strangest case of architectural assassination.

St Front, who seems to have been Egyptian, was sent here by St Peter himself and became Vesunna's first bishop. In the sixth century, a church was built to house his relics. The current church, probably begun between 1100 and 1150, was one of the biggest in southwest France. Though the five-domed plan is most likely a copy of St Mark's in Venice, the rest of the architecture is solid, stocky western Romanesque.

Besides being a major stop on the pilgrims' route to Compostela, the church was a pilgrimage destination in its own right, thanks to the wonders worked by St Front, who had chased out demons and cured lepers by the thousand. The cathedral's downfall began with a sacking by Protestants in 1575, in which the saint's tomb was destroyed and his bones scattered. It was left to moulder for centuries, but the real damage would come with its restoration.

Paul Abadie, a collaborator and eventual rival of Viollet-le-Duc, got the job of restoring the cathedral

Essentials

Getting around Périgueux is small enough to reach all the sights on foot. The big boulevards encircling the medieval centre – cours Fénelon, cours Montaigne and allée de Tourny – mark the course of the old walls, and when the city demolished them it laid out plenty of gardens. These are now largely car parks, unfortunately, but they make parking relatively easy.

Taxis The main taxi stand is in place Bugeaud. You can ring there for a cab (T05 53 53 27 00), or try **Allo Taxi** (T05 53 09 09 09).

Trains The SNCF station (train information T36 35) is 1 km west of the centre on rue Denis Papin. For details of regional train services see page 278.

Buses For regional services see page 279.

Hospital **Centre Hospitalier de Périgueux** (av Georges Pompidou, T05 53 45 25 25), 1.5 km north of the centre on the continuation of cours Montaigne.

Post office Place André Maurois.

Tourist information 24 place Francheville, T05 53 53 10 63.

Tip...

Ask at the tourist office about guided *visites-découvertes* (€5-10), which include night tours with entertainment, bike tours through the city's parks, courses in ancient Roman cuisine and even a treasure hunt.

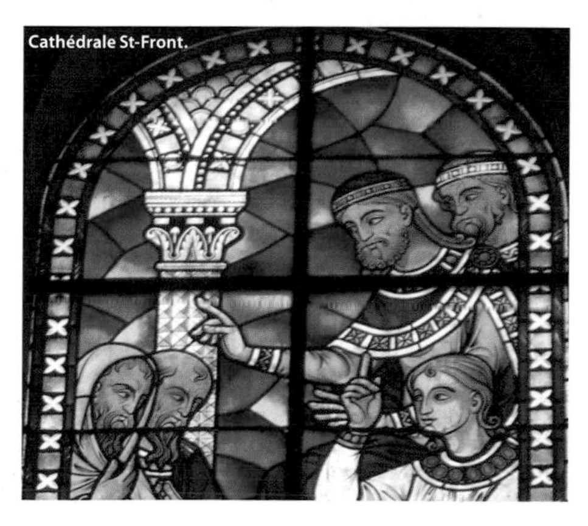
Cathédrale St-Front.

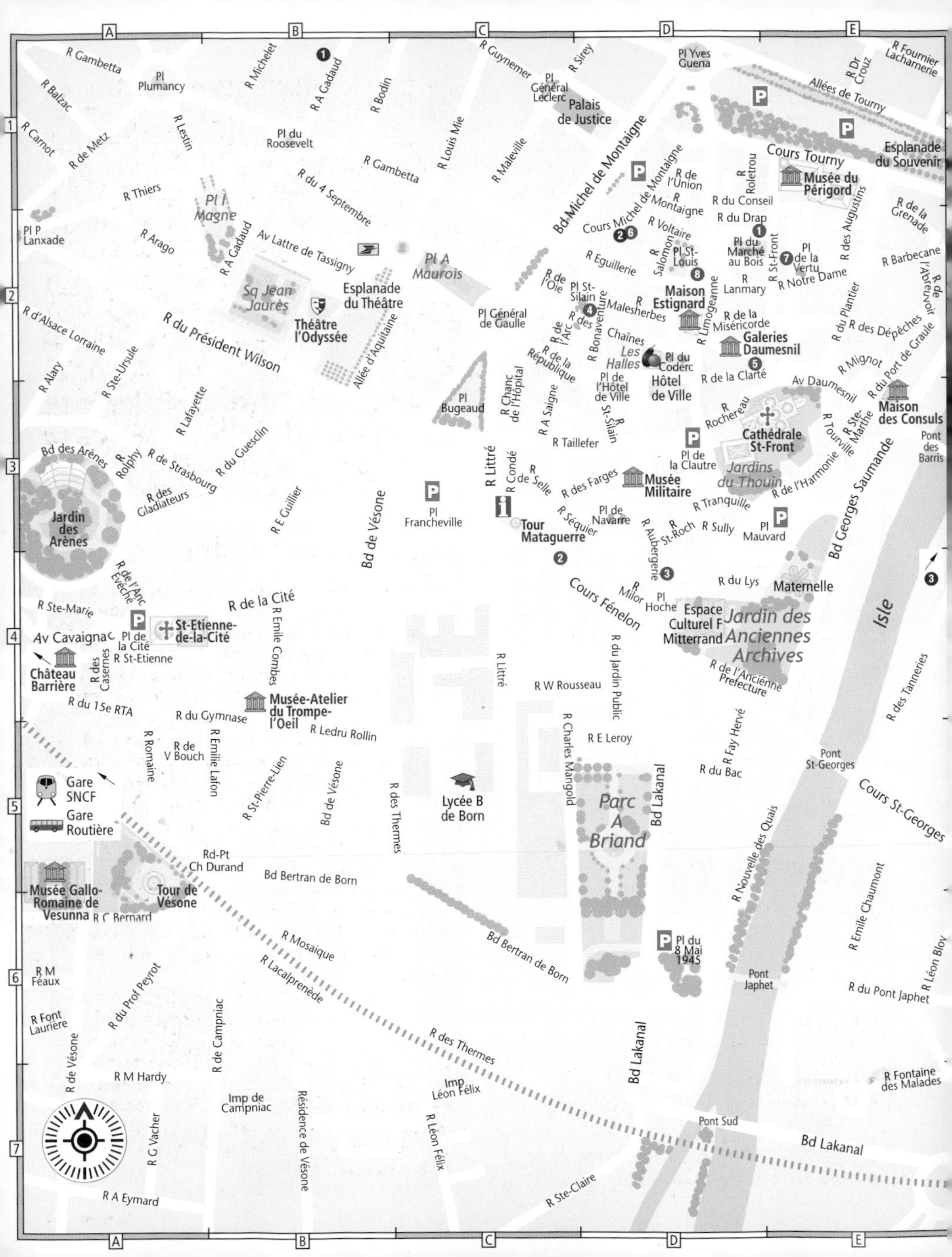

A
B
C
D
E
1
2
3
4
5
6
7
R Gambetta
Pl Plumancy
R Michelet
R A Gadaud
R Bodin
R Guynemer
R Sirey
Pl Yves Guena
R Fournier Lacharnerie
R Dr Crouz
Allées de Tourny
R Balzac
R Carnot
R de Metz
R Lestin
Pl du Roosevelt
R Louis Mie
R Maleville
Pl Général Leclerc
Palais de Justice
Bd Michel de Montaigne
Cours Tourny
Esplanade du Souvenir
R Gambetta
R du 4 Septembre
R Thiers
Pl I Magne
R de l'Union
R Montaigne
Cours Michel de Montaigne
R Roletrou
Musée du Périgord
R du Conseil
R du Drap
R de la Grenade
R des Augustins
Pl P Lanxade
R Arago
R A Gadaud
Av Lattre de Tassigny
Pl A Maurois
R Voltaire
R Eguillerie
R Salomon
Pl St-Louis
Pl du Marché au Bois
R St-Front
Pl de la Vertu
R Notre Dame
R Barbecane
R de l'Abreuvoir
Sq Jean Jaurès
Théâtre l'Odyssée
Esplanade du Théâtre
R de l'Oie
Pl St-Silain
R Malesherbes
Maison Estignard
R Limogeanne
R Lanmary
R d'Alsace Lorraine
R du Président Wilson
Allée d'Aquitaine
Pl Général de Gaulle
R de l'Arc
R des Chaînes
R Bonaventure
Les Halles
Pl du Coderc
R de la Miséricorde
Galeries Daumesnil
R du Plantier
R des Dépêches
R du Port de Graule
R Alary
R Ste-Ursule
R de la République
Pl de l'Hôtel de Ville
Hôtel de Ville
R de la Clarté
R Mignot
Av Daumesnil
R Lafayette
Pl Bugeaud
R Chanc de l'Hôpital
R A Saigne
R St-Silain
R Rochereau
Cathédrale St-Front
R Ste-Marthe
Maison des Consuls
R du Guesclin
R Taillefer
Pl de la Clautre
R Tourville
Pont des Barris
Bd des Arènes
R Rolphy
R de Strasbourg
R Littré
R Condé
R de Selle
R des Farges
Musée Militaire
Jardins du Thouin
R de l'Harmonie
Bd Georges Saumande
R des Gladiateurs
Jardin des Arènes
R E Guillier
Bd de Vésone
Pl Francheville
Tour Mataguerre
R Séquier
Pl de Navarre
R St-Roch
R Tranquille
R Sully
Pl Mauvard
R Aubergerie
R de l'Arc Evêché
Cours Fénelon
R du Lys
Maternelle
R Ste-Marie
R de la Cité
R Milor
Pl Hoche
Espace Culturel F Mitterrand
Jardin des Anciennes Archives
Isle
Av Cavaignac
Pl de la Cité
St-Etienne-de-la-Cité
R St-Etienne
R Emile Combes
R Littré
R du Jardin Public
Château Barrière
R des Casernes
R de l'Ancienne Prefecture
R W Rousseau
R des Tanneries
Musée-Atelier du Trompe-l'Oeil
R du 15e RTA
R du Gymnase
R Ledru Rollin
R Charles Mangold
R E Leroy
R Fay Hervé
R Romaine
R de V Bouch
R Emilie Lafon
R St-Pierre-Lien
Bd de Vésone
R des Thermes
Lycée B de Born
Bd Lakanal
Parc A Briand
R du Bac
Pont St-Georges
Cours St-Georges
Gare SNCF
Gare Routière
Rd-Pt Ch Durand
Bd Bertran de Born
R Nouvelle des Quais
Musée Gallo-Romaine de Vesunna
Tour de Vésone
R C Bernard
R Mosaique
Bd Bertran de Born
Pl du 8 Mai 1945
R Emile Chaumont
R M Feaux
R Lacalprenède
R du Prof Peyrot
Pont Japhet
R du Pont Japhet
R Léon Bloy
R Font Laurière
R de Campniac
R des Thermes
Bd Lakanal
R de Vésone
R M Hardy
Imp Léon Félix
R Fontaine des Malades
Imp de Campniac
Résidence de Vésone
R Léon Félix
Pont Sud
R G Vacher
Bd Lakanal
R A Eymard
R Ste-Claire

in 1852. Abadie was devoted to medieval architecture, but devoted perhaps even more to his own ego. He demolished most of the existing church and rebuilt it, largely after his own designs. There's nothing medieval about the peculiar scaly domes and their knobby lanterns: they're pure Abadie.

The people of Périgueux, who had no say in the state-run restoration, hated it from the start, and not many have a good word to say about it today. But for all its sheer awfulness, the work was much praised in its day, and Abadie became a favourite at the famously philistine court of Napoleon III; he would later copy his Périgueux domes for the new basilica of Sacré-Coeur on Montmartre in Paris.

The squarish 56-m **bell tower**, at least, is almost entirely original, built in a style unique for the Middle Ages. Abadie replaced almost all the sculptural decoration, but some of the original work can be seen on the **west portal**. The cavernous, dismal interior, with its fake painted masonry joints, is mostly Abadie's work too, though the enormous cut-out pillars were part of the original plan. Highlights include the huge chandeliers, which were first hung in Paris's Nôtre-Dame for Napoleon III's wedding in 1853, and a bombastic Baroque wooden retable. Another survivor, reached by a side door, is the simple **cloister**; the 'pine cone' at its centre – a copy of a common Roman decorative motif – originally topped the bell tower.

Périgueux listings

Sleeping

1 Bristol *37-39 rue Antoine Gadaud* B1
2 Hôtel de l'Univers *18 rue cours Montaigne* D2
3 Hôtel des Barris *2 rue Pierre Magne* E3

Eating & drinking

1 Café de la Place *7 place du Marché au Bois* D2
2 Délices de Russie *11 cours Fénelon* C4
3 L'Eden *3 rue Aubergerie* D4
4 L'Espace du Sixième Sens *place St-Silain* D2
5 L'Essentiel *8 rue de la Clarté* D2
6 Le Cercle *3 rue Eguillerie* D2
7 Le Clos Saint-Front *5 rue de la Vertu* E2
8 Tea for Tous *28 rue Eguillerie* D2

Medieval street, Périgueux.

A tale of two cities

Roman Vesunna, a prosperous metalworking city of elegant temples and baths in its heyday in the second century AD, lay to the west of the current city centre. Unfortunately, it got an early taste of the barbarian invasions. In 275 the Alemanni raided Gaul and gave Vesunna a thorough sacking. It never really recovered, shrinking in size and cannibalizing its public buildings for stone to build a defensive wall.

Through the Dark Ages, Vesunna reverted to its alternate name of Civitas Petrocorii, and eventually just **La Cité**. By then it was little more than a robber's nest for local barons. But a new settlement was growing up around the nearby pilgrimage church of St-Front. The two towns fought like dogs and cats, but the new **Puy St-Front** had the future on its side. By the 12th century it was a thriving merchant town, and started building a wall of its own. It was St Louis, the king famous for his justice, who finally decreed Périgueux reunified and gave it a charter.

Along with the rest of the region the city suffered through the Hundred Years' War and the Wars of Religion. By 1790 it was a backwater again. In that year the Périgourdins couldn't decide whether Périgueux, Bergerac or Sarlat should be capital of the new Dordogne department. The revolutionary government in Paris threw up its hands and decided they should take turns. Périgueux got the honour first – and never gave it up.

Medieval streets

Down the cobbled streets behind St-Front lies Périgueux's somewhat neglected riverfront. The 15th-century **Maison des Consuls**, the old seat of the city government, reflects Périgueux's late-medieval and Renaissance heyday. It is flanked on either side by noble palaces, the Hôtel de Lur and the Hôtel Lambert. Behind them, the picturesque rue Port de Graule and rue du Plantier have changed little since the 1600s.

Place de la Claütre, at the front of the cathedral, is the main market square. From here, rue Salinière leads north, turning into **rue Limogeanne**, the narrow, intimate shopping street of old Périgueux, now closed to traffic and a favourite promenade of the Pétrocoriens. There are a number of fine Renaissance buildings in and around this street. Halfway up, the **Maison Estignard** dates from 1520; note the salamanders carved on the lovely main portal – a way of flattering King François I, whose emblem they were. Across the way, don't miss the charming series of palaces and courtyards called the **Galeries Daumesnil**.

Musée Militaire du Périgord

32 rue des Farges, T05 53 53 47 36.
Apr-Sep Mon-Sat 1300-1800, Oct-Mar daily 1400-1800. €3.50, €1.75 concessions, under 10s free.
Map: Périgueux D3, p84.

Founded and staffed by the Veterans of Périgord, this museum has a big collection of arms and armour, battle flags, wild Zouave uniforms and everything else military, dating from the Middle Ages up to the Resistance and the war in Algeria. There are mementos of General Daumesnil and Périgord's other heroes, and the Germans are well represented, notably by a whole cabinet of *pickelhauben* – those old spiky Prussian helmets. The museum also has a collection of folk art brought back by soldiers serving in France's colonies.

Musée du Périgord

22 cours Tourny, T05 53 06 40 70, musee-perigord.museum.com.
Oct-Mar Mon and Wed-Fri 1000-1700, Sat-Sun 1300-1700, Apr-Sep Mon and Wed-Fri, 1030-1730, Sat-Sun 1300-1700. €4 (free Oct-May weekdays 1200-1400), under 18s free.
Map: Périgueux E1, p84.

A grand beaux-arts palace is the setting for the department's big museum. The collection of paintings isn't overwhelming, though there is a Canaletto and some Dutch works, but there are plenty of other things to catch the eye. Sprinkled among the paintings are decorative artworks of all kinds: Limoges enamels, bronzes and ceramics, and especially works made in Périgord. The medieval collection has Merovingian relics and some of the original sculpture from St-Front. Thanks to Périgord's caves, the prehistory section is one of the best in France. There's also an ethnographic collection specializing in Oceania and Africa, much of it provided by Admiral Bougainville, who sailed around the world in 1768 and brought the French their first bougainvilleas.

La Cité

After Perigueux's two centres had merged to become one city in 1240, the Cité dwindled in importance. The final indignity came in the 19th century when a rail line was built right through it, but in recent years archaeological excavations and the opening of a brilliant new museum have brought old Vesunna back to life.

Tour de Vésone

Map: Périgueux A5, p84.

According to ancient writers, this fantastical ruin once stood in the exact centre of Vesunna, in the middle of a colonnaded square. It was the temple of the city's tutelary deity, some murky Celtic

Rue Limogeanne.

goddess who didn't like to be named.

Today it stands alone in a park, an enigmatic stone and brick cylinder 25 m high. The huge breach in the tower is explained by a pious legend. Among the many miracles attributed to St Front, the hagiographers wrote that he smashed the wall himself, to chase all the pagan devils out of the tower.

The tower was only the *cella*, or inner chamber, of the temple. Imagine this great cylinder as it must have appeared in the Middle Ages, still surrounded by some of its circle of columns. Note the row of sockets about 6 m from the top; beams projected from here to hold up the cornice and roof, which would have been domed or conical. If you've been paying attention in Périgueux, this may seem familiar. Look again at the uniquely odd circular lantern on the top of St-Front's bell tower: it's the very image of the Tour de Vésone. This iconic, almost magical building must still have held Périgueux in its spell, and the Romanesque builders were able to finally capture it and Christianize it.

The hero of Vincennes

The men of Périgord have an especially proud military history. Not far from the Musée Militaire, on the cours Montaigne, you can see a fierce-looking statue of Périgueux's famous son, the gruff, peg-legged General Pierre Daumesnil. In 1815, after Napoleon's defeat, Daumesnil was in charge of the biggest arsenal in France at the Château de Vincennes. The Allies – and his own superiors – ordered him to surrender it, and when that failed they offered him a million-franc bribe, which was also ineffective.

When the Prussian negotiator arrived, Daumesnil waved a lighted paper in front of the mountain of gunpowder he was guarding, frightening the daylights out of the Prussian. Daumesnil finally told the Allies that he had lost one of his legs to them at the Battle of Wagram, and he wouldn't surrender Vincennes until he got it back. He refused to give up the keys until the new king, Louis XVIII, came to accept them in person. In a beaten and humiliated France, Daumesnil's defiance made him the hero of the day. Later on the old rascal confided: 'That refusal was my heritage to my grandchildren.'

More Roman ruins

From the museum, if you cross over the rail tracks on to rue Turenne you'll find the ruined **Château Barrière**; built into the old Roman fortifications, which are still clearly visible, it was once the headquarters of one of those robber baron families that made life in the medieval Cité so interesting. Further on are surviving stretches of the **Roman wall** and Vesunna's western gate, called the **Porte Normande** since the ninth century, when west was the direction that spelled danger – the norsemen, the Vikings, coming up the rivers.

Cross rue Chanzy and you come to the **Jardin des Arènes**, a circular park landscaped around the ruins of Vesunna's amphitheatre. Unlike the Greeks and other conquered peoples, the Gauls enjoyed gladiatorial shows and animal fights as much as the Romans themselves; this place could seat 20,000, nearly the town's entire population. The amphitheatre was turned into a castle for the Comtes de Périgord at some time in the Dark Ages, and it has been plundered for its stone for centuries.

Musée Gallo-Romain de Vesunna

Parc de Vésone, T05 53 53 00 92, vesunna.fr.
Apr-Jun and Sep Tue-Fri 0930-1730, Sat-Sun 1000-1230 and 1430-1800, Jul-Aug daily 1000-1900, Oct-Mar Tue-Fri 0930-1230 and 1330-1700, Sat-Sun 1000-1230 and 1430-1800. €6, €4 concessions, under 6s free.
Map: Périgueux A5, p84.

Since 1960, archaeologists have been busy in the area around the Tour de Vésone, and they've uncovered a lot. When the city decided to build a museum to house it all, the job went to a native of

Tip...

The museum sometimes opens on Thursday evenings in summer: ring ahead to check.

Château Barrière.

Musée Gallo-Romain.

the southwest (born in Fumel on the Lot), and France's most celebrated contemporary architect, Jean Nouvel. The museum is based on a clever idea: take the sumptuous Roman villa just unearthed, and make it the setting to display everything the archaeologists found in and around it. Nouvel's airy glass pavilion does the job perfectly.

The star attraction is of course the villa itself, with its paintings, central courtyard and fountain, and that poshest of Roman mod cons, a hypocaust (underfloor central heating). The finds displayed include a little bit of everything, divided into sections on public and private life, and there are models of Vesunna and its most important buildings.

Eglise St-Etienne-de-la-Cité

Place de la Cité.
Daily 1000-1800.
Map: Périgueux A4, p84.

We can get a better idea of what St-Front originally looked like from this church, its rival, begun about the same time. St-Etienne, built over what had been a Roman temple to Mars, may have been just as impressive a sight in its day, with a single long nave covered by four domes. The Protestants destroyed half of it during the Wars of Religion; two of the domes survive.

Originally this was Périgueux's cathedral; now it's a quiet and somewhat lonely building, often used for concerts during the city's summer music festival. Stripped to its bare bones, St-Etienne is still impressive, and the elegant stone arcading, inside and out, gives an idea of how grand it must once have been. Like St-Front, it has an ornate wooden retable of the 1600s. The original baptismal font and part of a bishop's tomb survive, along with one medieval curiosity: a carved calendar for calculating the date of Easter.

Musée-Atelier du Trompe-l'Oeil et du Décor Peint

5 rue Emile Combes, T05 53 09 84 40, museedutrompeloeil.com.
May-Sep Tue-Sat 1030-1230 and 1430-1830, Sun 1500-1800, Oct-Apr Tue-Sat 1400-1730, Sun 1500-1730; hourly guided tours (booking recommended). €5, €3.50 concessions, under 6s free.
Map: Périgueux B4, p84.

On a quiet side street near the Musée Gallo-Romain, this is not quite a museum but a workshop-exhibition space, the collaborative effort of a number of artists who are trying to recapture the old Renaissance love of illusionistic painting. They're good at it, and you'll enjoy learning the history of trompe-l'oeil on the tour. There is a shop, and they run workshops in case you want to learn their tricks yourself.

Périgueux cathedral.

Dordogne Valley

The stretch of the river between Le Buisson and Bergerac is scenic and peaceful. It may not have the castles and museums of the part that runs through Périgord Noir, but it's a great place to relax after touring Périgueux, and the riverside villages of Limeuil and Trémolat are ideally suited for that. You can get in some sightseeing too, at the Renaissance Château de Lanquais and at the Abbaye de Cadouin, which has some of the best medieval sculpture in Périgord.

Twin bridges at Limeuil.

Le Buisson-de-Cadouin

Life can't be easy for a village called 'the shrub', but Le Buisson's position on the river makes it a busy spot in summer, with campsites, canoes and beaches. Just 1 km from the village, from which they are well signposted, are Périgord's most recently opened caves, discovered in 2000.

Grottes de Maxange

T05 53 23 42 80, maxange.com.
Daily, Apr-Jun and Sep 1000-1200 and 1400-1800, Jul-Aug 0900-1900, Oct-Nov 1000-1200, 1400-1700. €7.20, €4.80 child (4-12).

So far no traces of habitation have been found here, only some bear claw marks, but the attraction is the rare 'eccentric' concretions – stalactites that due to capillary action refused to grow straight down as they're supposed to. In some places the effect is like frost on a windowpane, in others more like a coconut cake.

Abbaye de Cadouin

T05 53 63 36 28, semitour.com.
Feb-Mar and Nov to mid-Dec Mon, Wed-Thu and Sun 1000-1230 and 1400-1730; Apr-Jun and Sep-Oct Wed-Mon 1000-1230 and 1400-1800; Jul-Aug daily 1000-1900; mid-Dec-early Jan Wed-Mon 1000-1230 and 1400-1800.
€5, €3 child (6-12).
6 km south of Le Buisson on D25.

The most important monastery in Périgord grew up here for only one reason: the presence of the St-Suaire, said to be nothing less than the head-cloth put on Jesus for his burial. A brother of King Louis VI bought it in Antioch during the Crusades, and it later fell into the hands of a cleric from these parts, who brought it to Cadouin hidden in a barrel.

In 1115, canons from Périgueux founded a monastery to house it, which became affiliated with the new Cistercian Order. Pilgrims, including several French and English kings, poured in to see the relic, and soon an imposing church was erected. Fortunately, there were no killjoy scientists around to spoil the fun: modern analysis has found that the St-Suaire is nothing more than an 11th-century Muslim's turban, and the decorative border is really an Arabic inscription in fancy calligraphy.

Abbaye de Cadouin.

The **church**, big as it is, is heavy and austere, the way the early Cistercians liked them. This reforming order put their principles in stone, eschewing carved decoration in favour of a minimalist aesthetic that depended on the elements and proportions of the architecture alone. The best thing in it came much later: a truly beautiful marble Madonna from the 15th century.

The **cloister** is an entirely different story. Louis XI, one of the royal pilgrims, paid for its rebuilding in lavish Flamboyant Gothic. The sculpture here is excellent work, with a bit of the cartoonist's spirit; the more the pity that so much of it was damaged

Madonna at Cadouin.

Limeuil.

in the Wars of Religion and the Revolution. What's left is a wild hodgepodge of sacred and profane, scripture and legend. There's a monster or two, the tale of Lazarus, merchants fighting over a goose, and anti-female tableaux of cautionary tales, beginning with Samson's.

Limeuil

When the river was the main highway across Périgord, this village counted for something. Standing on its height overlooking the confluence of the Dordogne and the Vézère, Limeuil was the key to the valley, and always well defended. Parts of its walls and gates survive today, though the castle on the hill is long gone. With its steep roofs and winding alleys, Limeuil is one of the most beautiful villages in Périgord – but those alleys can get pretty crowded in July and August.

Parc Panoramique de Limeuil

T05 53 57 52 64, perigord-patrimoine.com. Apr-Jun and Sep-Oct Sun-Fri 1000-1230 and 1430-1800, Jul-Aug daily 1000-2000. €5, €4 child (5-18).

In a perfect setting overlooking the confluence of the rivers, Limeuil has turned its old castle hill into a unique park: it has an arboretum with over 60 species of tree, gardens containing herbs, ornamental and edible plants, and panoramic views over the surrounding countryside. In summer an artisans' organization called Au Fil du Temps puts on arts and crafts classes, exhibitions, concerts and storytelling.

Cingle de Trémolat

After Limeuil, the die-straight Dordogne takes it into its head to pretend it's the Lot for a while, and starts meandering about. The *cingles* (oxbow loops) of the river make for some good scenery as they brush up against the hills. For cars there's a signposted **Route des Cingles**; hikers can enjoy the views on the GR6 starting from Limeuil. **Trémolat** itself has a nice *plan* *d'eau* (bathing place) for a swim, and a rugged 12th-century church, St-Nicolas.

Lalinde & around

Though the Dordogne gives up meandering after Trémolat and runs straight and sensible again, it was still no picnic for the boatmen. The worst rapids along the river are here, and medieval **Lalinde** made its living largely by piloting boats through them. In the 19th century the tree-lined Lalinde Canal was built around the rapids. Lalinde itself is a bastide (see box, page 97), founded by the English. Across the river, the town of **Couze** has been a centre for papermaking from the 1500s to modern times.

Moulin à Papier de la Rouzique

Couze, T05 53 24 36 16.
Apr-Jun and Sep-Oct 1400-1830, Jul-Aug 1000-1900. €4.50.

This surviving paper mill has been restored to offer visitors a chance to see how it was done in the old days. There's a small museum and a shop selling their products. They recommend you ring ahead outside the holiday months to avoid the large numbers of school groups that visit.

Château de Lanquais

T05 53 61 24 24, chateaudelanquais.fr.
Apr and Oct Wed-Mon 1430-1800, May-Jun and Sep Wed-Mon 1030-1200 and 1430-1830, Jul-Aug daily 1000-1900, late Jul-late Aug, night visits Fri until 2100. €6.
South of the river, 4 km west of Lalinde.

This hyper-elegant Renaissance manor was built over the foundations of a medieval castle during the Wars of Religion, but being new did not save it from attack: they'll show you the holes musket balls made in its walls in 1577. This is one of the most completely furnished châteaux in Périgord, with many pieces dating back to the 16th and 17th centuries. From the outside, the heavy pediments and arches around the doors and windows betray an Italian hand, and it is believed that Italian craftsmen were brought to help with the design and carve the beautiful *grottesca* details on the fireplaces inside.

Papermaking with rags, Moulin à Papier de la Rouzique.

Bastide Country

It's a rich land: rolling hills covered in orchards, vines, grain, tobacco – a little bit of everything. And every 20 km or so, with unusual precision, the road will take you through a neatly planned village built around an arcaded square.

Because it's so lush, it's hard to imagine how this region could have been so empty 800 years ago. That is when the kings in faraway Paris and London decided to fill it. To house a booming population and put it to work for them, they turned this patch of Périgord into a new frontier, one of many in the southwest. Starting with a blank slate, medieval civilization got a chance to build and plan a whole region from scratch, and the result is not so medieval-looking as you might assume.

Château de Biron.

Monpazier

Once you've had a look round Monpazier, you won't be surprised to hear that it was founded by the English in 1284. The English are still here, mostly doing crosswords in the cafés, and looking so at home you'd think they had never left.

It's not your average bastide. *Le shopping* here is better than in Bergerac or Périgueux; galleries and boutiques crowd the main streets alongside the boulangerie and the boucherie. An old farmer, hearing I was headed that way, complained he couldn't afford a haircut there any more: *"Monpazier,"* he laughed, *"C'est le petit Paris."*

Monpazier's promoters call it the 'architecturally perfect bastide'; that's a stretch, but it is an attractive place. It had a rough history, climaxing perhaps in the famous night during the Wars of Religion when its militia went off to attack Villefranche-du-Périgord just as Villefranche's men were coming to Monpazier. Both captains were delighted to find their objectives undefended, and the two bastides merrily sacked each other.

After all the troubles, not much of historical interest is left, but the arcaded **Place des Cornières** is lovely, with a timbered covered market and buildings from the 13th to 15th centuries. Just off the square, the **Eglise St-Dominique** retains a curious piece of political propaganda from the Revolution. Carved into the façade you can still make out the inscription 'The People of France recognize the existence of a Supreme Being and the Immortality of the Soul.' After the church burnings during the Terror, by 1795 the leaders in Paris were trying to settle things down and get the pious provincials behind the new regime.

On rue Jean Galmot, the **Atelier des Bastides** (T05 53 22 60 38) has material and photos relating to Monpazier's history, along with exhibits by contemporary artists.

Bastides

If the village around you has crooked streets that simply meander about, it most likely grew up slowly and organically. But if it has a grid of nice straight streets like Chicago's, you are in a planned city: a bastide. Surprisingly, whenever people have founded new settlements – all the way back to the Indus Valley civilization 5000 years ago – this is how they've usually done it. Right angles make surveying and selling property so much easier and less subject to dispute.

And property was the name of the game, in the great medieval land boom in southwest France. Any underpopulated area became prime development land in the 13th century, and the kings of France and England jockeyed for position, trying to grab as much of it as they could by creating new settlements.

Altogether over 700 bastides were founded, most here in the southwest. Most followed the same simple, elegant plan: a central market square surrounded by stone arcades. The church, interestingly, is always off in a corner, implying that business, not religion, was the centre of bastide life.

Many of the settlers in these new towns were former serfs, breaking feudal bonds and sometimes acquiring land of their own. For the kings, the advantages were obvious: the settlers owed their loyalty and their taxes not to a local feudal baron, but to the crown. We might see this as an early image of our modern world, expressed in streets and squares.

Tip...

Almost every bastide with a tourist office puts on guided tours by appointment, as at **Eymet** (T05 53 23 74 95) and **Molières** (T05 53 22 39 12). **Beaumont-du-Périgord** (T05 53 22 39 12) and **Lalinde** (T05 53 61 08 55) also offer night tours in summer. **Monpazier** (T05 53 22 68 59) is the most ambitious. You can take their regular tours in summer (Tue and Fri 1100, ring ahead), or rent an audio guide, and there are even special tours for the blind.

Château de Biron

T05 53 63 13 39, semitour.com.
Feb-Mar and Nov-Dec Sun and Tue-Thu 1000-1230 and 1400-1730, Apr-Jun and Sep-Nov Tue-Sun 1000-1230 and 1400-1800, Jul-Aug daily 1000-1900. €6, €4 child (6-12).
8 km south of Monpazier.

Most of the great Périgord châteaux are the unified creations of a single architect. Biron is different. Over the eight centuries they owned it, succeeding generations of the powerful Gontaut family (see page 138) built bits and pieces, leaving an ensemble of buildings and styles that manages to be rather grand and rather charming at once.

In its isolated setting it certainly makes an impression. Biron never quite made the complete transition from castle to château. Simon de Montfort was just one of many who besieged it, and the quarrelsome Gontauts seldom lacked uninvited guests to test its stout walls. Much of the best of Biron dates from the Renaissance, especially the unique two-storey **chapel** built into the walls near the main gate. The ground floor, with an outside entrance, was for the villagers; meanwhile the Gontauts would be celebrating their own mass upstairs, accessible only from inside the castle. Added in the late 15th century, it's a remarkable building, one in which late Gothic meets the dramatic forms of the Italian early Renaissance.

Inside, the first sight is the delightful little **Pavilion de la Recette**. Across the courtyard are a wonderful Renaissance **staircase** and **gallery**, and the 12th-century keep called the **Tour Anglaise** – the Gontauts always maintained good relations with the English. They flirted with heresy too, first with the Cathars and later with the Protestants. Though they may have been the most powerful of the four baronies of Périgord, such behaviour kept them in the King of France's doghouse.

Inside, there's a fully fitted out medieval **kitchen** and **dungeon** – courtesy of the many films that have been shot here over the years.

Beaumont-du-Périgord

15 km northwest of Monpazier.

Edward I Longshanks founded this bastide in 1275. It still has one of its gates and fragments of its walls, along with the stoutly fortified **Eglise St-Laurent-et-St-Front**, with a remarkable 13th-century portal depicting hunting scenes, saints and a mystic mermaid.

To the north is one tremendous Renaissance château you'll have to be content with admiring from the outside, the **Château de Bannes**, and the peaceful hamlet of **Molières**. A few bastides, such as Montauban down in the Tarn-et-Garonne, grew into big cities; some, like Beaumont, are still much as they were in the Middle Ages. Most never really thrived at all: Molières with its 295 people is just a monument to lost expectations.

East of Beaumont, the lush valley of the River Couze offers a chance for a scenic detour. The D26 follows the Couze through the tiny but charming village of **Montferrand-du-Périgord**, with a medieval covered market and some fascinating medieval frescoes in the Eglise St-Christophe: the sun, moon and stars, a gaping mouth of hell, and a chubby, chilled-out *Christ in Majesty* who looks disconcertingly like Barry White.

The GR36 from here is a nice, easy route for hikers, and there are innumerable quiet green spaces for a picnic. Just north of the Couze, **St-Avit-Sénieur** began with a fifth-century soldier named Avitus who moved into a cave and became a holy hermit. The monastery that grew up on the spot was a stop on the pilgrimage route to Compostela. The huge 11th-century church survives, its half-wrecked steeple having provided a surreal landmark ever since Simon de Montfort passed through.

Issigeac.

Eymet.

Bastides over the border

Bastide country continues into the plum orchard territory of the Lot-et-Garonne, and if you're planning an excursion you might want to dip over the border. **Castillonnès** is one attractive bastide, another is **Villeréal**, with its 14th-century market. If you wanted a textbook example of a bastide with all its elements intact, Villeréal would be it: it's a lively place, not too tarted up for tourism, and home to a hippodrome that runs a schedule of races in summer. The most beautiful bastide here is **Monflanquin**, set on a commanding hill with a romantic twin-steepled church. It's an arty place, with a few galleries and occasional concerts.

Issigeac

18 km southeast of Bergerac.

In the land of rectangular bastides, this is the odd one out. Neatly circular Issigeac seems to have always been here. They've dug up signs of a Celtic village, along with a Roman villa and some Merovingian sarcophagi. Medieval Issigeac rebuilt itself around a monastery, and as a special favour Jean XXII, the pope from Cahors, made it a bishopric in place of Sarlat. The legacy of those heady days is the imposing **Eglise St-Félicien**. This was finally completed in 1527, just in time for the Issigeacois to turn Protestant and start whacking it with hammers. The only other sight is the 16th-century **château** that replaced the archbishops' palace, but Issigeac is a very amiable place, worth a stop just for a walk around.

Eymet

20 km west of Issigeac.

You can't tell a French bastide from an English one – the same builders worked for both sides. Eymet happens to be one of the 50 founded by Alphonse de Poitiers, the indefatigable brother of Louis IX. The English couldn't seize it in the Hundred Years' War, but they've got it now. Nowhere else in Périgord is the expat community so prominent: the ladies' shoe shop specializes in extra-wide fittings. Eymet may be the prettiest of the bastides, with a green setting on the little River Dropt and all its arcades and half-timbered buildings intact. Having lots of modest local shops helps keep it a busy, cosmopolitan, bilingual place.

Bergerac & around

Like London and Paris, Bergerac grew up around a bridge – the first one ever built over the Dordogne, in the 12th century. That helped make it a port too, and the new settlement grew up into a proper city, making its fortune first on wine and later on tobacco. Its people tended to be practical and sober-minded penny biters, and when the Protestant Revolution hit, Bergerac became one of the Huguenots' biggest strongholds in France.

That was probably a mistake. Cardinal Richelieu cut down the city's walls to leave it defenceless, and when Louis XIV put an end to tolerance and started his policy of forced conversions, most of the population simply packed up and left for new lives in England, Holland and Prussia. Bergerac remained a backwater for centuries.

The arrival of the low-cost airlines at its newly expanded Roumanière Airport in the 1990s, however, gave the old town, and its economy, a good jolt. The presence of so many tourists has persuaded Bergerac to smarten itself up considerably, and the old medieval centre, long neglected, is coming back to life.

Bergerac

Musée d'Anthropologie du Tabac

Place du Feu, T05 53 63 04 13, ville-bergerac.com.
Tue-Fri 1000-1200 and 1400-1800, Sat 1000-1200 and 1400-1700, Sun 1430-1830 (mid-Nov to mid-Mar closed Sat afternoon and Sun). €3.50, €2 child (10-17).

Bergerac was once France's tobacco town, with a big cigarette factory that perfumed the entire city with the pong of old-time Gauloises. Now there's only the museum and the memories. Housed in the **Maison Peyrarède**, an elegant 17th-century mansion, the tobacco museum takes you back to the days when the Olmecs and Aztecs were using the evil weed to dry evil humours, cure migraines and keep sorcerers at bay.

You can learn a lot here – the fascinating story of the American Indian cult of the calumet, or about the first historical wave of tobacco prohibitionism, back in the 1600s, and how it ended. There are collections of everything from carved African pipes to snuff boxes to early pipe-making machines. No smoking in the building!

Musée du Vin et de la Batellerie

5 rue des Conférences, T05 53 57 80 92.
Mid-Mar to mid-Nov Tue-Fri 1000-1200 and 1400-1730, Sat 1000-1200 and 1400-1700, Sun 1430-1830, mid-Nov to mid-Mar Tue-Fri 1000-1200 and 1400-1730, Sat 1000-1200. €2.50.

Wine and boats are what Bergerac is all about, and this museum brings them together with old photos, memorabilia and scale models of the traditional sailing barges, known as *gabarres*, that carried the river trade from medieval times up to the 1920s.

Essentials

Getting around Bergerac is small enough to reach all the sights on foot.

Taxi Outside the station, or T05 53 23 32 32.

Trains Bergerac is on the Bordeaux-Sarlat line running along the Dordogne Valley. For details of regional train services, see page 278.

Buses Most buses leave from outside the train station. For regional services, see page 279.

Hospital 9 boulevard du Professeur Albert-Calmette, T05 53 63 88 88.

Post office 36 rue de la Résistance, T05 53 63 50 00.

Tourist information 97 rue Neuve d'Argenson, T05 53 57 03 11, July-August Monday-Saturday 0930-1930, Sunday 1030-1300 and 1430-1900, rest of year Monday-Saturday 0930-1300 and 1400-1900.

Tip...

Bergerac tourist office will have details of guided walks around vineyards and visits to *chais*, wine tastings and lessons in wine appreciation, or you can contact the Maison des Vins de Bergerac (T05 53 63 57 55) or the Maison du Tourisme et du Vin de Monbazillac (T05 53 58 63 13).

Vleux Bergerac.

A walk through Vieux Bergerac

It all begins down on the river, where scores of wine barges once lined the quays. Today it's quiet enough down there, but you can take a boat trip up the Dordogne on a **gabarre**, to see the city and also the herons, cormorants and turtles in a bird sanctuary downstream; contact Périgord Gabarres (T05 53 24 58 80, gabarres.fr; Mar-Oct Tue-Sun on the hour 1100-1200 and 1400-1600, until 1800 in summer; €7.50, €4.50 child 2-12). Just off the quay is the **Cloître des Recollets**, the grey and sombre monastery of the order Louis XIV installed in the centre of Bergerac to burn prohibited books and convince the Bergeracois to be good Catholics again. Now the building is the **Maison des Vins** (T05 53 63 57 55, Jun-Sep daily 1000-1900, Oct-May 1030-1230 and 1400-1800), with exhibits, a film and tastings of Bergerac wines.

Walk inland from here to place du Docteur Cayla, where the strange, chilly **Temple Protestant de Bergerac** says more about the city's past than the histories could ever express. The adjacent **place de la Myrpe**, lined with half-timbered houses and shaded by old trees, is a delight; it's where the old folks of the neighbourhood like to sit and gab under the long nose of the **statue of Cyrano de Bergerac**.

Or, we should say, one of the statues, for there's another one in living Technicolor just to the north in **place Pelissière**, the lively centre of old Bergerac, with plenty of beer to drink and café tables to sit at. Just off this square is a very pretty bauble: the 17th-century **Eglise St-Jacques**, a medieval work rebuilt as a monument to King Louis's Catholic restoration.

From here it's a block north to the carrots and courgettes on display at the **Marché Couvert**, or a block east to **rue des Fontaines** and some of the palaces of Bergerac's past, such as the 14th-century **Vieille Auberge** or the **Maison Doublet**, where Henri IV stayed during the Wars of Religion.

Maison des Vins, Bergerac.

Cyrano de Bergerac

A lot of people are still surprised to learn that Cyrano wasn't just a fictional character. And a lot of the Bergeracois wouldn't believe it if you told them that their hometown hero wasn't from Bergerac at all, and probably never even visited. The model for Edmond Rostand's stirring tale was Hector Savinien de Cyrano, born near Paris in 1619. Cyrano was fully the man for his picaresque times – poet, playwright and soldier: a perfect combination, especially if one happened to be gay. On the literary side, Cyrano was successful and popular, writing among many other works a satire called *L'Histoire comique des Etats et des Empires de la Lune*, which is considered one of the precursors of science fiction. He was good with the sword too, a renowned duellist who served his king in a number of battles.

When Cyrano was young he joined a company of Gascons, the boys with all the flash and style in those days. Among his family's estates was a little village near Paris called Bergerac, and so to sound like a fellow southwesterner he started calling himself Cyrano de Bergerac. (There may have been another reason. Bergerac in those days was still a hard-headed Protestant town, and Cyrano was a brave freethinker who had more than a few brushes with the censor.)

As for the schnozzola, the few surviving likenesses suggest it was big, but not quite *that* big.

Monbazillac

You catch your first glimpse of it on the N21 just south of Bergerac: after the suburban sprawl on the plain fades away, a sudden patch of hills closes in on the right. It catches the sun, glinting off endless rows of well-tended vines in intricate patterns. It seems a different world up there, serene and aristocratic, its vines arrayed around the stunning Renaissance château that brings order to the scene. You would expect the wine that grows here to be special, and Monbazillac is one of the southwest's finest.

Château de Monbazillac

T05 53 63 65 00, chateau-monbazillac.com.
Apr daily 1000-1200 and 1400-1800; May, Jun, Sep and Oct daily 1000-1230 and 1400-1900; Jul-Aug daily 1000-1900; Nov to mid-Jan and mid-Feb to Mar Tue-Sun 1000-1200 and 1400-1700. €6.

The car park is impressive enough, set among the ancient trees of the château's park. A classic *allée* leads straight toward the entrance, the château's forest of gables, turrets and frilly weathervanes appearing through a sea of vines. You would think a grand duke lives here, but the château is really the property of the Monbazillac wine growers' cooperative.

This is one of the most imposing of the great châteaux. The Aydies, Vicomtes de Bergerac, built it in 1550, and it hasn't much changed since. Inside, it is completely furnished, partly in the *grand siècle* manner of Louis XIV and partly with whatever bits and bobs came to hand over the centuries. One room is dedicated to books, portraits and memorabilia of French Protestantism for, strangely enough, just after the family built this ultimate symbol of conspicuous consumption they got religion and converted.

You'll get to see the château's monumental wine cellars, and as you leave you'll be offered a tasting of Monbazillac (in seven degrees of sweetness!) or if you prefer, a bit of Bergerac.

Monbazillac vineyards.

Monbazillac: it's the fungus that makes it famous

With such an aristocratic eyrie for a vineyard, it isn't surprising that Monbazillac is the wine most favoured to go with foie gras. It was prized in the Middle Ages, and there are records of shipments to England as early as 1250. We probably owe Monbazillac in its present form, made mostly from Sémillon grapes, to the Dutch, who had a taste for sweet wines in the 18th century and were happy to buy it from their fellow Protestants in Périgord. It has been AOC since 1936.

The growers favour north-facing slopes, for it is here that they get the right humidity and temperatures to encourage the 'noble rot' that makes Monbazillac so special. This is a fungus, *Botrytis cinerea*, which lives by sucking water out of the maturing grapes, thus concentrating the sugars inside. You can learn all about it, and pick up a few bottles to take home, at the **Cave de Monbazillac**, a brash modern building next to the château.

Monbazillac may be the star, but it's hardly the only fine wine in this fertile area. From the belvedere behind the château you can see the vineyards of four appellations. Everyone knows AOC **Bergerac**, though living in the shadow of the more famous Bordeaux its wines perhaps don't always get the praise they deserve. There are many wines from smaller areas worth seeking out: **Pecharmant**, a strong, tannic wine with a lot of character, grown only in a few villages east of Bergerac, or **Saussignac**, another sweet wine made from Sémillon grapes, from just west of Monbazillac. **Rosette** comes from north of Bergerac, while **Montravel**, **Haut Montravel** and **Côtes de Montravel** grow in a broad area along the north bank of the Dordogne.

Musée André Voulgre.

Mussidan

Musée André Voulgre

2 rue Raoul Grassin, T05 53 81 23 55, museevoulgre.fr.
Apr-May Sat-Sun 0930-1200 and 1400-1800, Jun-Sep daily 0930-1200 and 1400-1800; rest of year by appointment. €3, €2.50 concessions, under 13s free.
25 km north of Bergerac.

A lot of French villages have museums full of old farm tools and such, but this one north of Bergerac is serious. André Voulgre was a local doctor who spent decades assembling the collections, which include working farm machinery, a reconstructed forge, even a fully furnished house of a century ago.

Moncaret

Site Archéologique de Montcaret

T05 53 58 50 18, montcaret.monuments-nationaux.fr.
Jun-Sep daily 0945-1230 and 1400-1830, Oct-May Sun-Fri 1000-1230 and 1400-1730. €3, €2.50 concessions, under 18s free.
36 km west of Bergerac, just off D936.

Back in the shabby end-days of the Roman Empire, when a very small elite owned all of the property and most of the people, there were rural villas like this all over Aquitaine – the only buildings kept up when everything else was falling apart. Enough of this one survives to give an idea of the layout, and many floor mosaics have been excavated, including that favourite Roman status touch, a mosaic of fish at the bottom of the little pool in the courtyard.

St-Michel-de-Montaigne

Château de Montaigne

T05 53 58 63 93, chateau-montaigne.com.
Feb-Apr and Nov-Dec Wed-Sun 1000-1200 and 1400-1730, May-Jun and Sep-Oct Wed-Sun 1000-1200 and 1430-1830, Jul-Aug daily 1000-1830. €6, €4.50 concessions/child (10-15), under 10s free.
44 km west of Bergerac, off D936.

It's a long way from anywhere, tucked into Périgord's furthest southwestern corner, but anyone who cares about good books and great thoughts might consider a pilgrimage here to visit one of the most civilized places on the planet. Michel Eyquem de Montaigne was the model of the erudite Renaissance essayist. His great knowledge and his attitude of tolerance and amused scepticism inspired readers all over Europe.

Montaigne's status as a country gentleman gave him all the time in the world to write essays. In 1571, after a busy public career, he retired here – not to his château so much as to his **tower**, a round medieval relic that Montaigne converted into a library, his refuge from the world. The books are gone now, but the proverbs and bons mots in Greek and Latin he inscribed on the beams can still be seen. The château itself is still lived in and not open to visitors.

Sleeping

Périgueux

Château des Reynats €€€€-€€€
15 av des Reynats, Chancelade, T05 53 03 53 59, chateau-hotel-perigord.com.
Closed Jan.
6 km west of Périgueux.
This turreted château from the time of Napoleon III stands in the middle of a spacious park full of big old oaks. Each of the classically furnished rooms is named after a famous Périgourdin, and each has a character of its own. There is a fine restaurant, tennis courts and a pool, and they'll make reservations for you at the 18-hole golf course a few minutes away.

Bristol €€
37-39 rue Antoine Gadaud, T05 53 08 75 90, bristolfrance.com.
Map: Périgueux B1, page 84.
You won't find a non-chain upscale hotel in the centre of Périgueux, but the Bristol has air conditioning, parking and broadband, and the rooms are everything they should be. It's a gosh-awful modern building, but you don't have to look at it once you're inside.

Château d'Escoire €€
Escoire, T05 53 05 99 80, escoire-lechateau.com.
12 km east of Périgueux.
And quite a grand château it is, with a stately rotunda and expansive grounds. Four spacious, brightly decorated rooms are available; it's good value, with breakfast included and a pool. (We ought to mention the château was the site of one of the most sensational triple-murder cases in France, back in 1941 and still unsolved.)

Hôtel de l'Univers €€
18 cours Montaigne, T05 53 53 34 79, hotelrestaurantlunivers.fr.
Map: Périgueux D2, page 84.
A grand name for an establishment with only nine rooms, but they're comfortable and convenient; this universe includes broadband and parking.

L'Ecluse €€
Route de Limoges, Antonne-et-Trigonant, T05 53 06 00 04, ecluse-perigord.com.
10 km east of Périgueux on N21.
It's a new building, and a little startling at first – a sort of traditional Périgord farmhouse translated to the size of a 47-room hotel. It could be kitsch, but is actually quite attractive, aided by a lovely setting among trees on the banks of the Isle. The rooms are plush and comfortable, and look as if they've had grandmère's personal attention. The restaurant does the usual traditional dishes, in a room with a panoramic view over the river.

Hôtel des Barris €
2 rue Pierre Magne, T05 53 53 04 05, hoteldesbarris.com.
Map: Périgueux E3, page 84.
Right on the bridge, facing St-Front across the river: when you book, try to get one of the rooms with a view. It's a modest establishment, but a good solid budget choice in a great location.

Self-catering

Les Lilas
Chemin de Puyrousseau, T09 61 46 58 84 or 06 60 38 39 29, gite-leslilas.fr.
An unusual alternative for seeing the city, this is a modern-rustic gîte on a hill overlooking Périgueux, five minutes from the centre, simply furnished and with a garden. For an overnight stay it's €60-155 depending on accommodation and season; per week in high season €700.

Camping

Barnabé
80 rue des Bains, T05 53 53 41 45, barnabe-perigord.com.
Mar-Oct.
A campsite, and so much more. See page 114.

Trémolat

Le Vieux Logis €€€€
T05 53 22 80 06, vieux-logis.com.
A Relais & Châteaux member, the Vieux Logis is a Périgord inn for the elite: a 17th-century manor with beautiful gardens and a

pool, 17 rooms and nine apartments individually decorated in a manner that is utterly posh without pretension. Its real distinction, however, is that it has one of the southwest's best restaurants (see page 112).

Couze-St-Front

Relais de Belle Vue €€
T05 53 61 75 70, relaisdebellevue.com.
Tranquillity is assured in this lovely home in a huge forested park, convenient to the Dordogne and the bastide country. Four good rooms with breakfast included, and a pool. Minimum stay two nights.

Monpazier

Edward 1er €€€
5 rue St-Pierre, T05 53 22 44 00, hoteledward1er.com.
Closed mid-Nov to mid-Mar.
On a quiet bastide side street, this is a 19th-century mansion modelled on the Renaissance châteaux and now converted into a variety of rooms and suites. The rooms are comfortable, though not notably cheerful, and they lay on some clever package deals: romantic weekends, golf and riding holidays, and one where they send you off on a day trip in a ragtop Citröen 2CV with maps and a picnic basket.

Le Prieuré du Château de Biron.

Biron

Le Prieuré du Château de Biron €€€
T09 60 47 46 07, leprieurebiron.com.
Closed mid-Nov to Mar.
A serene, luxurious B&B in the 500-year-old residence of the priests of Biron. There are stunning views from the five spacious and elegantly furnished rooms with big oak beams, and a pretty garden with comfy chairs – perfect for sitting out with a good book.

Montferrand-du-Périgord

Auberge Lou Peyrol €
La Barrière, T05 53 63 24 45, hotel-loupeyrol-dordogne.com.
Closed Oct-Easter.
A sweet and simple country inn, with a restaurant, in the quiet and pretty valley of the Couze. If you want an inexpensive base for enjoying the countryside while still conveniently close to the major destinations, this could be the place. They also offer tailor-made walking holidays, with a guide if you wish.

Bergerac & around

Château les Merles €€€
Tuilières, T05 53 63 13 42, lesmerles.com.
12 km east of Bergerac on D660.
This stately 17th-century manor has been reincarnated as a golf resort, with a challenging course (but only nine holes). The interior is decorated in a modern style that is minimalist but sharp; there's a spa for golf widows and one of the department's top restaurants, La Bruyère Blanche (see page 113).

Hôtel de France €€
18 place Gambetta, T05 53 57 11 61, hoteldefrance-bergerac.com.
Solid, comfortable city centre hotel with broadband, a garage and a small garden and pool.

Le Colombier de Cyrano et Roxane €€
17 rue du Grand Moulin, T05 53 57 96 70.
On the prettiest square in Bergerac, a British-run B&B in a brightly painted storybook house, decorated inside with a touch of whimsy.

Le Logis Plantagenet €€
5 rue du Grand Moulin, T05 53 57 15 99, lelogisplantagenet.com.
Another gracious chambre d'hôte just nearby in the historic centre, and also British. Beautifully furnished rooms in a medieval half-timbered building with a small garden.

Self-catering

Au Lézard Doré
Lamonzie-Montastruc, T05 53 27 14 72, aulezarddore.com.
12 km northeast of Bergerac.
This is a modest gîte out in the country that sleeps four in two rooms, but it's a gîte with a difference: there's a personal balneotherapy spa, with a Turkish bath and sauna; California and traditional massage and other treatments are on offer. €625 per week; shorter stays are available.

Les Domaines du Château des Comtes d'Estissac
Saussignac, T05 53 23 24 83, gites-ruraux-perigord.com.
Closed Dec-Mar.
18 km west of Bergerac.
Three charming and comfortable restored farmhouses on a working wine estate. Two of them accommodate six people (€990 and €1360 per week) and the other will fit 12 (€2125). The three share a pool. When available they also let for short stays, even one night.

Le Colombier de Cyrano et Roxane.

Eating & drinking

Périgueux

Le Clos Saint-Front €€€€
5 rue de la Vertu, T05 53 46 78 58, leclossaintfront.com.
Tue-Sun lunchtime.
Map: Périgueux E2, page 84.
There's a touch of the avant-garde in the kitchen here, with a bit of foam here, an emulsion of young nettles there and a hint of smoked tea, and some critics accuse them of trying a little too hard, but Le Clos is still one of the top tables in Périgueux. You can choose between an elegant room with an 18th-century air or a pretty garden terrace.

L'Essentiel €€€
8 rue de la Clarté, T05 53 35 15 15, restaurant-lessentiel.com.
Tue-Sat.
Map: Périgueux D2, page 84.
The ambience isn't much, but habitués are perfectly happy to avoid distraction and concentrate on the cooking, with a range of menus from €25 up. The city's new trendy favourite features an impressive wine list and some innovative cooking to go with it.

L'Eden €€
3 rue Aubergerie, T05 53 06 31 08, leden restaurant.com.
Tue-Sat.
Map: Périgueux, D4, page 84.
One of the more bright and cheerful rooms in this city, with a cuisine to match. You'll find some unexpected dishes, like duck and seafood risotto or a saffron-scented seafood couscous. The €25 menu is a treat, and the €13 lunch menu one of the best bargains in town.

Le Cercle €€
3 rue Eguillerie, T05 53 53 34 79, hotelrestaurantlunivers.fr.
Daily, bar open until 0200.
Map: Périgueux, D2, page 84.
A chic and very popular wine bar and brasserie-style restaurant, with plates of tapas, charcuterie or oysters to help the Bordeaux and Bergerac go down. Part of the Hotel de l'Univers (see page 108).

Café de la Place €€-€
7 place du Marché au Bois, T05 53 08 21 11.
Daily 0800-0200, restaurant service until 2230 (Sat-Sun 2300).
Map: Périgueux, D2, page 84.
A Périgueux institution, this cosy and comfortable old-style brasserie is the place for a late-night drink, or an early one out on the square watching *tout-Périgueux* pass by. The cooking is hearty and simple and fits the ambience: steak tartare, *ris de veau*, snails or whatever's on the slate.

Délices de Russie €€-€
11 cours Fénelon, T05 53 09 37 51.
Tue-Sat.
Map: Périgueux, C4, page 84.
Not, perhaps, what you came to Périgord for, but this charming establishment might make you forget all about foie gras and ris de veau for a while. It's a Russian food shop, an art gallery and a simple restaurant, where you can have a hearty soup and a selection of different Russian specialities on small plates, along with wines from Georgia or the Crimea.

L'Espace du Sixième Sens €
6 place St-Silain, T05 53 09 24 29.
Tue-Sun, closed Sun evening and Feb.
Map: Périgueux, D2, page 84.
Part restaurant, part delicatessen, great for an *assiette* of various treats and a glass of wine whenever you need it. They serve all day, and stay open as late as 2300 in summer.

Cafés & bars

Tea for Tous
28 rue Eguillerie, T05 53 53 92 86.
Daily until 1900, 0100 on Wed, Fri and Sat in summer.
Map: Périgueux, D2, page 84.
More different teas than you ever dreamed existed, along with home-made apple crumble and tables outside on place St-Louis to enjoy it. Good for light lunches too, with bruschette, salads and quiches.

Cadouin

Auberge de la Salvetat €€
Route de Belvès, T05 53 63 42 79, lasalvetat.com.
Closed Sun evening and Mon lunch.
A very likeable restaurant that explores Périgord's traditional cooking a little more deeply than most: snails, *ris de veau*, quail, Cabecou cheese with walnuts and honey. It's also a hotel with 14 well-appointed rooms (€€).

Limeuil

Le Chai €€
Place du Port, T05 53 63 39 36.
Closed mid-Nov to Jan, and Wed except Jul-Aug.
Set in a gracious old house down on the port, this restaurant serves plenty of duck – even duck with mushrooms on pasta, because here the Périgord cooking sometimes gives way to Italian: a choice of fresh pasta dishes, pizza, and tiramisù for dessert.

Trémolat

Le Vieux Logis €€€€
T05 53 22 80 06, vieux-logis.com.
An exquisite setting for one of the region's finest. Chef Vincent Arnould has a way with scallops, foie gras and many other good things, and he likes to throw in a truffle or two. Weekday lunches offer the best deals: a €40 *menu du marché* or a special tapas menu at €38. At the other end of the kitchen you'll find the Bistrot d'en Face (T05 53 22 80 69), which does duck and other traditional fare (€€).

Monpazier

Chez Minou €€-€
55 rue Notre-Dame, T05 53 22 46 59.
Right by the town gate, with a little garden, a good spot for a light lunch: pizza, salads and omelettes.

Restaurant la Bastide €€-€
52 rue St-Jacques, T05 53 22 60 59.
Not many places in the bastides give you a choice beyond the usual stuff. Here they offer couscous, samosas and *brik* (Maghrebian stuffed pastries), prawns *au pastis* and salads.

Issigeac

La Brucelière €€
Place de la Capelle, T05 53 73 89 61, bruceliere.com.
Thu-Tue, closed Jan.
The emphasis here is on seafood: *coquilles St-Jacques* (scallops), lobster and langoustines. They also do a nice roast pigeon, and everything is presented with art and panache. This building was once the post house, and it has been an inn for 120 years; today there are five inexpensive air-conditioned rooms (€).

Bergerac & around

La Bruyère Blanche €€€€
Tuilières, T05 53 63 13 42, lesmerles.com.
12 km east of Bergerac on D660.
For a guy who learned how to cook in the Dutch Navy, Albert Kooy ain't bad. Between writing books and winning prizes, he runs this ethereal, silvery room full of candelabras, and serves up a real *cuisine de maître* with influences from Japan, Provence and half the places in between. It's part of the Château les Merles golf resort (see page 110), and many of the ingredients come from the chateau's own gardens, while its vineyard supplies the house wine. There's also a *bistrot* (€€) serving the chef's interpretation of more traditional dishes.

L'Imparfait €€€
8 rue des Fontaines, T05 53 57 47 92, imparfait.com.
Tue-Sat, closed mid-Dec to mid-Jan.
Maybe the best of the restaurants in Bergerac's historic centre, with some unexpected delights on the menu: Vietnamese *nems* (spring rolls) with red tuna carpaccio, a steak with foie gras, almonds and hazelnuts. It gets a little crowded inside but they put tables out in summer.

La Scala €€
29 rue des Conférences, T05 53 22 72 10.
Tue-Sun.
You can eat pizza, salads and bruschette on tables outside on place Pélissière, with the best view in town.

Le Rouge Ardoise €€
14 rue St-Clar, T05 53 22 37 26.
Closed Tue evening, Wed out of season.
It's hardly a year old, but already making a reputation for itself around Bergerac. The ambience is informal and *branché*, which fits the cooking well: lots of duck, but also dishes with an oriental touch and a hazelnut dacquoise for dessert.

La Bodega €
4 rue de la Brèche, T09 64 28 34 82.
Mon-Sat.
Spain isn't that far away after all; in this cosy corner of the historic centre you can get tapas (about €3 each, or a nice assortment for €9.80), or a full dinner built around ribs, chops and brochettes.

Monbazillac

Le Tour des Vents €€€€
Moulin de Malfournat, T05 53 58 30 10, tourdesvents.com.
Jul-Aug closed Mon, Sep-Jun closed Sun evening and Mon-Tue lunch; closed Jan.
An essential part of the Monbazillac experience, and probably a great spot for a marriage proposal, this could well be the most stylish food you can get in the Dordogne, and in the most stylish setting, around an old windmill on a terrace with tremendous views over the valley. It's not too stylish to eat though: chef Marie Rougier's cooking rates highly with the experts. Flaming crêpes Suzette top a truly decadent dessert list. Menus from €25-45 seem a bargain.

Entertainment

Périgueux

Bars & clubs

Barnabé
80 rue des Bains, T05 53 53 41 45, barnabe-perigord.com.
How to explain it? Well, it's a listed historical landmark, and it's a campsite with an incredible mini-golf course decorated with miniatures of the famous buildings of Périgord. There's a garden on the riverfront and a billiards room too. Barnabé is really a *guinguette* – one of those places fashionable a century ago where city people went to enjoy a Sunday outing in the country. And it's a very special *guinguette*, with a 1930s art deco pavilion, still run by the family that built it and almost perfectly preserved. Come for a drink just to see the place, or check the listings: Barnabé does occasional jazz nights. It's on the south bank of the Isle, about a 20-minute walk east of the centre.

Le Mellow
4 rue de la Sagesse, T05 53 08 53 97.
Mon-Sat 1700-0100, 0200 in summer.
Périgueux's most sophisticated room, with a lot of jazz, frequent theme nights, exotic cocktails and a wide choice of beers and wines.

Music

Espace Jaune Poussin
33 rue du Président Wilson, T05 53 06 90 70, jaune-poussin.com.
This venue has a big hall it uses for regular concerts and shows. Mostly they're jazz nights, including groups from the USA, but they also put on dinner-dances and other entertainments; usually €30-40 for dinner and a show, less for concerts only.

Le Sans Réserve
192 route d'Angoulème, T05 53 06 12 73, sans-reserve.org.
It's the best Périgord can do, and it's so noisy they've put it out by the train tracks west of town on the D939. This old tractor garage hosts a regular schedule of concerts: straight rock, indie, reggae, ska, hiphop and more.

Bergerac

Bars & clubs

Bay Bar
33 rue des Fontaines, T05 53 61 69 87, bay-bar.com.
Tue-Sun 1800-0300.
A very sophisticated joint, in a tastefully restored medieval building. There's a wide choice of cocktails, and it seems so civilized getting stewed here while contemplating the big jade Buddhas around the bar. They put on occasional exhibitions and other events.

Music

Le Music Hall
109 rue Neuve-d'Argenson, T05 53 22 58 11, le-music-hall.fr.
Jun-Sep.
Yes, music hall, laid on every summer by the Cosmopolitan Company. All-inclusive tickets are €50-70 per person for the show and dinner (usually on Saturdays). In 2009 it was 'French Cancan', with a full troupe of dancers, acrobats, comics and singers. Other shows include an Andalucian revue, and they do pantos at Christmas.

Shopping

Périgueux

Food & drink

La Gaveuse d'Oie
6 rue Salinière, T05 53 02 92 63, lagaveusedoie.fr.
Daily 0900-1900.
When you're looking for treats to take back home, have a look in this one-stop shop: foie gras in all its forms, vacuum-packed cured duck magrets (great in salads), preserves and the house speciality – prunes, peaches and other fruits stuffed with foie gras.

Gifts

Coutellerie Favie
5 rue Limogeanne, T05 53 53 48 83.
Tue-Sat 0900-1200 and 1400-1900.
A delightfully old-fashioned cutlery shop, with its giant pair of scissors hanging out over the street as if it were still the 14th century. There are glittering displays of Laguiole and Nontron knives, also fancy tableware and some unusual gifts.

Markets

The big markets take place on Wednesday and Saturday mornings, filling up the three little squares and surrounding streets near St-Front. In summer there are farmers' markets every morning in place de Coderc, and in winter (mid-Nov to mid-Mar) a Saturday morning *marché au gras* in place St-Louis, selling ducks and geese, foie gras and charcuterie, and sometimes truffles.

Cadouin

Art & antiques

Galerie Art'Cad
Place de l'Abbaye, T05 53 73 02 52, art-perigord.com.
Daily 1000-1200 and 1500-1800.
Over 30 artists place their work here: paintings, jewellery, ceramics and much more. The best bits are the modern pottery, both frivolous and useful, with a sense of humour as well as design.

Tip...

Apart from Périgueux and Bergerac, other good markets are Tuesday: Beaumont-du-Périgord, Trémolat; Wednesday: Cadouin; Thursday: Eymet, Lalinde, Monpazier (see page 97); Fridays: Le Buisson; Saturday: Lalinde, Beaumont-du-Périgord; Sunday: Issigeac, Limeuil (in summer), Couze-St-Front.

Monpazier & around

Art & antiques

Atelier Marqueterie
Place Cornières (place Centrale), T05 53 23 20 74, marqueterieplanchon.com.
Tue-Sun 1000-1230 and 1500-1930.
Christophe Planchon is a master of marquetry (inlaid wood), but his work is nothing like the familiar souvenirs they make in Italy. These are real art, done with a sensibility with a touch of Dali in it. There are grand works and also small, inexpensive gifts.

Claudie's Galerie
30 rue St-Jacques, T05 53 28 49 62, medievalatelier.com.
Open when it's open, more likely in summer.
Monpazier is the perfect place for Claudie Maigrot, a woman in love with the Middle Ages who creates strikingly beautiful 'fabric murals' that resemble scenes on stained glass. Her work is reasonably priced, and the gallery is well worth a look even if you haven't any more room in your bags.

Jewellery

Bijoux d'Email
Biron, T06 83 18 90 27, bijouxdemail.fr.
Almost in the shadow of the great château, Delphine Geoffray runs a little shop that glitters like the cave of the Forty Thieves. She makes and sells handmade enamelled jewellery of all kinds, at attractive prices.

Bergerac

Gifts

Les Folies de Sophie
41 rue Bourbarraud, T05 53 27 10 59.
Tue-Sat 1000-1230 and 1430-1900.
A very modest establishment with some very nice things inside: paintings, jewellery, bags, shoes and fashions, all the work of local artists and craftspeople.

Markets

Market days in Bergerac are Tuesday (organic farmers' market), Wednesday and Saturday. There is a **truffle market** (Dec-Feb) on Wednesday and Saturday, and a **flea market** in the centre on the first Sunday morning of each month.

Activities & tours

Excursions

Autorail Espérance
In summer, the SNCF operates a special tourist train, running up the Dordogne Valley between Sarlat and Bergerac, passing Beynac and some of the other castles along the way. A guide provides a running commentary, and a tasting of local foods and Bergerac wines is on offer. (The line was closed for maintenance in 2009, and at time of writing timetables, rates and services for 2010 have not been decided. Contact SNCF or the Sarlat or Bergerac tourist offices for more information.)

Les Attelages de Monsacou
Lamonzie-Montastruc, T05 53 27 14 72, attelagesdemonsacou.com.
11 km northeast of Bergerac on D21e.
The *attelage* is an antique carriage called a *calèche*, and it's a pleasure to meet Roland Lagorce and his horse Albert for tours around the countryside. Tours last 90-120 minutes, from €10-17 per person.

Golf

Golf Club de Périgueux
Saltgourde, T05 53 53 02 35, golfdeperigueux.com.
5 km west of the city on D6089.
Périgueux has one of the best and most attractive courses in the department: par 72, 6029 m with plenty of traps and swans in the water hazards. Fees are reasonable and there are some special offers (see their website). It's always busy though: book ahead.

Horse racing

Hippodrome de Pesquié-Bas
Villeréal, T05 53 36 62 14.
32 km southeast of Bergerac.
In the lovely bastide of Villeréal, the local Société Hippique puts on a summer schedule of racing, mostly in sulkies. It's not Longchamp but it can be great fun; you can sit in the grandstand or get a good duck-and-potatoes lunch and lots of wine at bargain prices in the marquee while you watch the nags run. Champagne is available in magnums if you're lucky, but first try to corral a regular and get him to explain how French betting works. Ask at the Villeréal tourist office (T05 53 36 09 65) for the current schedule.

Water sports

One of the best bases for canoeing and water sports is Trémolat. At their 'Base Nautique', **Aquafun** (T05 53 57 72 27) rents canoes and kayaks and will bus you out for junkets of two to nine hours to Limeuil, Siorac or Le Bugue. They also do the popular new 'surfbikes'. From the port in Limeuil, **Canoe Rivières Loisirs** (T05 53 63 38 73) will take you up to La Roque-Gageac or Beynac and let you float back past the castles.

Autorail Espérance.

Lakes and good spots along the river are rather few in this area, so **swimming** opportunities are limited. Le Buisson has supervised river swimming at the Plage du Pont de Vicq (Jul to mid-Aug), and there are good *plans d'eau* at Pombonne, just north of Bergerac on the D21, and Lanquais. The latter also has electric boats for kids to ride at the **Port Miniature 'Le Ligal'** (T06 83 16 15 92, Apr to mid-Jun and Sep-Oct Sat-Sun 1400-1800, mid-Jun to Aug daily 1100-1900).

Périgord Vert

Contents

Château de Hautefort.

Introduction

They say it was Jules Verne who first gave 'Green Perigord' its name, and green it certainly is – a jumble of forested hills and farms that stretches across the northern edge of the department.

Tranquillity, as the French like to say, is assured. There isn't a town in Périgord Vert with more than 3500 people. It has exactly 15 km of N (national) road in it, just passing through a corner on its way somewhere else. There are more sheep and cows than people, and if the ducks knew how badly they had us outnumbered they might rebel against getting turned into foie gras.

But Périgord Vert has its charms, and there's nothing at all rustic about them. It is the place where the aristocratic ethos of old Périgord comes through most clearly. Above the trees you can see the turrets of great châteaux: Hautefort, Bourdeilles, Jumilhac, Mareuil; these, along with the equally aristocratic town of Brantôme, provide the best reasons to visit. Recently, though, a new one has appeared: the Voie Verte, a disused rail line now recycled as a hiking and cycle path that runs through some of the best parts of the countryside.

Hay bales, Périgord Vert.

What to see in...

...one day
No one should miss **Brantôme** when they're in the area. After a tour of the abbey and maybe a boat ride around this water-girt town, there will still be time for a trip to the exquisite **Château de Bourdeilles**.

...a weekend or more
After Brantôme, you could spend an entire day on the 17-km **Voie Verte** and visiting the sights around it; after that you might want to tour around to see the châteaux: along with Bourdeilles, **Hautefort** and **Jumilhac** are the most spectacular.

Brantôme & the Dronne Valley

To get the full effect, it's best to enter Brantôme from the west. Follow the signs for the abbey, and your first sight will be its gleaming white façade reflected in the river, in a wonderfully urbane townscape of parks, pavilions and fountains.

Brantôme makes a neat bookend to Sarlat, over on the other side of Périgord. Both were essentially aristocratic preserves – the latter, a place where the elite built their townhouses, the former where they parked their younger sons in a five-star monastery. The setting is perfect. Beneath the cliffs and forested hills, the town centre is an island in the River Dronne, and the water lazily flowing on all sides has given it the nickname of 'the Venice of Périgord'. Altogether, the result is one of the most celebrated and beautiful towns in France.

Brantôme has been here a long time, though little is known about what it was like in Celtic or Roman times. The medieval chroniclers say the Benedictine abbey was founded in 769, and endowed by Charlemagne himself with the relics of the rather obscure St Sicarius. As a village grew up around it, the abbey thrived in spite of some occasional troubles. The Vikings sacked it twice in the ninth century, the English turned it into a fortress in the Hundred Years' War, and it had more narrow escapes during the Wars of Religion.

Brantôme

Abbaye Troglodytique et Musée Fernand Desmoulin

T05 53 05 80 63.
Feb-Mar and Oct-Dec Wed-Mon 1000-1200 and 1400-1700, Apr-Jun and Sep Wed-Mon 1000-1230 and 1400-1800, Jul-Aug daily 1000-1900. €4, €2 concessions/child (7-18).

The abbey church now serves as Brantôme's parish church, and is open during normal church hours. There isn't a lot to see in any case. It suffered a lot over the centuries and Paul Abadie was hired to do a restoration; the result is not quite as ham-fisted as the job he did on Périgueux's St-Front.

The rest of the abbey (the part you buy a ticket for) is on the left; it also houses the town hall and the tourist office. Its imposing Renaissance façade conceals a load of surprises – directly behind it stands the rough cliff face, with the caves that have made this a holy site since Celtic times and provided shelter for the monks in Charlemagne's time.

At the door they'll hand you a plan with an explanation of all the sights along the cliff, including Dark Age crypts and a spring that still flows, the **Fontaine de St-Sicaire**; this probably provided the original, pre-Christian reason for the veneration of this site. Built atop a spur of the cliffs is another wonder, the abbey's slightly tipsy **bell tower** (Jun-Sep Mon-Fri 1000-1230 and 1400-1800, Sun 1000 1230). With its Merovingian foundations,

Bell tower, Brantôme Abbey.

it's claimed to be the oldest bell tower in France. Most of it is 11th century, and its rugged architecture hints at early Romanesque. Its marble columns are probably from a Roman temple that previously occupied the site.

All this is a prelude to something ancient and strange, so uncanny and cinematographic that you'll half expect Douglas Fairbanks or Indiana Jones to leap out with a flaming torch. A huge temple carved out of the cliff focuses on a colossal relief known as *The Last Judgment*. No one knows its exact age or what the complex composition really represents. The huge shadowy figure that dominates the scene is said to be Christ, but looks more like some emanation from the prophetic works of William Blake. The rows of heads recall the Celts, like the carved heads on the corbels of Romanesque churches. Saints or angels look up towards the deity from both sides, their faces too eroded for identification. The *Crucifixion* carved on an adjacent wall is believed to be from the 17th century.

After all this, you won't be too surprised when the tour ends with the slightly eerie galleries of the

Tip...

The river view of this lovely place is an experience in itself. Rent canoes from **Brantôme Canoë** (Route de Thiviers, T05 53 05 77 24, brantomecanoe.com, May-Sep) or **Allo Canoë** (Bas Chatenet de Près, T05 53 06 31 85, allocanoes.com, Apr-Oct). If you're too pooped to paddle, the **Arche de Noé** is a little electric pleasure boat that leaves from place du Marché for a 50-minute tour around the town (daily in season at 1115, 1400, 1500, 1600, 1700, 1800. €7).

Brantôme Abbey.

The Abbot of Brantôme

Pierre de Bourdeille (c 1540-1614), from the family and château of the same name, was one of those younger sons who ended up in abbeys. First, though, he managed to find time for a very picaresque life – travelling to Morocco and England, where he met Elizabeth I, and running off to help the Knights of Malta fight the Turk. A fall from a horse put an end to his soldiering, and leisure made a writer of him; his *Memoirs* were read all over Europe.

Just by chance, Pierre also happened to be Abbot of Brantôme. In those days the French Church was so decadent that benefices were like any other noble property, to be bought or sold or inherited. The Abbey gave him his pen name, Brantôme, and plenty of feudal rents.

Not many people read such works as *Les vies des dames galantes* or *Les vies des hommes illustres et des grands capitains* any more, which is a shame: they're pretty spicy stuff. Brantôme was a one-man tabloid, and much of his popularity came from his insider's account of what was really going on behind the arrases of the great palaces. He is still celebrated for his wit and worldly cynicism, but mostly survives in French books of quotations, imparting such louche epigrams as *'D'une vielle poule on fait le meilleur bouillon'* ('An old chicken makes the best soup'), and *'Toute belle femme s'estant une fois essayée au jeu d'amour ne le désapprend jamais'* (or, as we might say, 'Once you learn to ride a bike you never forget').

Musée Fernand Desmoulin. Born in 1853 in Javerlhac, near Nontron, this artist and spiritualist was popular in his day, a friend to such luminaries as Emile Zola. Around 1900, he began consulting mediums and letting his unconscious draw for him in the dark. The results can be seen here.

Outside the abbey are its worldly embellishments, all lovely works added by the wealthy abbots. The **Fontaine Médicis**, with a relief of the famous Abbot of Brantôme, stands just on the edge under the cliffs. The **Pont Coudé** (crooked bridge) and the delightful **Pavillon Renaissance** were both added by his predecessor, Pierre de Mareuil. The utterly picturesque **Moulin de l'Abbaye**, its mill wheel still turning, is now a luxury hotel with an excellent restaurant (see page 142), and in the park along the river are three elegant stone *reposoirs* (temporary altars for church festivals).

The Pont Coudé will take you into the town itself, a throbbing place on Friday – market day – and just a little sleepy otherwise. In summer you can have a look at the **Château de la Hierce** (T05 53 05 87 17, Jun-Oct Sat-Thu 1430-1800, €5), a very charming Renaissance hideaway begun in 1530; its grounds are a botanical garden with all the flowers and plants of Périgord in attendance.

The Abbot of Brantôme.

Bourdeilles

You could say that Brantôme and Bourdeilles are really part of the same place, the two poles of a little world apart, separated by 10 lovely, forested kilometres of the Dronne Valley. Their histories have always run together; often one member of the family ran the abbey at Brantôme while his brother looked after more worldly affairs from Bourdeilles, seat of the first of the four baronies of Périgord.

As at Brantôme, the aristocratic graces of the old days still scent the air. The little village that grew up around the château is effortlessly cute. After the château, walk down to the handsome medieval bridge over the Dronne.

Château de Bourdeilles

T05 53 03 73 36, semitour.com.
Feb-Mar and Nov to mid-Dec Sun-Mon and Wed-Thu 1000-1230 and 1400-1730; Apr-Jun and Sep to mid-Nov Wed-Sun 1000-1230 and 1400-1830, Jul-Aug daily 1000-1900. €6, €4 child (6-12).

Most of Périgord's castles offer you either a stout medieval *château fort* or a Renaissance palace that succeeded one. Here at Bourdeilles you get both, one on top of the other. The older model is first mentioned in 1183, when the Abbots of Brantôme used it as a refuge from trouble. The English grabbed it in 1360 and held it on and off for a century.

The famous Abbot of Brantôme was born here, and while his sister-in-law Jacquette de Montbron was in charge of it she built the new palace in the castle's huge courtyard. Jacquette knew what she wanted, and she taught herself architecture so that she could oversee the works. The story goes that she created it to attract a visit from Catherine de' Medici, and when the queen failed to show Jacquette was so furious she moved out and never lived in it again. (Historians suggest that Catherine was afraid of being captured by a band of Protestants.)

Later on, Bourdeilles fell into the clutches of those anachronistic bad boys, the Comtes de Périgord, who turned it into a robbers' hideout. The King of France confiscated it as soon as he was able. For a while in the 18th century Jacquette's proud palace was reduced to a silkworm farm, and in the Revolution they used it to make saltpetre for the army. Bourdeilles was in a sad state until recently, when a wealthy descendant of the original family bought it, fixed it up, filled it with Renaissance furnishings and then gave it all to the Dordogne department.

Though it is well preserved, there isn't a lot to see in the medieval castle and its eight-sided **keep**. Jacquette's delightful formal **gardens**, however, have been perfectly restored, and a small labyrinth added. The view over the walls is as paradisiacal as Périgord gets; on the western side it looks straight down on the château's 17th-century **mill**, shaped like a boat in the river.

Griffins of Bourdeilles

In Bourdeilles you'll notice an unusual device on the town's arms. Those aren't chicken feet; they belong to griffins.

According to an old legend, Marcomir, King of the Franks, was married to a princess of the Angles named Bourdeille. Their three sons went off in their ships to raid the rich land of the Romans, and in the mouth of the Garonne they landed on a magic island where the inhabitants were all savages. The brothers killed them all, but in turn were set upon by griffins. Two succumbed, but the youngest prevailed. He cut off their claws and put them on his banner at his new home in Périgord, which he named after his mother.

There really was a Marcomir, one of what French historians call the *roitelets* (little kings) of the Franks in the fourth century, and he is claimed as the ancestor of the Merovingian kings. And as for griffins, with the body of a lion and the head, wings and talons of an eagle, in the Middle Ages they were still visible on surviving Roman art. Everyone believed in them, but they always lived out yonder, just beyond those hills…

Bourdeilles.

As an architect, Jacquette didn't do a bad job, though typically of the French of her time she had a nice, medieval contempt for the new Italian-style symmetry. The main floor contains an **armoury**, with some wonderfully decorative weapons and armour from Germany, Spain and the Islamic world. The two floors above are furnished with a rich hoard of furniture, wedding chests, tapestries and portraits. Highlights include a German Renaissance polychrome wood group of *The Dormition of the Virgin*, the Gilded Room, with some of Jacquette's original furnishings, and a bed fit for an emperor – in fact, the bed of that megalomaniac Renaissance scoundrel Emperor Charles V.

Château de Mareuil

Mareuil, T05 53 60 99 85.
Guided tours, Apr-Jun Wed-Sat 1015-1200 and 1400-1715, Sun 1400-1715; Jul-Aug Wed-Sat 1015-1200 and 1400-1815, Sun 1400-1815; Sep to mid-Oct Wed-Sat 1015-1200 and 1400-1700, Sun 1400-1700; mid-Oct to mid-Nov Wed-Sun 1400-1700; mid-Nov to Mar Sun 1400-1715. €5. 19 km northwest of Brântome.

Mareuil-sur-Belle is a slightly bedraggled corner of Périgord, and this may be the most bedraggled of its great châteaux. Once one of the four baronies of Périgord, it began as a medieval castle standing alone on the plain. Its transition to a residential château began after the Hundred Years' War, and among the many owners who have held it since was the famous Baron Talleyrand.

Inside there are dungeons, some furnished rooms and a Flamboyant Gothic chapel, along with a museum dedicated to Maréchal Lannes, an ancestor of the current owners. Jean Lannes was a country boy from the Gers who worked his way up through the ranks, serving the Grande Armée across Spain, Italy, Egypt and central Europe. In 1809 he was famously recorded as complaining: "This Napoleon is going to get us all killed." He died after a battle only a few months later, his legs crushed by a cannonball.

Following the Dronne

Sometimes, instead of trailing around the big sights and enduring guided tours, it makes a refreshing change just to head for some terra incognita and see what a day's exploring might turn up, some place where the roads are a little twisty and merit green 'scenic route' lines on the map.

One of these is an area that can make a fine day trip from either Brantôme or Périgueux. The Dronne is a charmer, and it has had its way with all the drowsy villages along its length. **Bourdeilles** is the first stop on the river after Brantôme, then it's a leisurely drive through the villages of **Creyssac**, **Lisle** and **Montagrier**, where you can visit the **Maison de la Dronne** (by appointment, T05 53 90 01 33), a medieval water mill that was turned into an electricity generator in the 1900s. Montagrier also has a little riverside beach called the **Baignade de Salles**.

The biggest village in this part of the valley is **Ribérac**, where you can rent a canoe or visit the Romanesque **Eglise St-Pierre de Faye**. Besides Ribérac's there are at least a score of Romanesque churches in this area, and you could easily spend the whole day tracking them down. Perhaps the best is St-Cybard at **Cercles**, 21 km north on the D99, which has a wealth of good sculpture. Others worth seeking out (all north of the Dronne) are at **Celles**, **Grand-Brassac**, **Allemans**, **St-Paul-Lizonne**, **St-Martin-Viveyrol** and **Cherval**, where the church has five domes, like Périgueux's St-Front.

In the same area, you could visit **Petit-Bersac** to see the Roman-era relics in the Musée Gallo-Romain (T05 53 90 27 02, Jul-Aug daily 1430-1800, otherwise by appointment; €2) or a tiny village acclaimed as one of the most beautiful in Périgord, **Lusignac**. The village and everything around it has been a protected area since François Mitterand owned a country house here while he was president.

There has been a purpose to all this touring, and that was to get you to **Aubeterre-sur-Dronne**, just over the border into the Charente. Aubeterre is an exquisite village famous for its outlandish **Eglise Monolithique** (T05 45 98 65 06, daily 0930-1230 and 1400-1800, 1400-1900 in summer; €4.50), an entire 20-m-high church carved out of a rocky cliff; it was begun in the fifth century, over a Roman-era temple of Mithras, and expanded in the 12th century. Aubeterre also has a more traditional Romanesque church, **St-Jacques**, with some fine sculpture on its façade and capitals.

Tip...

Once you start taking a good look at churches of the 11th-12th centuries, the little mysteries in their sculpture and sacred geometry can become addictive. Much of the Romanesque is a lost world to us, but you can find some keys to understanding it on a fascinating website created by two locals: The Green Man of Cercles (green-man-of-cercles.org).

Eglise Monolithique.

Nontronnais & Haut Périgord

It's a quiet region, even by Périgord standards, as far removed as you can get from the tourist hotspots of the Dordogne valley. But it has a number of attractions, and enough natural charm to make at least a few people come back each year to make it their own personal Périgord.

The Nontronnais is the patch of country around the hard-working town of Nontron, famous for making knives. Haut Périgord, draped over the northern edge of the department, includes three of the greatest Périgord châteaux: Hautefort, Jumilhac and Puyguilhem. Most of the area is part of the Parc Naturel Régional Périgord-Limousin – not really a park at all, merely a government organization promoting tourism and sustainable development. Just the same, it is a great place for hiking or biking, around the newly opened Voie Verte and the gorges of the Auvézère.

Nontron

It's a funny old name for a funny old town. Nontron has been around forever (its name comes from a Celtic word that means 'ash trees') and unlike the other Périgord towns, sprawling lazily on the riverbanks, this one perches high on a hilltop, one of the few Celtic *oppida* to survive into modern times.

One other thing sets Nontron apart. While the rest of Périgord sometimes seems to get by just cooking confits for the tourists, this busy little town actually works for a living. The Nontronnais have a long tradition of skilled manufacturing; they make fine saddles, pewter ware, porcelain, neckties and plenty of other things. The town, though tiny (with a population of 3500), is the biggest in Périgord Vert.

Mostly though, Nontron is famous for blades. Since the 1400s its knife-smiths have had a reputation all over France, and they'll sure try to sell you one today. At the tip of the town on place Paul-Bert, the **Coutellerie Nontronnaise**, in business since 1653, has opened a big, modern workshop-showroom (see page 144). From here, avenue Général Leclerc follows the top of the hill, passing first the **Espace Paul-Bert**, where this hot-for-culture town puts on some interesting art exhibitions, and then the 18th-century neoclassical **Château de Nontron**, now the town hall and tourist office (3 av Général Leclerc, T05 53 56 25 50).

Near this is the entrance to the **Jardin des Arts**. The long-neglected gardens of the château, recently restored and enlarged, hang down the hillside with views over the Bandiat Valley. The restorers did a fine job, with plenty of fountains and flowers and, unlike Périgord's other new urban garden, at Terrasson (see page 178), it's free and open for people to enjoy all the time.

Varaignes

Varaignes is famous for turkeys all year round, but especially so on 11 November, when thousands of people from all over France descend on the village for the annual **Foire des Dindons**. The members of the Confrérie des Dindons lead the festivities, dressed up in period costume (just what period isn't entirely clear), and they parade their flocks of birds through the village. Turkeys being rather independent-minded, this isn't always easy, but the gendarmes are there to keep them in line. There is music, a gobbling contest, and of course last year's birds make a return appearance for a big communal turkey dinner in the evening.

Château de Varaignes – Atelier-Musée des Tisserands et de la Charentaise

T05 53 56 35 76.
Apr-Jun and Sep-Oct Wed-Sun 1400-1700, Jul-Aug Mon-Sat 1000-1200 and 1430-1830, Sun 1430-1830, rest of year by appointment. €3.80, €2.30 child.

Before there were turkeys, Varaignes was famous for felt slippers, called *charentaises*, produced by the farmers' wives. The village's modest Renaissance château has been fitted out as a museum to this cottage industry and to fabrics in general, with antique looms, knitting machines and felt presses.

Abbaye de Bussière-Badil

18 km north of Nontron.

In a village tucked away in some pretty countryside on the border with the Charente, a Benedictine abbey was founded in about 768. Its 12th-century church survives, and provides a chance to see the Limoges and Charente styles of Romanesque sculpture. The extravagant main portal has a wealth of decoration, with mythical beasts hidden among the lush foliage. The church was rebuilt more than once, and the rest of the portal's sculptures seem to have been rearranged at random. Inside, there are some fine capitals, carved in more Périgourdin style.

La Voie Verte

East of Brantôme, along the valleys of the Dronne, Trincou and Côle, lies some of the choicest countryside in Périgord Vert. Decades ago when the old Nontron-Excideuil branch line closed, people thought it was just another nail in the coffin of rural life. But today, those rusted tracks have given way to something new with a lot of promise for the future.

Between Excideuil and Thiviers the tracks are still in place, and you can pedal down them in the special rail cars of **Vélorail du Périgord Vert** (see page 145). From Thiviers to St-Pardoux-la-Rivière, however, they've tried a different strategy. The old right of way is now the **Voie Verte**, or 'green way': a 17-km dedicated trail for hikers, cyclists and horses.

There's plenty to see in the area, and the route offers the possibility of hitting the sights in a way that is serene and civilized. The **Grotte de Villars** is a couple of minutes off the route, and the **Château de Puyguilhem** only 3 km beyond that. Right in the middle, the lovely village of **St-Jean-de-Côle** offers a lunchtime break, or even an overnight stay if you're not in a hurry.

Following the Voie Verte is fun in itself. Nature grew back around the line after it closed; now it seems more like a park, with plenty of stately stone and iron bridges to cross. Keep in mind that it's only a few years old, and the infrastructure hasn't yet grown up around it (for one thing, there's still no convenient place to rent bikes). Eventually it will. Voies Vertes are springing up around Europe and beyond, and they are increasingly popular. They give a hint of what holidays in the future will be like.

Saut de Chalard

At the beginning of the Voie Verte, 4 km outside St-Pardoux-la-Rivière, there is a scenic area around this small waterfall (*saut*) with a 2-km nature trail; you can get a guide to the plants and animals along it from any of the local tourist offices.

Grotte de Villars

T05 53 54 82 36, grotte-villars.com.
Apr-Jun and Sep daily 1000-1200 and 1400-1900, Jul-Aug daily 1000-1930, Oct-Nov daily 1400-1830. €7.50, €4.50 child (5-12).
2.5 km from Voie Verte on D82.

Discovered only in 1953, this is one of the few caves to offer both natural and manmade wonders (and they have recently added a sound and light show to make it even jazzier). The stalagmites are pretty good, especially in the 'Grand Balcon', and there are Palaeolithic drawings of bison, galloping horses and a rare human representation.

Château de Puyguilhem

Villars, T05 53 54 82 18, puyguilhem.monuments-nationaux.fr.
May-Aug daily 1000-1230 and 1400-1830, Sep-Apr Tue-Sun 1000-1230 and 1400-1730. €5, €3.50 concessions, under 18s free.

Puyguilhem could be the perfect château on the Loire, a little brother of Chambord or Azay-le-Rideau. In fact, it predates most of them and influenced their architecture. It was built in 1510 for a very important gentleman, Mondot de la Marthonie, President of the Parlement de Paris in the reign of François I.

Château de Puyguilhem.

The château was on the verge of collapse when the state bought it in 1939. The Compagnons de Devoir, that wonderful institution dedicated to training artisans and keeping traditional building methods alive, worked on it for 20 years, and the result has been furnished with 17th- and 18th-century pieces from France's Mobilier National. There are some fine Aubusson and Flanders tapestries – in one you'll notice what may well be the first embroidered image of a rhinoceros. But the best thing here is an original Renaissance relief of the *Labours of Hercules* on an upstairs fireplace.

Outside, it is difficult to tell what the original gardens were like; a maze of box hedges was added in 1950. If you come in June and no one else has found them first, you can pick wild strawberries around the car park.

Just 1.5 km from Puyguilhem on the D98, you can visit the romantic but roofless ruin of the Cistercian **Abbaye de Boschaud** (begun in 1145), standing in an open meadow.

St-Jean-de-Côle

Yes, it's another of those official *plus beaux villages de France* that run so thick on the ground in Périgord. But it is a lovely place, popular with summer visitors, with a Romanesque church and priory, half-timbered houses, a 15th-century humpbacked bridge, and the 12th-17th-century **Château de la Marthonie** (T05 53 82 30 21, Jul-Aug daily 1000-1200 and 1400-1900, €4.50), which includes a small museum with exhibits on the history of papermaking and advertising posters of a century ago.

As if St-Jean isn't pretty enough, every year on the second weekend in May they cover it in flowers for a festival called **Les Floralies** that attracts visitors from all over.

Thiviers & around

At the eastern end of the Voie Verte lies the busy market town of Thiviers. Surrounded by ducks, it's a big foie gras producer, with a few factories to bring just a slight touch of urban grit to this bucolic corner of the world. It has a Renaissance church with some good sculptural work, and the **Musée du Foie Gras** (place Foch, T05 53 55 12 50, daily 1000-1300 and 1400-1800, closed Sun Oct-Apr), with a very didactic exhibition that will teach you more than you ever wanted to know about ducks and geese.

Château de Laxion

T06 73 88 64 08, chateaulaxion.blogspot.com.
Daily Jul-Aug 1000-1900, mid to end Jun and beginning to mid-Sep 1000-1230 and 1400-1830. €5, €4 concessions, €3 child (5-16).
5 km south of Thiviers on D76 between Eyzerac and Corgnac.

One of the most imposing of the region's Renaissance châteaux, Laxion was allowed to fall into total ruin in the 1960s, helped along by fires. Today, its new owners François and Gaëlle Dumy are gamely trying to restore it with the help of the people of Corgnac. The worksite is open for visits in summer, and they throw in a schedule of mock jousts, medieval dinners and such to help the cause; if you want to learn how to build dry stone walls, they'd be grateful for the help.

Château de Jumilhac

Jumilhac-le-Grand, T05 53 52 42 97.
Guided tours only, Dec-Easter Sun 1400-1700 or by appointment, Easter-May and Oct daily 1400-1800, Jun-Sep daily 1000-1900, plus Tue (and Thu Jul-Aug) 2130-2330. Château and gardens €8, €7 concessions, €6 child (5-12).
19 km northeast of Thiviers.

This château lords it over the village of Jumilhac like a true aristocrat; a long *allée* built through the

Château de Jumilhac.

centre of the village nicely frames its famous roofline, crowded with steep gables and turrets, and roofed in black slate topped with a forest of iron figures: birds and angels, the sun and moon, and figures supposed to be allegorical references to the history of the Jumilhacs.

These are only fitting, since it was iron that built this château, mostly in the 16th century – the profits from Antoine Chapelle de Jumilhac's iron furnaces and forges made it possible. In those days, metallurgy wasn't far removed from magic in the common mind, and Jumilhac's great wealth gave him a reputation as an alchemist; some have read alchemical symbolism into the figures on the rooftops.

Inside are furnishings from the 16th-19th centuries, a well-equipped kitchen and plenty of paintings, including a series of hunting scenes in the Grand Salon. The present château sits atop the old feudal castle. One of the dungeons here, the Chambre de la Fileuse, where some early frescoes were recently discovered, recalls the fanciful story of a lady of the castle who was locked up here by a jealous husband; she spent her time spinning and smuggling out love letters to her sweetheart, a shepherd, hidden in the bobbins.

Jumilhac has extensive gardens, restored to look something like the Renaissance originals, and the designers have attempted to weave in alchemical allegory here too, with plantings to represent the seven planets and the four types of gold. The latter theme is brought out further in the **Galerie d'Or** (T05 53 52 55 43, open informally), a little museum built into some of Jumilhac's *chais* and dedicated to the history of the precious metal. Gold is found in the River Isle, and the museum puts on half-day courses in summer to teach you how to pan for it.

Excideuil & around

Place Maréchal Bugeaud is the centre of Excideuil, named for yet another Périgourdin military hero. Thomas Bugeaud was a Napoleonic veteran who, through speed, daring and sheer brutality, won France its new colony Algeria in the 1830s and 40s. The statue of him that adorns the allée André Maurois used to stand in the centre of Algiers. Bugeaud grew apples on his farm at nearby Lanouaille when he wasn't torturing, starving and slaughtering Algerians, and he gave Excideuil the pretty fountain on the square as a present.

Behind it stands the **Eglise St-Thomas**. You've probably noticed it already: the unique open steeple that looks like a crown on its head is visible for miles around. St-Thomas has suffered a lot; its rebuilding after the English burned it down in 1420 (along with the rest of the town) explains its mixture of Romanesque and Flamboyant Gothic styles, but it doesn't explain that crazy steeple – made of reinforced concrete and added in 1936.

Excideuil's **château** stands on a hill at the edge of town. It's a handsome castle, with a fine Renaissance gate and bits and pieces from other periods, and it's had a busy history. Richard the Lionheart, who spent a lot of time in this part of Périgord, besieged it no less than three times but couldn't get in; the English would be more successful later on. Today, part of it houses the town hall and they put on some big-name art exhibitions each summer.

Gorges de l'Auvézère

East of Excideuil the scenery becomes a little wilder as it climbs up towards the mountains of the Corrèze. The geology is different too; you'll begin to see houses made of dark metamorphic schist. The gorges around the hamlets of St-Mesmin and Payzac aren't dramatic, but there are nice walks everywhere along the River Auvézère and on paths between the villages. You'll also find two relics of this rustic corner's surprising industrial past.

Excedeuil.

Forge de Savignac

Savignac-Lédrier, T05 53 62 50 06, tourisme-lanouaille-perigord.com.
Guided tours May-Jun Sat 1000-1230, Jul-Sep Tue-Fri 1000-1230, Sat 1000-1230 and 1430-1830, also May-Sep 2nd and 4th Sun of each month 1500-1800. €2.

In Périgord and elsewhere around Europe, wherever ore was present, iron used to be produced in small-scale forges like this one, which is mentioned in records as early as 1521. Most of the machinery here is 19th-century and powered by charcoal. It's all still in good working order, the only one of its kind in France.

Papeterie de Vaux

Payzac, T05 53 62 50 06, tourisme-lanouaille-perigord.com.
Guided tours May-Nov Tue-Sat 1000-1230 and 1430-1830, Sun 1500-1800, rest of year by appointment. €4, €2.50 child.

This little rustic factory started as a forge too, but in 1861 it was converted to make paper out of straw. The original machinery is still present.

Ecomusée de la Truffe

Sorges, T05 53 05 90 11, ecomusee-truffe-sorges.com.
Mid-Jun to Sep daily 0930-1230 and 1430-1830, Oct to mid-Nov and mid-Feb to mid-Jun Tue-Sun 1000-1200 and 1400-1700, mid-Nov to mid-Feb Tue-Sun 1400-1700. €4, €3 concessions, €2 child (10-15). 16 km west of Excideuil.

This unprepossessing village likes to call itself the 'World Capital of Truffles', so the opening of a truffle museum was only a matter of time; the visit includes a trip through a cultivated truffle zone.

Château de Hautefort

Hautefort, T05 53 50 51 23, chateau-hautefort.com.
Mar and beg-mid-Nov Sat-Sun 1400-1800, Apr-May daily 1000-1230 and 1400-1830, Jun-Aug daily 0930-1900, Sep daily 1000-1800, Oct daily 1400-1800. €8.50, €4 child (7-14).

In its first incarnation, as a fortress, Hautefort belonged to the Lastours, one of whom entered Jerusalem with Godfrey de Bouillon on the First Crusade; later it passed to a family that included the famous troubadour Bertran de Born. The Gontaut family of Biron acquired it in the 15th century; they styled themselves Marquis de Hautefort and began the process of converting it into a palace.

The Gontauts had money and taste enough to make Hautefort the greatest of Périgord's châteaux, as much a symbol of the *grand siècle* – the age of Louis XIII and XIV – as Versailles itself. Dominating the countryside from its hilltop, Château de Hautefort can also be seen as a symbol of the magnificent aristocratic arrogance that would one day lead to revolution.

The entrance to the château runs through the expansive **Parc à l'anglaise**, still recovering from the 1999 winter storm that flattened millions of trees all across the southwest. The **Jardin à la française** that borders the other three sides, with its nervously perfect topiary bushes and flowerbeds, is a 19th-century addition that probably gives a good idea of the original plan. The overall effect is breathtaking, though understandably there isn't a lot to see inside: acres of marquetry, period furnishings, a lot of somewhat faded tapestries and a remarkable domed neoclassical chapel.

Tip...

Come on a Wednesday evening in July or August, when Hautefort puts on its 'summer spectacle', with music and dramatizations evoking the life and times of Jacques-François and Marie. It begins at 2100 and lasts two hours; the ticket office opens at 2015.

The luck of Hautefort

Hautefort must have had a special talisman, for few châteaux have endured so many narrow escapes. Bertran de Born, the noble troubadour who owned it, loved war so much he was constantly stirring up trouble between the kings of England and France and inciting the Plantagenets to fight each other. When he helped Henry Court-Mantel rebel against his father Henry II, the king took Hautefort by siege, and Bertran needed all his charm to avoid ending up in the dungeon.

Jacques-François de Gontaut, who oversaw the end of the rebuilding in the 17th century, had a reputation as the biggest miser in France (he may have been the model for Molière's miser in *l'Avare*). But his sister Marie was the darling of the Paris court. Everyone called her 'Aurore', except Cardinal Richelieu and his agents; for them, her code-name was 'the Creature'. The high point of her career of troublemaking was the conspiracy of Cinq-Mars, a plot to get rid of Richelieu that had the support of Louis XIII's queen, Anne of Austria. Richelieu was too smart to let himself be kidnapped, yet when he took his terrible revenge he spared Hautefort, and Marie too.

Hautefort survived the Revolution thanks to the pluck of the Gontauts, who personally manned the cannons when a mob came from Excideuil to sack it. When the revolutionaries finally took control they kept it up to use as a prison.

By 1929 the château seemed on its last legs, but it found an angel in the person of Baron Henri de Bastard, who fell in love with it and spent the rest of his life restoring it. In 1968, with the work almost finished, Hautefort suddenly had to face its most dangerous enemies of all – two teenagers, whose careless smoking started a fire that could be seen 40 km away in Périgueux. Nothing was left but the stone, but the Baron's indomitable widow Simone de Bastard immediately started planning the rebuilding. With a little help from the state she saw it through, and was able to move back in before she died in 1999, at the age of 96.

Château de Hautefort.

Musée de la Medicine de Hautefort

T06 85 52 29 75, musee-medecine-hautefort.fr. Easter-May daily 1000-1200 and 1400-1800, Jun-Sep daily 1000-1900, Oct Mon-Fri 1000-1200 and 1400-1800. €5, €3.50 concessions, under 12s free.

Jacques-François de Gontaut wasn't really such a miser after all. While it was the fashion of the day, encouraged by Louis XIV, to throw fortunes away on extravagances and mock those who wouldn't play along, the Marquis de Hautefort preferred to spend his money on more useful things. The great domed hospice he built, nearly as impressive as the château itself, was intended for the care of the sick and indigent (but only 33 of them at a time).

Now, the building and its grand chapel are an interesting and quite comprehensive museum of medicine through the ages, with rooms set aside for dentists and veterinarians too. There's also a garden of medicinal herbs.

Gardens at Château de Hautefort.

Sleeping

Brantôme

Hôtel Coligny €€€
8 place Charles de Gaulle, T05 53 05 71 42, hotel-coligny.fr.
The rooms are modern and nothing special, but if you can get one with a balcony overlooking the river it's worth a go. There's a sauna and jacuzzi, and a restaurant where they serve duck, cassoulet and a pretty good plate of *escargots* on a terrace with a view.

Les Arômes €€
13 av André Maurois, T05 53 08 53 46, aromesperigord.com.
Right in the centre, an elegant 18th-century townhouse with a pool and garden. As well as B&B accommodation they offer evening meals, with some quite fancy cooking on menus of €25 and €28.

Maison Fleurie €€
54 rue Gambetta, T05 53 35 17 04, maison-fleurie.net.
There are flowers everywhere in this welcoming, British-run city centre B&B, with five beautifully decorated rooms and just enough space out back for a small courtyard and pool. The same family also owns gîtes, including one of the oldest, half-timbered houses in the town (sleeps 2, €550 per week) and two others, one in Brantôme and one in the country (both sleep 6, €750 per week).

Hôtel Coligny.

Bourdeilles

Hostellerie les Griffons €€€
T05 53 45 45 35, griffons.fr.
The pretty house with blue shutters has stood on the banks of the Dronne since the 1500s. Now it is one of the most elegant inns in the Dordogne, capturing the mood of this aristocratic little village perfectly. The 10 rooms are beautifully decorated without being at all pretentious. There's a pool, and a fine restaurant (see page 142).

Lusignac

Self-catering

Font Losse
T+49 (0) 89-989947, lusignac.com.
Font Losse is one of four houses around Lusignac and Petit-Bersac, with three to eight bedrooms, owned by Jacqueline and Dirk Fleischer. Each is beautifully decorated and has a pool. Rates range from €1520 (sleeps 5) to €3690 (sleeps up to 16).

St-Saud-Lacoussière

Hostellerie St-Jacques €€€€-€€
T05 53 56 97 21, hostellerie-st-jacques.com.
St-Saud is an absolutely peaceful place far off the beaten track east of Nontron, and its luxury inn has been thriving under three generations of operation by the

same family. The ivy-covered building is charming enough to be in all the 'charming hotel' guides; it has a heated pool and jacuzzi, gardens and a tennis court. There is a wide choice of rooms, suites and apartments at widely differing prices, all furnished with a lot of effort and loving care; book far enough ahead and you can get a bargain here. There's also an exceptional restaurant (see page 143).

Camping

Kawan Village Château le Verdoyer
Champs-Romain, T03 59 59 03 59 (reservations), T05 53 56 94 64 (site), verdoyer.fr.
Mid-Apr to Oct.
5 km west of St-Saud on D96.
A campsite in the extensive grounds of a château, this is part of a chain but has a lot to offer. There's a bar, a good restaurant, shops and lots for children, including games, three pools and a waterslide. They lay on every sort of activity, including excursions and theme nights with local entertainment. Accommodation runs from simple pitches to chalets and mobile homes (sleeping up to 6), and even rooms in the château (€).

La Coquille

Hôtel des Voyageurs €
12 rue de la République, T05 53 52 80 13, hotelvoyageurs.fr.

Hostellerie les Griffons.

A nice budget choice, with a pool and garden, and a restaurant that's popular with the locals (€€).

Mavaleix

Château de Mavaleix €€
T05 53 52 82 01, chateau-mavaleix.com.
12 km north of Thiviers on N21.
While you're touring around looking at châteaux, why not stay in one too? Mavaleix is a lovely Renaissance specimen, but it's not snooty, rather an informal and friendly place offering nice, simple rooms. There are extensive grounds to play in, ponies for the children to admire, a pool and tennis courts, along with a bar and a restaurant (€€) offering local and some Italian dishes.

Next to the castle is an elegant gîte in a separate house with three bedrooms (€1150 per week).

Thiviers

Hôtel de France et de Russie €€
51 rue Général Lamy, T05 53 55 17 80, thiviers-hotel.com.
The grandiose name celebrates the 1893 Franco-Russian alliance; apparently the Russian ambassador had a house in the Dordogne and was quite a celebrity. This is an old post house, not so grandiose but friendly, comfortable and interesting, at unbeatable rates.

Excideuil

Le Fin Chapon €€-€
3 place du Château, T05 53 55 14 42, lefinchapon.com.
A modest establishment, but with some style; it's been here since 1751, but has recently been remodelled. If you like accordion music you will swoon for this place. Opt for the *chambre nuptiale* – you won't forget it. The restaurant (see page 143) is excellent.

Eating & drinking

Brantôme

Le Moulin de l'Abbaye €€€€
1 route de Bourdeilles, T05 53 05 80 22, moulin-abbaye.com.
Mid-Apr to mid-Nov open daily for dinner, plus Sat-Sun lunch.
The abbey's 18th-century mill, on the banks of the Dronne, enjoys perhaps the most gorgeous setting in Périgord. Now converted into a luxury hotel (€€€) of 19 rooms, it also houses a restaurant considered by many to be the best in the department. The chef comes up with some combinations never before seen – lobster and pigeon, turbot with goat's cheese and truffles – but the results have them coming down from Paris and beyond.

Les Saveurs €€€
6 rue Georges Saumande, T05 53 05 54 23, restaurant-les-saveurs.com.
Closed Wed, and Mon-Thu evenings out of high season.
It doesn't look like much from the street, but there's a wonderful secret garden at the back under a weeping willow. The duck and steaks share the menus with some fancy seafood.

Au Fil du Temps €€€-€€
1 chemin du Vert Galant, T05 53 05 24 12, fildutemps.com.
Mar-Dec, closed Mon-Tue outside high season.
A popular choice with the Brantômais. You'll do just as well here with the €12 lunch menu or a €35 splurge, with good things from the rotisserie and grill and afterwards, perhaps, something rather English that seems to have become a traditional southwestern dessert – apple crumble.

Bourdeilles

Hostellerie les Griffons €€€
T05 53 45 45 35, griffons.fr.
Open daily for dinner, closed for lunch Mon-Sat except Easter and Jul to mid-Sep.
One of the most gracious rooms anywhere, and of course there's a terrace overlooking the river. You can enjoy a very nice millefeuille with asparagus and a hint of truffle, rabbit with apricots wrapped in prosciutto, or a *fondue périgourdin*. The dessert compositions are entirely too beautiful to eat.

Le Moulin de l'Abbaye

St-Jean-de-Côle

Le Saint-Jean €€
Route de Nontron (D707), T05 53 52 23 30.
Closed Tue evening.
There's not much fancy along the Voie Verte, but the €11-15 lunch menus in this old family establishment go down nicely on the terrace.

St-Saud-Lacoussière

Hostellerie St-Jacques €€€€
T05 53 56 97 21, hostellerie-st-jacques.com.
Part of the luxury inn in this remote corner east of Nontron (see page 140), and well worth seeking out. The cuisine *très soignée* includes lobster and other seafood, on menus that change with the seasons. A beautiful garden terrace makes the experience complete.

Excideuil

Le Fin Chapon €€-€
3 place du Château, T05 53 55 14 42, lefinchapon.com.
Tue-Sun, closed Sun evenings and Jan.
Part of a 250-year old hotel (see page 141), this is the real southwest, with good cooking at bargain prices: big meaty salads as they like them here, *escargots*, *ris de veau* and all the duck you could want.

Sorges

L'Auberge de la Truffe €€€
T05 53 05 90 11, auberge-de-la-truffe.com.
Closed Sun evenings and Mon lunch out of season.
Périgord's truffle capital deserves one first-class restaurant, and fate has landed it here in this unassuming roadside hotel. There is a €100 truffle menu, but you needn't splurge: the breast of guinea fowl with girolles or the venison steak with a hint of truffle in the sauce are enough of a treat. The hotel (€) is just fine and a good bargain (with a billiards room); try to get a room facing the back garden.

Hautefort

L'Auberge du Parc €€
Place René Lavaud, T05 53 50 88 98, aubergeduparc-hautefort.fr.
Thu-Tue, closed Sun evening and mid-Dec to Feb.
Just outside the walls of the château, a nice spot with tables outside for lunch. There is a wide choice of *salades composées* and omelettes, a €16.50 lunch menu and other menus heavily weighted towards duck and foie gras. The Auberge also has five simple rooms (€).

Shopping

Brantôme

Food & drink

Cellier des Moines
4 bd Charlemagne, T05 53 04 10 24.
This is an outlet for the quality farm products of Périgord Vert: everything from foie gras to jams to ostrich and buffalo steaks.

Market

Brantôme has the biggest market in the area on Friday, picturesquely lining the riverbanks and even the bridge by the Abbey; unlike most markets, it runs all day.

Nontron

Knives

Coutellerie Nontronnaise
Place Paul-Bert, T05 53 56 01 55.
Mon-Fri 0900-1200 and 1330-1815, longer hours in summer.
The classic Nontron design in all manner of knives and tableware, not to mention souvenir miniatures. You can also see knives being made here.

Le Périgord
23 place Agard, T05 53 56 62 78, couteau-leperigord.com.
Mon-Sat 1000-1200, 1400-1800.
The Nontronnaise's worthy competition, with carved handles in a dozen different fine woods.

Both these firms also have shops in the centre of Brantôme.

St-Jean-de-Côle

Art & crafts

La Dame Blanche
Rue du Fond de Bourg, T05 53 62 38 88.
May-Sep Tue-Sat 1000-1900.
An interesting shop that sells the works of local artists and artisans: ceramics, painting, stained glass, clothing and accessories.

Tip...

Other markets in the area: Tuesday – Thiviers (summer only), Mareuil); Wednesday – Hautefort; Thursday – Excideuil, La Coquille, St-Pardoux-la-Rivière; Saturday – Nontron, Thiviers.

Activities & tours

Adventure sports

Vert-Auvézère
Le Bourg, Cherveix-Cubas, T05 53 52 72 90, site.voila.fr/vert.auvezere.
Open all year.
The valley of the Auvézère is a great place for wild exploring. Here (just north of Hautefort) you can rent off-road bikes, canoes and kayaks. They'll take you out for river trips, and they also offer equipment and advice for caving and rock climbing.

Balloon rides

Hautefort Montgolfière
Hautefort, T06 83 43 36 01, montgolfiere.fr.
A one-hour trip over the château and gardens and the surrounding countryside for €170.

Horse riding

Ferme Equestre Hippocamp
Lempzours, T05 53 52 61 99, hippocamp.fr.
South of St-Jean-de-Côle.
Open all year.
Hire horses and ponies from the stable closest to the Voie Verte: €60 for a full day. They also run trekking holidays.

Vélorail

Le Vélorail du Périgord Vert
Corgnac-sur-l'Isle, T05 53 52 42 93, velorail24.com.
Open all year, advance booking essential.
7 km south of Thiviers.
It looks like hard work to us; let's see if the idea catches on. Over the disused rail line between Thiviers and Excideuil you can travel on specially constructed pedal cars that fit on the tracks; each one seats five, with two people pedalling. Rent one from the station in this village for €25 (or €15 for a shorter, 50-min trip) and see the countryside; there are tunnels and some impressive viaducts to cross along the way.

Périgord Noir

Contents

Beynac-et-Cazenac.

Introduction

When the French up in the northern cities dream of Périgord and its charms, it's usually Black Périgord they're thinking of. 'Black' is for the truffles of course, but the colour conjures up so much more: the dark walnut and chestnut groves, the caves and the dark night of time – and the top of a properly grilled *magret du canard*.

Besides its fully justified reputation for natural beauty and easy living, Périgord Noir also claims an unfairly large share of the department's attractions. The Vézère Valley, 'World Capital of Prehistory', draws crowds from around the world to see the astonishing works of some of humankind's first – and most talented – artists.

And the choicest stretch of the Dordogne is the one that flows past Domme and La Roque-Gageac: a mini-Rhineland where the castles are planted so thickly you can see four or five at a time. Not far from these is the region's little capital, Sarlat, a town that won't ring a bell with most people, though it is one of the most beautiful and distinctive cities in France.

Shaved whole black truffles.

What to see in...

...one day

Cavemen or castles? The gems of Périgord Noir are concentrated in two surprisingly small regions, and you can take your pick. The **Vézère Valley** offers **Lascaux** and a dozen more famous sites of Palaeolithic art – the best is **Font-de-Gaume**, but remember to book ahead. If you prefer to stay in daylight, head for **Sarlat**; just 10 minutes from there you can commence a tour down a very short stretch of the Dordogne between **Domme** and **Beynac** that includes some of the region's best scenery and most interesting sights.

...a weekend or more

In three or four days you can see the best of both these areas. Take some time for the lesser-known sights: spectacular classical gardens at **Marqueyssac** and **Eyrignac**, a lesson in medieval warfare at **Castelnaud**, or the inspiring story of Josephine Baker at her home, **Les Milandes**.

Sarlat-la-Canéda

When you come to this lovely town, you might feel a little underdressed. What you'll really want is a tunic and cuirass, a cape and a pair of big saggy musketeer boots, and a broad-brimmed hat trimmed with a *panache* (that's the name for those big feathers they wore). You wouldn't look more out of place than the tourists in their shorts and bum bags, and if you're lucky you might get to be an extra in a film.

Sarlat is a dream of the ancien régime, a town with an aristocratic air and an ensemble of listed buildings as impressive as any in France. It looks more like the Paris of Cardinal Richelieu's time than Paris itself, which is what draws the directors every couple of years or so for another costume drama.

Périgueux – bigger and flashier – may be the capital, but there's no place more Périgourdin than Sarlat. It's as if the region's very essence had been distilled and concentrated here. Above all, this is a town devoted to the duck and the goose: there seems to be a shop on every corner offering foie gras, confits, smoked *magrets* and pâtés, not to mention truffles, walnuts, liqueurs and all the rest. The town's covered market, a real temple of local produce, fittingly occupies what was once a church.

Sarlat rooftops.

Cathédrale St-Sacerdos

Place du Peyrou.
Daily except during Mass, Jul-Aug 0800-1900, rest of year 0800-1215 and 1315-1900.
Map: Sarlat, p154.

Sacerdos was a local boy who became a monk here in the seventh century and went on to become Bishop of Limoges. Because of his reputation for curing lepers, his tomb became the object of a pilgrimage in the Middle Ages, and an important church was built. Nothing of that Romanesque original is left, save the distinctive squarish **bell tower**, similar to that of Périgueux. The stately 17th-century replacement church isn't really a cathedral any more; the diocese was merged with Périgueux in 1821.

Walk through the **cloister** to see the **Cour des Fontaines**, one of the town's loveliest squares, and don't miss Sarlat's most peculiar and intriguing monument, directly behind the church: a bullet-shaped 21-m stone tower called the **Lanterne des Morts** (see box, opposite).

Essentials

Getting around Sarlat's historic centre measures only 1 km across, so you can do it all on foot. Trying to drive through can be impossible in summer, and simply annoying at other times. Fortunately, there are two big, convenient car parks: at the southern end of the main drag (rue de la République), the one at place de la Grande Regaudie is closest to the sights; at the northern end, the car park on avenue Général de Gaulle is only a little further from the action.

Taxis **Allo Allo** (T05 53 59 02 43) or **Allo Philippe** (T06 08 57 30 10, allophilippetaxi.monsite.wanadoo.fr). Philippe Mouret speaks English and also offers customized tours around Périgord.

Buses For regional services see page 279.

Train station The train station is 2 km south of the centre on avenue de la Gare, with trains to Les Eyzies, Bergerac and Souillac. For details of regional train services see page 278.

Hospital **Centre hospitalier Jean Leclaire** (T05 53 31 75 75), 2 km north of the centre.

Post office Place du XIV Juillet.

Tourist information 2 Rue Tourny, T05 53 31 45 45, daily 0900-1200 and 1400-1800, July and August 0900-1900.

Sarlat.

Lanterns of the dead

Sarlat's may be by far the biggest and boldest, but it is only one example of a medieval enigma. *Lanternes des morts* are found all over France, though they're concentrated most thickly in what, in the 12th century when they were built, was the Duchy of Aquitaine.

A *lanterne* is round or sometimes square, with at least three small windows near the top; some later versions had a small colonnade on top. In the old days a light would be hoisted up on a pulley to shine through the slits. They were said to be like lighthouses, guiding the souls of the dead.

They are indeed most commonly found in cemeteries, though they were also sometimes built into churches; the strange cupola on Périgueux's St-Front may be one. They also appear at crossroads, or as slender little steeples perched incongruously on an old wall. Beyond hints from folklore, we have no idea what purpose they served, but we can guess that it is something genuinely old and strange – perhaps a survival of the old Celtic religion: the tower with small windows at the top is a form reminiscent of the cella in a Gallo-Roman temple.

The most fascinating thing about Sarlat's *lanterne* is its upper chamber. It's completely sealed off, and no one alive knows what's in it.

Place du Peyrou

Many of Sarlat's fine *hôtels particuliers* (mansions) are on or around this central square, beginning with the bishop's palace: the **Ancien Evêché**, next to the cathedral, was built by an Italian cardinal in 1533. It now houses the tourist office. Across place du Peyrou stands the city's most elegant building, the 1525 **Hôtel de la Boétie**, with its ornately carved windows and chimneys. This was the birthplace of Etienne de la Boétie, friend of Montaigne and author of the *Discours de la servitude volontaire*, a profound attack on France's royal tyranny.

Behind the house is a picturesque network of medieval courtyards and alleys called the **passage Henri de Segogne**, now largely occupied by cafés and restaurants, and beyond that another fine *hôtel particulier*, the 1557 **Hôtel de Maleville**.

Marché Couvert/Eglise de Ste-Marie

Mid-Apr to mid-Nov daily 0830-1400 (Fri 0830-2000), mid-Nov to mid-Apr Tue-Wed and Fri-Sat 0830-1300.

This church's story would make a great melodrama. Having been sacked in the Revolution, it was turned into a tenement house and then a warehouse for saltpetre. Then a builder tore down its façade and made its chapels into shops. For a while it was a post office, and finally a dispensary,

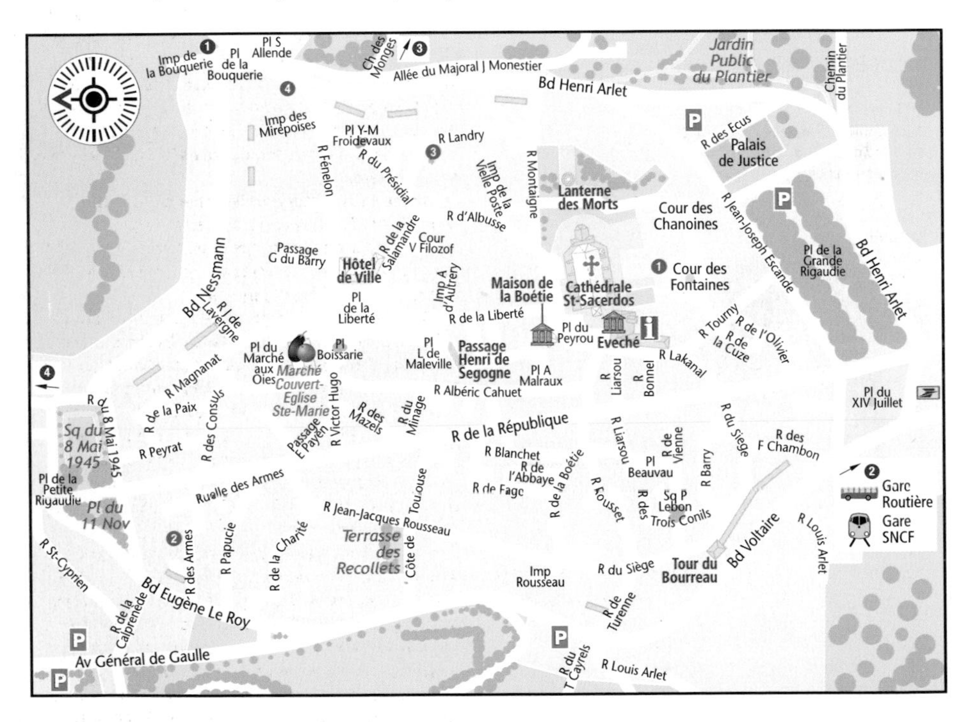

before being locked up and abandoned altogether.

In the 1990s Sarlat decided to recycle it as a market, and hired the famous architect Jean Nouvel (see page 90) to make the transformation. The colossal doors he added to close off the open end add a bit of surreal spice to the square's *grand siècle* dignity. The market space inside, though small and crowded, is tremendously popular with the Sarladais. This is the place to pick up gifts for foodie friends – foie gras, stuffed duck necks, confits and liqueurs – and to forage for a decadent Périgourdin picnic (see page 189).

Across the way, note the shallow staircase leading up to **rue Magnanat**. It's the perfect spot for a sword fight, and locals say it's been used as a film set dozens of times.

Sarlat listings

Sleeping

1 La Couleuvrine *1 place de la Bouquerie*
2 La Hoirie *rue Marcel Cerdan*
3 La Maison des Peyrat *Le Lac de la Plane*
4 Le Jardin *14 rue du Jardin de Madame*

Eating & drinking

1 Créperie des Fontaines *4 place des Fontaines*
2 Criquettamu's *5 rue des Armes*
3 Le Présidial *6 rue Landry*
4 Le Rossignol *15 rue Fénelon*

Getting to know Sarlat

Just how did this aristocratic jewel appear in one of the wildest, unlikeliest corners of Périgord? Like so many other cities in this book, it owes a lot to the church. Sarlat grew up around a monastery, which may have been founded as early as the sixth century. It flourished in the Middle Ages, with the help of commerce and some iron deposits found nearby and smelted here.

In the 14th century, while other cities in the region were starting to decay, Sarlat began to accumulate the collection of beautiful buildings that are its pride today. Seeing them, you'd guess that old Sarlat was a thriving, happy place.

Hardly. As rural Périgord grew poorer and more backward with each century, Sarlat became more of an island-oasis – a place where royal officers, high clerics and local barons could build showy mansions and live a decorous, genteel life in safety. They endowed Sarlat with a strong circuit of walls, and during the Croquant rebellions of the 1600s (see page 35) it seemed as if these were there to protect the city against its rustic neighbours rather than any possible foreign invaders.

Sarlat's lush life and privileges came to a rude end with the Revolution. It dwindled until a century ago fine palaces were being sold for a few hundred francs. And that, oddly enough, is what made the city's fortune. With no pressure from new growth, almost nothing was demolished, and Sarlat held on to its unique architectural patrimony without really trying. It got its big break with the 1962 'Malraux Law', under which it became the showcase for France's first national effort at historic preservation.

Best potatoes in the galaxy

We never thought of ourselves as the kind of people who would keep a tub of goose fat in our fridge, but down here everyone does it. It goes into a proper *tourin* (garlic soup) and many other things, but mostly it's for spuds – *pommes de terre sarladaises*, the perfect accompaniment for your *magret* or confit, and perhaps the most exalted use of the humble potato ever devised.

Some Périgourdin specialities require real skill, but with a little practice anyone can make Sarlat potatoes. So this is how to do it.

Get some nice, firm, floury potatoes, and slice them however you fancy. The fat (duck or goose) is available in any supermarket; a tin of confits will have more than enough in it. Heat it in a heavy frying pan. The result will depend on how much fat you use; a thin layer will make the potatoes a little burnt and a little white (most people's favourite); 15 mm (never more) gives you golden brown potatoes that are more evenly cooked.

If they stick, you've got inferior spuds, but keep scraping them off the bottom and hope for the best. Salt and black pepper early and often. Stay near the stove, turning them occasionally for about 20 minutes; reduce the heat if they're browning too fast. Finely chop some garlic (1-1½ cloves per person) and when the potatoes are about done, clear a space and throw the garlic in. Let it brown a tiny bit and then mix it around. Tilt the pan as you remove the potatoes so they drain a little, and then toss some chopped fresh parsley on top. And there you are.

Gorodka

La Canéda, T05 53 31 02 00, gorodka.com.
Daily 1400-1800, Jul-Aug 1000-2400.
€8, under 10s free.
4 km south of Sarlat.

At the entrance there's a hat rack and a sign inviting you to hang up your *idées fixes*. Beyond that, you've got 2 ha of art in the woods, presided over by a giant neon dragonfly. Gorodka is the life's work of Parisian artist **Pierre Shasmoukine**, and he's been at it since the 70s, building and landscaping the place almost single-handedly. Behind the art there's a message involving self-reliance, creativity and communion with the land, all encapsulated in the idea of 'habitable sculpture'.

Shasmoukine's *folies plastiques*, paintings and sculptures number in the hundreds, and there's still plenty of room in this artistic village for the works of scores of other artists of all kinds, outdoors and in several galleries. There are artists in residence too, some of whom might be musicians, dancers or performance artists, so you never know what to expect. There's a lot to see and no café – visitors are encouraged to bring a picnic. Try to come on a summer night, when the follies are illuminated; if you want to stay over and see it all, there's an inexpensive chambre d'hôte (€35 for a double room).

Around Sarlat

Château de Puymartin

T05 53 59 29 97, chateau-de-puymartin.com.
Jan-Jun and late Aug to Sep 1000-1200 and 1400-1800, Jul 1000-1200 and 1400-1830, 1-20 Aug 1000-1830, Oct-Nov by reservation only 1430-1700. €7, €5 concessions, €3.50 child (6-12).
8 km west of Sarlat on D47.

This 15th-century manor house, set in a beautiful park, is furnished with priceless antiques, mythological trompe l'oeil paintings and Aubusson and Flemish tapestries. The highlight is the unique **Cabinet Mythologique**, a room painted around 1660 with eight grisaille tableaux of mythological subjects: the hundred-eyed Argus killed by Hermes, the myth of Bellerophon, Helios and Aeolos among others. There may be some mystic purpose behind it, but no one today can explain it. Later owners turned it into a children's room.

Puymartin is also well and truly haunted. The story goes that Thérèse de St-Clar was caught in flagrante by her husband coming home unexpectedly from the wars; she was imprisoned in one of the towers, with only one small window and a trapdoor, until her death 15 years later, when her pitiless husband had her body walled up there. The 'Dame Blanche' has been putting in occasional appearances, usually around midnight, for the last 400 years.

Jardins d'Eyrignac

T05 53 28 99 71, eyrignac.com.
Jan-Mar and Oct-Dec 1030-1230 and 1430-sunset, Apr 1000-1900, May-Sep 0930-1900. €9.50, €4 concessions/child (7-13); audioguide (in English) €1.
14 km northeast of Sarlat off D47.

The first thing to know about Eyrignac is that it has been in the same family for over 500 years. And while you're exploring these 4 ha of classic *jardin à la française*, you might conclude that current owner Patrick Sermadiras and the 21 generations that preceded him were put on earth for no other reason than to make this lovely thing possible.

Like many great French gardens, this one isn't about flowers. There are a few in each season, mostly white and discreetly placed, but the emphasis is on grand axes and patterns of sculpted bushes and hedges. Here, the main axis has had a modern revamp; the **Allée des Charmes** is a complex topiary composition of hornbeams (*charmes*) and yew, incorporating a folly castle and its reflecting pond. This is paralleled by the more secluded and intimate **Allée des Vases**; both lead

Spices.

Five of the best

Gardens in Périgord

Jardins d'Eyrignac.

to the terraced **Jardin Française**, built to be seen from the château windows.

The exception to the design, and for many the most delightful part of the gardens, is the **Roseraie**, with its abundance of pure white roses and frog fountain to complement the views over the countryside.

Carlux

This tiny village has a *lanterne des morts* poking above the roofline of its old houses, and a castle that is finally getting some restoration work over 600 years after the English wrecked it.

Along the river, near the bridge and the Jardins de Cadiot, you can catch a glimpse of the elegant 16th-century **Château de Rouffillac**, still a private residence.

Jardins de Cadiot

Carlux, T05 53 29 81 05, lesjardinsdecadiot.com.
May-Oct daily 1000-1900. €6.30.

This is a modern garden, begun only in the 1980s by Bernard and Anne-Marie des Cottagnies. They've put an immense amount of time and care into it, and its two terraced hectares will be a treat for garden lovers: 400 varieties of roses, nearly as many peonies, a 'Tuscan garden', a small labyrinth and much more, including a gallery of works by contemporary artists from Africa.

Château de Fénelon

Ste-Mondane, T05 53 29 81 45.
Feb and Nov Sat-Sun 1400-1700, Mar and Oct Tue-Sun 1400-1700, Apr-May and Jun-Sep Tue-Sun 1030-1230 and 1430-1800, Jul-Aug daily 1000-1900. €7.50, €5 child.
7 km south of Carlux.

For all its airs and graces, there's something solidly medieval about this château; the double ring of fortifications seems to say to invaders: 'Just go ahead and try.' The beautiful Renaissance residence that grew out of the medieval keep seems incongruous, like a top hat on a carthorse. Still, it's a fine château to visit, furnished simply and honestly as the great man born here would have liked it.

François de Salignac de la Mothe-Fénelon was a cleric and theologian in the time of Louis XIV; his family had provided bishops of Sarlat for most of a century. The enormous cedar of Lebanon by the main entrance was planted to celebrate Fénelon's birth in 1651. He preached his first sermon at 15, and became so renowned for wisdom and integrity that he was chosen as tutor to the king's grandson. From that exalted position he would aim a surprise satirical shot right at his boss: *Les Aventures de Télémaque*, an assault on the tyranny of Louis and all absolute monarchs, disguised as a novel written for the instruction of his royal pupil. Like La Boétie, Fénelon was a hero to the *philosophes* of the following century. His little book inspired them all; it was the first great work of the Enlightenment.

The castle is still inhabited, and completely furnished with items dating from the Renaissance to the Second Empire, including a collection of arms and armour, tapestries and a cabinet of curiosities.

Carsac-Aillac

9 km south of Sarlat.

Back on the north side of the Dordogne, this village has a small but interesting Romanesque church. **St-Caprais** was built in the 12th century on a site that had been holy to the Celts; the nearby wood was a sacred grove. The church has a small dome and some unusual capitals (such as the baby Hercules strangling the snakes in his cradle). After a sacking by the English the nave was rebuilt in the Gothic style, with some dramatic rib vaulting.

Jardins d'Eau

St-Rome, T05 53 28 91 96, jardinsdeau.com.
May-Aug daily 0900-2000, Sep-Oct 1100-1900.
€5.50, child €2.50, under 10s free.
3 km downstream from Carsac.

In these gardens the accent is on aquatic plants, with plenty of lotuses (16 varieties) and water lilies in bloom in the summer months, and no end of frogs and dragonflies to keep them company.

St-Caprais.

Castles on the Dordogne

Each château has its own character and moods: Beynac is dark and forbidding, Castelnaud alert and seemingly still looking out for invaders, Les Milandes a gracious and welcoming home. But they are all neighbours, on a stretch of the river less than 15 km long. From the roof of one castle you can usually see three or four others. Throw in the unique towns of Domme and La Roque-Gageac – one atop a tall cliff, the other underneath one – and you have the biggest attraction in Périgord. In summer, not surprisingly, this part of the Dordogne is packed, not just with castles but with people.

Château de Castelnaud.

Domme

When the fog rolls in along the river valleys, as it does so often in the autumn and winter, Domme seems like a city in the clouds. Medieval bastides were built all over Périgord, but until King Philippe le Hardi founded Domme in 1281 no one had thought of parking one on top of a mountain.

The town's tourist office takes pains to point out that 'We are not a *piége à touristes* (tourist trap)!' and that's the truth. Though it is smack in the middle of the tourist-trappiest corner of southwest France, Domme remains a gracious and unspoiled town, proud of its title as 'the acropolis of Périgord'.

Place de la Halle

The covered market in the centre of Domme is a French classic, constructed from stone and heavy timbers with the town hall upstairs – a style of building that began in the Middle Ages. Domme's market, in its most recent incarnation, dates from the 17th century. Quite a few towns and villages knocked theirs down in the late 20th century to make space for parking cars, and this is one of the best of the survivors, still hosting stalls selling everything from turnips to turkeys every Thursday morning.

Some of the other buildings on the square go back to the 16th century, including the **Maison du Gouverneur**, now the home of the tourist office. On its edge stands the church, rebuilt after the original was burned down during the Wars of Religion, and behind that is the **Belvédère de la Barre**, a shady viewpoint overlooking the Dordogne.

Grotte de Domme

Place de la Halle, T05 53 31 71 00, ot-domme.com.
Feb-Mar and Oct-Nov Sun-Fri 1100-1430 and 1530-1630, Apr-Jun and Sep daily 1015-1200 and 1415-1800, Jul-Aug daily 1015-1840. €8.

Henry Miller & the Dordogne

Henry Miller, normally a pretty hard-boiled guy, went all mushy whenever he wrote about Périgord, as when he described looking down over the Dordogne from Domme in *The Colossus of Maroussi*: 'The vision of the black and mysterious river, down from this beautiful cape, is something for which you are grateful for the rest of your life.'

Domme's market has a truly unique feature – from inside it you can take a lift down into one of the Dordogne's best stalactite caves.

As at La Roque-Gageac (see page 162), the upper levels of this cave were used as a fortress and refuge, probably even before the bastide was founded. The lower levels were discovered only in the 1950s. There are no prehistoric paintings here, only glistening limestone reflected in clear pools – a fairy grotto running right under the streets of the town.

L'Oustal: Musée des Arts et Traditions Populaires

Place de la Halle, T05 53 31 71 00.
Apr-Jun and Sep daily 1030-1230 and 1400-1800, Jul-Aug Sun-Fri 1030-1900, Sat 1030-1230 and 1430-1900. €4.

Costumes, farm gear, furniture and crafts of the last two centuries in Périgord. Like any good town museum, this has some curiosities (including a mammoth's tooth) and a small collection of prehistoric finds.

Prison des Templiers

Feb-Dec, guided visits by reservation with Domme tourist office (T05 53 31 71 00). €6.50, €4 child.

Bits of Domme's walls and three of the town's original gates survive. Most impressive of these is the **Porte des Tours**, flanked by two squat towers. Some 70 Knights Templar were locked up in one of them after the suppression of the order in 1309, and they covered the walls with mysterious scratchings of crosses and other symbols. No one has yet made sense of it all, but don't be surprised if you find yourself next to some furtive Templar treasure-seeker taking notes.

West of Domme

La Roque-Gageac

It's somehow just too peculiar to be real; tourists might think it was put up just for them. La Roque-Gageac is a line of classic Périgourdin buildings, squeezed into a single narrow row with the river in front and impossibly tall vertical cliffs behind. It grew up in the Middle Ages as a community of fishermen and boatmen, protected by a castle cut into the cliffs. Now, officially listed as one of *les plus beaux villages de France*, it's full of ice cream and Perrier, the place where everyone congregates after visiting the castles or paddling a canoe on the Dordogne. Do they worry about falling rocks? Not much: the last big chunk of cliff to fall was way back in 1957, and it only crushed six houses.

The main tourist attraction here is a cruise in a *gabarre*, a replica of a traditional river barge; trips last about an hour, and take you past all five of the castles on this stretch of the Dordogne: La Roque-Gagaec; Beynac and Castelnaud (page 164); and Milandes and Marqueyssace (page 166). But spare some time to climb up the back alleys. La Roque, under its south-facing cliff, enjoys a warm microclimate, and the villagers have taken advantage of it to grow palms, citrus and banana trees and a riot of tropical flowers. The **Fort Troglodytique** (T05 53 31 61 94, Jan-mid-Nov Mon-Fri 1030-1800, also Sat in summer; €4) was La Roque's ready-made natural castle in the cliffs. It first appears in the records in the 13th century, a nearly impregnable fortress owned by the bishops of Sarlat.

La Roque-Gageac.

A perfect day in the Dordogne

Dani Chouet made an adventurous trip from her home in Vélines to Australia in 1969, and with Trish Hobbs she opened that country's first real French restaurant. 'Cleopatra', up in the Blue Mountains, made them famous, and probably changed Australian cooking forever (Dani's cookbook comes out in 2010). Now retired, they're back in their beloved Périgord, and shared some thoughts on their favourite things.

The perfect day in the Dordogne begins with a trip to a local **marchè**. Monpazier's is crowded and buzzing in the summer months: foie gras, wine, vegetables, country bread, goat's cheese and honey from local producers, straw hats, tablecloths and cotton skirts all vie for attention. Take a coffee in one of the pleasant cafés around the square, pop into the 12th-century church and wander the grid of lanes adorned with climbing roses.

For lunch a local *ferme-auberge* is a must. **Chez Ilse** (La Mothe, T05 53 29 43 84, ilse.xceed.be, booking essential) is just off the route from Monpazier to Belvès, and almost everything is produced at the farm: foie gras, terrines, poultry, pork and fruits. The servings are more than generous. It's an experience – and you will need a bit of exercise afterwards.

The most impressive of the many local châteaux is **Beynac** (see page 164) not too far from Belvès. The view is fabulous and climbing around the interior great fun. There are guided tours in English, but it is easy to take the English printed guide and explore, taking your own time.

Next, it's down to the village of **La Roque-Gageac** (see page opposite), where you can take a trip on the Dordogne in a *gabarre*, an ancient-style flat-bottomed sailing boat (see page 193). The 65-minute tour, floating past châteaux, towering cliff faces and postcard villages in the soft late afternoon light is unforgettable. After a lunch chez Ilse a light supper will be in order; the cafés of La Roque-Gageac have outdoor terraces and local rosé. Finish the day at nearby **Marqueyssac** (see page 166) with the magical Thursday evening **Marqueyssac aux Chandelles**. The beautiful topiary gardens are candlelit on summer evenings and the views are breathtaking.

The Fort Troglodytique, La Roque-Gageac.

Château de Beynac

Beynac-et-Cazenac, T05 53 29 50 40, beynac-en-perigord.com.
Daily Mar-May 1000-1800, Jun-Sep 1000-1830, Oct-Nov 1000-sunset, Dec-Feb 1200-sunset.
€7, €3 child (5-11).

Grey and forbidding, this castle clinging to the cliffs over the river seems to dare anyone to attack it. You would think no one could get in, but Richard the Lionheart did, in 1199, by sending his men to scale the 200-m cliff walls. Only 15 years later it was Simon de Montfort's turn to break in. As the seat of one of the four baronies of Périgord, Beynac was a busy place, though the Barons of Beynac always managed to win it back in the end.

Tip...

It's a stiff climb up from the village; if you're driving there's a well-signposted road to the car park at the top.

Spears, Château de Beynac.

Château de Beynac.

Beynac can still give castle fans a lesson in medieval defence: there's a stout, squarish 12th-century keep, a clever use of a natural ravine on one side, double walls, moats and barbicans at the weak points. Inside, the rooms and furnishings date from the 14th to the 17th centuries. The best parts are the tapestries and painted wooden ceilings, particularly in the Renaissance **Salle des Etats**, with its adjacent frescoed oratory. Downstairs you'll find a well-restored and suspiciously well-stocked kitchen, which may look familiar to film fans: most recently Beynac was used as a set for the latest *Jeanne d'Arc*, by Luc Besson, and the popular 1993 comedy *Les Visiteurs*.

Château de Castelnaud: Musée de la Guerre au Moyen Age

Castelnaud-la-Chapelle, T05 53 31 30 00, castelnaud.com.
Daily mid-Nov to Jan 1400-1700, Feb-Mar and Oct to mid-Nov 1000-1800, Apr-Jun and Sep 1000-1900, Jul-Aug 0900-2000.
€7.80, €3.90 child (10-17), under 10s free.

History doesn't explain why there should be two big castles so close to each other. The sheer bloody-mindedness of the owners might have something to do with it, and Périgord's battling barons never lacked for that. Castelnaud ('new castle') was built in the 12th century by a family that later converted to Catharism. That made them a target for Simon de Montfort, who gave the place a thorough bashing in 1214. Quickly rebuilt,

Castelnaud kept a wary eye on its arch-rival Beynac for the next four centuries. In the Hundred Years' War its owners, the Caumonts, sided with the English (usually), while Beynac stuck with the King of France.

The Caumonts gave up their draughty old home for the more comfortable Les Milandes in the 16th century, leaving Castelnaud to serve as a base for the hell-raising Protestant captain Geoffroy de Vivans. After that it gradually fell into ruin; when you see the old photos inside you'll be amazed how much work had to be done to get the place back in shape.

Since 1985, Castelnaud has housed the Medieval Warfare Museum, which has made it one of the most visited sights in France. It's an impressive effort: there are rooms full of weapons, audiovisuals and demonstrations and, best of all, life-size working reproductions of medieval siege weapons, including a huge trebuchet – a kind of sling-action catapult. In summer they wind it up to launch a ball or two against the curtain wall. Kids love it. There are guided tours on offer, during which they might teach your offspring how to shoot a crossbow or give them some tips on siege-craft.

The Black Venus

Josephine Baker was born in 1906 in East St Louis, Illinois, arguably the most desperate town in America, and grew up in a family so poor that at the age of 10 her mother sent her out to clean houses. For a while she was homeless, and danced on St Louis street corners for a living.

But she had talent. In the early 20s she made it to New York, where she worked with Eubie Blake, Sidney Bechet and other great jazz names, and the next stop was Paris, where she starred in *La Révue Negre*. With her erotic dancing, her famous banana skirt and pet cheetah she became a sensation; by 1927 she was the highest paid female performer in Europe.

The coming years would show the lady had a lot more to give. During the Second World War Baker worked for the Resistance in France and Morocco, and was later enrolled in the Légion d'Honneur. After the war she installed herself at Les Milandes with her 'Rainbow Tribe' of adopted orphan children from eight countries. Though she remained in France, she contributed a lot to the American Civil Rights movement, and even spoke before Martin Luther King at the March on Washington in 1963.

Baker was useless with money. Largely retired from show business, her finances got entirely out of hand, and in 1968 she found herself evicted from Les Milandes. An old friend – Grace Kelly – came to the rescue and got her on her feet again. A 1975 grand comeback tour began with a smash success in Paris. *Hélas*! Josephine died of a cerebral haemorrhage four days later. She was buried with full military honours.

Château des Milandes

T05 53 59 31 21, milandes.com.
Apr and Oct Sun-Fri 1000-1815, May Sun-Fri 1000-1830, Sat 1300-1830; Jun and Sep Sun-Fri 1000-1900, Sat 1300-1900, Jul-Aug daily 0930-1930. €8, €6.80 concession, €5.50 child (5-17).
5 km west of Castelnaud along the river.

It's easy to see what made the Caumonts move here from Castelnaud. Besides the glass windows and other Renaissance mod cons, Les Milandes is gorgeous, with its tall gables and ornate dormers. Once it had sumptuous interior decoration to match, but when the Caumonts became Protestants they destroyed most of its art.

For all that, the real fame of Les Milandes is as the home of Josephine Baker, and the château is maintained as a shrine to the great lady. Screens show rare film footage from the 1920s; there are some original furnishings, and an art deco tiled bathroom to die for.

Les Milandes has a big surprise. While visiting the gardens you may notice niches in the walls with barred doors, from which falcons, eagles and owls peek out at you. They're waiting for their moment on stage: the Spectacle de Rapaces, in which the birds of prey perform some amazing acrobatic feats on and over the château's esplanade. The show happens daily April to October, and is free with admission to the château; ring ahead for exact times.

Jardins de Marqueyssac

T05 53 31 36 36, marqueyssac.com.
Daily, Apr-Jun and Sep 1000-1900, Jul-Aug 0900-2000, plus candlelight evenings every Thu 1900-2400, Oct to mid-Nov and Feb-Mar 1000-1800, mid-Nov to Jan 1400-1700.
€7.20, €3.60 child (10-17), under 10s free; candlelight evenings €10/€5; booking recommended in summer.
North bank of the Dordogne, 5 km east of Beynac.

You've probably never seen 150,000 hand-clipped box trees in one place before. Marqueyssac is unique: a hilltop formal garden in a matchless setting overlooking the river. The original plan was by a student of the great André Le Nôtre, but when Julien de Cerval inherited the garden in the 1860s he turned it into an Italianate fantasy, following a visit to Rome. Long neglected – like so many things in the Dordogne – it was nearly lost altogether as the box trees grew into an impenetrable forest. As restorers patiently trimmed them back in the 1990s they were amazed to see Cerval's original design come back to life.

Box tree, Jardins de Marqueyssac.

At the tip of the gardens there's an aviary and a charming loggia; from here you can see four castles and La Roque-Gageac. On the eastern side, the **Bastion** has sinuously curvy swirls of topiary forming a kind of green mandala that provides Marqueyssac's famous postcard image. Just opposite, the château hides modestly among the groves; it is sweet and small and idyllic. There is another wild area of topiary nearby, called **Chaos**, an avenue of fragrant rosemary bushes, a hedge maze for children and a tea room for when you're done.

Marqueyssac is very fond of children: as well as the maze there are special children's nature trails, crafts classes, playgrounds, a wood turner's workshop (using the gardens' excess boxwood) and even rock climbing for six years and up.

South of the Dordogne

Belvès

Belvès is a mini-Domme, another of those *plus beaux villages de France*, enjoying its medieval daydreams high on a hill riddled with caves. A Celtic tribe called the Bellovaquii founded it around 300 BC; it thrived in Roman times (the town centre is still called 'Le Castrum') and again in the Middle Ages, from which it retains many monuments, including the romantically sagging 15th-century **Halle** – note the chains hanging from one pillar, a sort of pillory used to tie up criminals. The 15th-century **Maison des Consuls** (the old town hall) now houses the tourist office, while the new town hall occupies the digs of a 13th-century monastery. Parts of the medieval walls and towers can be seen around the edges.

Visit the tourist office to arrange a tour of the **Habitations Troglodytiques** (T05 53 29 10 20, guided tours in English mid-Jun to mid-Sep daily 1200, 1545 and 1800, bilingual tours mid-Sep to Mar Mon-Sat 1100 and 1530, Apr-mid-Jun 1100, 1500 and 1630; €4, €2 child). These caves beneath the town were used as refuges in times of danger, and as homes by the poor as late as the 18th century.

Belvès.

Vézère Valley

Why here? Of all the places on earth, why should primitive people have chosen this particular green valley to begin our modest human experiment in self-expression? We may never get an answer to that – more likely, new discoveries elsewhere will eventually make it a moot point.

The first sensational discoveries at La Madeleine (1862), Cro-Magnon (1868) and Le Moustier (1908) rewrote the books on early humans, and inspired others to scour the endless caves of the Vézère for more. What they found was even better: the painted caves at Font-de-Gaume and Les Combarelles (both 1901) and Lascaux (1940) revealed the greatest collection of Palaeolithic art in the world. We have to give this valley its due: with 25 painted caves and 147 prehistoric sites, it is indeed the 'World Capital of Prehistory', just as the tourist offices claim.

One of the most striking things about a visit here is the contrast between the lush domesticity of the landscape and the outlandish history hiding just beneath the surface – try to imagine this very civilized countryside with cavemen jumping all over it. Visiting is easy: most of the sights are spread out at convenient intervals along the two main roads (the D706 up the Vézère and the D47/48 towards Sarlat), and all are well signposted.

Le Bugue-sur-Vézère

Le Bugue, the first and biggest town on the river, is the gateway to the Vézère Valley and a good base. It can be lively, especially when its big Tuesday morning market fills the streets, and besides its caves it has become a magnet for the kind of roadside attractions that have grown up all through the valley to entertain visitors.

Le Bournat

Allée Paul-Jean Souriau, T05 53 08 41 99, lebournat.fr.
Daily Mar-Apr and Oct-Nov 1000-1700, May-Jun and Sep 1000-1800, Jul-Aug 1000-1900.
€12 (€10 in Oct-Nov). €10 (€8) concession, €9 (€7) child (4-12).
On D31 on northern edge of Le Bugue.

As roadside attractions go, this is an ambitious one: an entire village dedicated to recreating Périgord rural life around 1900, with a model farm and over 50 buildings. You can see traditional craftsmen working at everything from brewing to lacemaking. It's a family-friendly place where you can spend a whole day, with carousels, music and lots of animals for the children. Activities differ from day to day; check the website to see what's on.

Aquarium du Périgord Noir

Allée Paul-Jean Souriau, T05 53 07 10 74, aquariumperigordnoir.com.
Mid-Feb to Mar and Oct to mid-Nov Mon-Sat 1300-1700, Sun 1000-1800, Apr-May and Sep daily 1000-1800, Jun daily 1000-1900, Jul-Aug daily 0900-1900. €9.90, €7.20 child (4-15).
Opposite Le Bournat.

Bakery, Le Bournat.

They claim it's the biggest freshwater aquarium in Europe, and it's full of astonishing things. You could never imagine just how ugly the eels of the Dordogne and Lot are until you meet them face to face. Leave them, and instead visit the pavilions devoted to lake and river creatures of Africa, Asia and the Americas (plenty of piranhas). The newest feature is Iguana Park, home to misty Turtle Island and hosts of winsome serpents – at the end of the circuit the kids get to feed them.

Grotte du Bara-Bahau

T05 53 07 44 58, grotte-bara-bahau.com.
Daily, Feb-Jun 1000-1200 and 1400-1730, Jul-Aug 0930-1900, Sep-Dec 1000-1200 and 1400-1700. €6.40.
Just west of Le Bugue on D703.

There's a little bit of everything in this cave: stalactites, traces of ancient bears, and a number of drawings and carvings of animals and symbols.

Gouffre de Proumeyssac

T05 53 07 27 47, gouffre-proumeyssac.com.
Daily, Feb and Nov-Dec 1400-1700, Mar-Apr and Sep-Oct 0930-1200 and 1400-1730, May-Jun 0930-1830, Jul-Aug (booking recommended) 0900-1900. €8.40, €6.80 concession, €5.70 child (4-15). 4 km south of Le Bugue on road to Audrix.

Less poetically, this used to be called simply the Trou (hole) de Proumeyssac, and everyone believed it was the crater of a volcano because of the smoke issuing from it – really just vapour caused by condensation in winter. No one bothered to explore it until 1907, but with an entrance tunnel and some electric lighting, the 'crystal cathedral' is now one of the region's more popular sights. It's the biggest underground cavern yet discovered in Périgord, hung with thousands of gleaming stalactites: an unforgettable sight.

Tip...

For an adventure at Proumeyssac, pay a little extra (€16.50 or €11 for under 16s) and they'll send you down the old-fashioned way, in a sort of cage called a *nacelle*, which is lowered through the immense void on a cable.

Grotte du Sorcier

St-Cirq, T05 53 07 14 37, grottedusorcier.com.
Daily, Mar-Apr and Sep-Nov 1000-1800, May-Jun 1000-1830, Jul-Aug 1000-1930, Dec-Feb 1100-1700. €6.80, €5.50 concession, €3.40 child. 5 km east of Le Bugue.

He doesn't really look like a sorcerer to us, but he is extremely well endowed, which has made him something of a prehistoric celebrity. He shares the cave with a number of other engravings, mostly of animals.

Les Eyzies-de-Tayac

The village wasn't much, just a few houses sheltering under a beetling cliff, but it was fated to lie at the centre of the greatest concentration of prehistoric sites. The discovery of Font-de-Gaume and the others brought in visitors as early as 1910, and Les Eyzies has been happy to serve as Cro-Magnon man's maid, butler, cook and ticket-puncher ever since. Somehow they managed to squeeze the mammoth (sorry!) Musée Nationale between the main street and the cliffs. At the entrance, on the cliff face, a very unflattering statue of Mr Cro-Magnon provides Les Eyzies with its landmark.

Musée National de Préhistoire

1 rue du Musée, T05 53 06 45 45, musee-prehistoire-eyzies.fr.
Oct-May Wed-Mon 0930-1230 and 1400-1730, Jun and Sep Wed-Mon 0930-1800, Jul-Aug daily 0930-1830. €5, €3.50 concession.

They have six million items, and new ones are coming in at such a rate they can hardly keep up with the cataloguing. But don't worry, they only have space to display some 18,000. The circuit begins in the entrance hall, with exhibits detailing humanity's origins in Africa: zillions of flints and other rocky paraphernalia that make visitors to museums of prehistory go green.

The upper gallery concentrates on the details of our ancestors' daily lives – or at least, the scholars' best guesses as to what was going on. There are weapons and jewellery, exhibits on the rites of burial and a reconstruction of a religious sanctuary.

What really makes this museum so compelling is the art: small carvings on bone that are often as well executed as the paintings in the caves. Most famous of these is the *Bison licking its flank*, with a meticulous sense of line that recalls classical Greek art. Rather less classical are the celebrated plus-size 'Venuses': most likely figurines of the great goddess, and some of the earliest religious art yet discovered. These, along with other works depicting male and female genitalia, suggest that sex was very much on the Magdalenian mind.

Abri Pataud

20 rue du Moyen Age, T05 53 06 92 46, semitour.com.
Mid-Nov to Dec and Feb-Mar Mon-Thu 1000-1230 and 1400-1730, Apr-Jun and Sep-Oct Sun-Fri 1000-1200 and 1400-1800, Jul-Aug daily 1000-1900. €6, €4 child (6-12).

Just on the edge of Les Eyzies, a few blocks from the museum, this is one of the largest and most impressive of the *abris* (rock shelters) inhabited as early as 33,000 years ago. The original Cro-Magnon site is not far away, and Cro-Magnon man left plenty of clutter here to keep archaeologists busy: tools, ornaments, leftovers from dinner, all displayed in a small museum. The highlight is a finely carved bas-relief of an ibex.

Statue, Les Eyzies.

North of Les Eyzies

Grotte du Grand Roc

T05 53 06 92 70.
Daily Easter-Jun and Sep-Oct 1000-1800, Jul-Aug 0930-1900. €7.50, €3.50 child (6-12).
2 km north of Les Eyzies on D47.

There isn't much room for paintings, as this big cave situated halfway up a cliff is almost entirely full of accretions. It's one of Périgord's great stalactite caves, known for the unusual, gravity-defying formations inside.

Grotte de Rouffignac

Rouffignac-St-Cernin, T05 53 05 41 71, grottederouffignac.fr.
Daily, Apr-Jun and Sep-Oct 1000-1130 and 1400-1700, Jul-Aug 0900-1130 and 1400-1800. €6.30, €4 child (6-12).
18 km north of Les Eyzies off D32.

Rouffignac is one of the most popular of the valley's caves, probably because you get to ride an electric train through it. With 8 km of galleries to see, it's the only way to travel. Beside the train, this cave is famous for mammoths – 154 of them, about half the world total of depictions of mammoths, and no one knows why they should have been so important here. Other species get a look-in too, especially on the **Grand Plafond** (great ceiling), an enormous swirling composition in which over 60 animals of all types can be seen.

The cave used to be popular with bears; all along the way the guides will point out their scratch marks and comfortable, sandy bear beds.

Tip...

They don't take bookings at Rouffignac, and in high season it's a good idea to show up before 1000 to be sure of getting in.

Tip...

It isn't easy to see Font-de-Gaume. We recommend booking at least a month ahead; you may be asked to pay in advance. A few places are set aside for last-minute visitors – if you come before they open you might be able to make a reservation for that day.

East of Les Eyzies

Grotte de Font-de-Gaume

4 av des Grottes, T05 53 06 86 00.
Mid-May to mid-Sep Sun-Fri 0930-1730, rest of year Sun-Fri 1000-1130 and 1400-1700. Pre-booked guided tours only (some in English), limited to 180 visitors a day. €7, €4.50 concession, under 18s free.

With Lascaux closed to visitors, this is the greatest painted cave you can see in France (and there are constant rumours that this one too might close). The artists of 14,000 years ago really show off their talent here; among the 250 paintings are many that show a high artistic sensibility and attention to detail: a horse resting with one raised hoof, a stag confronting a doe in a pose that seems very affectionate, friezes of bison that seem to be herds thundering over the plain. The bison is the main subject here, with over 80 of them, though there are also plenty of mammoths, reindeer and horses, even some goats, bears and something believed to be a rhinoceros, along with the usual hand outlines and geometric designs. Many of the paintings, preserved by a thin layer of calcite formation, look glisteningly new, and the skill of the artists in shading and handling colour is on display everywhere.

Grotte de Combarelles

T05 53 06 86 00.
Hours and admission arrangements as for Font-de-Gaume; advance booking essential.
2 km east of Les Eyzies on D47.

Grotte du Grand Roc.

Around the region

Like Font-de-Gaume, this is a victim of its own popularity, which is a shame since it is one of the great caves, nearly the equal of Font-de-Gaume with its hundreds of engravings. Horses are a speciality here – some 150 of them – along with a large number of rare portrayals of people.

Grottes du Roc du Cazelle

T05 53 59 46 09, rocdecazelle.com.
Daily, Feb-Apr and Oct-Nov 1000-1800, May, Jun and Sep 1000-1900, Jul-Aug 1000-2000, Dec-Jan 1100-1700. €6.80, €5.80 concession, €3.40 child (5-13).
4 km east of les Eyzies on D47.

There's a touch of Disney in the air at this *abri*, where people lived from Palaeolithic times up to 1966. Not only have they completely reconstructed the rather cosy cave-farmhouse of the last days, filled with antique furniture and authentic farm clutter, but they've placed over 100 human figures around the grounds, dressed in prehistoric costume and demonstrating little everyday chores. There's a full-size woolly mammoth to keep them company, and if you book ahead you can participate in one of the workshops to learn the skills of cave painting, flint-knapping or kindling a fire.

Grottes du Roc du Cazelle.

Abri du Cap Blanc

T05 53 06 86 00.
Mid-May to mid-Sep Sun-Fri 0930-1730, rest of year Sun-Fri 0930-1230 and 1400-1730. €7, €4.50 concession, under 18s free.
6 km east of Les Eyzies on D48.

The painted caves are famous, but few people know there is also a sculpted cave. Cap Blanc's art consists of a frieze of nearly life-size running horses; though they have been damaged over time, and nothing of their original paint remains, there's enough left to see that the Magdalenians were just as accomplished as sculptors as they were with paint.

From Les Eyzies to Montignac

Maison Forte de Reignac

Tursac, T05 53 50 69 54, maison-forte-reignac.com.
Daily, Mar-Apr and Oct to mid-Nov 1000-1800, May, Jun and Sep 1000-1900, Jul-Aug 1000-2000. €6.80, €5.80 concession, €3.40 child (5-13).

In Périgord, castles grow out of the ground like *cèpes*. This site seems to have been in business for some 20,000 years. It began to emerge from its cliff face in the Middle Ages, and the building you see today was begun in the 15th century. There are some furnished rooms to see, but the real interest here is the cave-castle behind – a surprisingly big construction with some sophisticated defence features. The château's owners, not content with a good thing, have camped it up with a display of medieval instruments of torture.

La Roque St-Christophe

Peyzac-le-Moustier, T05 53 50 70 45, roque-st-christophe.com.
Daily, Feb-Mar and Oct to mid-Nov 1000-1830, Apr-Jun and Sep 1000-1830, Jul-Aug 1000-2000, mid-Nov to Jan 1400-1700. €7.50, €6 concession, €4.50 child (12-16), €3.50 child (5-11).
3 km north of Tursac on D706.

Five of the best

Caves & sites of the Vézère

❶ **Font-de-Gaume** The finest cave paintings anywhere open to the public, page 172.

❷ **Lascaux II** A copy, but such a skilful one it is a work of art in itself, page 176.

❸ **Proumeyssac** The 'Crystal Cathedral', a spectacular stalactite cave, page 170.

❹ **Rouffignac** The 'Cave of 100 Mammoths' along with plenty of horses, bisons and a rhino, page 172.

❺ **Roque St-Christophe** The invisible castle, 55,000 years old, see opposite.

Of all Périgord's underground wonders this may be the most impressive. La Roque is a sinuously curving cliff face 80 m high and nearly 1 km long. In the Middle Ages, its inner terraces and caverns were a proper city, with a population of 1000 and even its own church. Everywhere along the cliff, you'll see rows of square sockets where house beams were fitted into the rock.

A lot of archaeological work has been done here, and the finds go back to the Neanderthals, some 55,000 years ago. Someone seems to have been holed up here in every age since La Roque was first seriously fortified against the Vikings; its security made it a thriving spot in uncertain times. It took a pounding from the English in the 1350s, and was abandoned for good after a bloody sacking in 1588. An enormous wooden winch has been reconstructed, of the kind that would have been used in medieval times to hoist up goods, and on busy summer days they sometimes give a demonstration.

St-Léon-sur-Vézère

There's nothing prehistoric here, but for some St-Léon may be the highlight of the tour. It's an utterly dreamy village, and it's a wonder that the small population has succeeded in keeping it so unspoiled. There's a Renaissance château (not open), grassy banks along the riverfront that make a perfect picnic spot, and a beautiful medieval **church** with a broad square tower and three pointy-topped apses, more like a Burgundian church than one in Périgord. Inside, a learned priest left a beautifully made display explaining the sacred geometry behind the church's proportions.

Château de Losse

Thonac, T05 53 50 80 08, chateaudelosse.com.
May-Sep Sun-Fri 1200-1800. €7.50, €6 concession, €4 child (7-14).

This is an elegant château even by Périgord standards, with its tall gabled roof and turrets reflected in the water; among all those cavemen and their mammoths it seems a little out of place. Externally, Losse has changed very little since 1576. Inside it is richly furnished from the 17th and 18th centuries, but its real charm is the gardens: all the precision of classical French style on a very intimate scale, with tidy ranks of lavender bushes and box hedges everywhere.

Le Thot

Thonac, T05 53 50 70 44, semitour.com.
Feb-Mar and Nov-Dec Tue-Sun 1000-1230 and 1400-1730, Apr-Jun and Sep-Oct daily 1000 1800, Jul-Aug daily 1000-1900. €6, €4 child (6-12). 7 km south of Montignac on D706.

Le Thot is for kids, intended as a complementary attraction to Lascaux and the other sites. While it might seem a little hokey, the centre makes an honest attempt to bring something of the distant world of the cave painters to life. There are films and life-size dioramas, a small zoo containing the animals most closely related to those in the paintings (ibex, 'aurochs', bison, Przewalski horses) and educational workshops where children can learn painting techniques and everyday life skills of Cro-Magnon days.

Montignac & Lascaux

Montignac is a handsome town, spread out along both sides of the Vézère, and once it was a peaceful one – until 1948, when the painted cave at Lascaux was opened to visitors.

There's more to Montignac's past than just Lascaux, however. Once this town was nothing less than the capital of the region, the seat of those legendary bad boys, the Counts of Périgord. The very bijou 19th-century château (not open) that overlooks the centre stands on the ruins of what was once the most important of all the castles. Its Taillefer dynasty rulers smashed a bloody trail through the Middle Ages, each trying to outdo his dad in mayhem and treachery. Their downfall began when Archambault V fatally sided with the English in the Hundred Years' War. The last of the line, his son Archambault VI, ended his days as an exile in London.

Today, Montignac has a very pretty riverfront, perhaps more neatly coiffed small dogs than it really needs, and some elegant 18th-century streets and buildings, mostly on the east bank of the Vézère.

Lascaux II

T05 53 51 95 03, semitour.com.
Feb-Mar and Nov-Dec Tue-Sun 1000-1230 and 1400-1730, Apr-Jun and Sep-Oct daily 0930-1800, Jul-Aug daily 0900-1900. €8.50, €5.50 child (6-12). 2 km south of Montignac.

At first, the idea seemed too silly to be true; there was a general shaking of heads when the Dordogne's departmental council announced that since the world's most famous painted cave could no longer be visited, they would build a replica. An old quarry building nearby was purchased, and the cave walls reproduced accurately down to the millimetre using concrete over wire mesh. A team of artists led by Monique Peytral then worked for 11 years to reproduce the paintings, using the same methods and natural pigments.

Despite all the scoffers, when it opened in 1983 Lascaux II was a complete success with the public, and even the scholars were impressed. Today it is the department's top tourist sight. About 90% of the paintings have been reproduced, representing over 600 animals along with just one human figure and a rich collection of symbols: hooks and dots, squares and bars are the most common, and their significance remains a mystery.

The original Lascaux, just 200 m away, has been called the 'Sistine Chapel of Prehistory' for its brilliant colours and advanced artistic technique: subjects portrayed in difficult three-quarter views, skilfully drawn legs of running horses and delightful trickery such as the row of 'swimming stags', heads held high as they cross a river that is nothing but a reflection on a ledge of rock. But it may not be as well protected as the authorities claim. Around the Vézère, and among specialists, you'll hear horror stories about bad judgment and bureaucratic incompetence. It seems that in 2000 the authorities decided that the cave's natural ventilation wasn't good enough and hired a firm with experience in cooling supermarkets to give Lascaux a new air conditioning system. Now the calcite problem may be cured, but the cave has a new enemy – patches of a mysterious black mould for which no cure has so far been found.

Site Néandertal du Regourdou

T05 53 51 81 23, regourdou.fr.
Daily, Feb-Jun and Sep-Nov 1100-1800, Jul-Aug 1000-1900. €5, €3 child (6-12). 800 m from Lascaux.

Roger Constant, the landowner, discovered this provocative site in 1954. He carefully excavated the ritual burial of a bear, with its bones arranged around its severed head, all decorated with the same red ochre used for the cave paintings. A Neanderthal human burial was found just 2 m away. Over the years, until the jealous archaeologists got the state to make him stop digging, Constant discovered 20 more bear graves and bones of other animals that seemed to be

Lascaux II.

offerings to the bear; he made himself an expert on the subject and even turned his house into a museum to display his finds. So just who was getting sacrificed, and why? The answers unfortunately are not clear. M Constant grew so fond of bears that he brought three of them to the site; they and their descendants are still there to entertain visitors.

St-Amand-de-Coly

9 km east of Montignac.

Another *plus beau village de France*, St-Amand is an amiable, tiny place full of crusty-looking *lauze* (stone tile) roofs. It grew up around an abbey that, though long gone, left it a great **church** (Jul-Aug Wed-Sun 1100-1300 and 1400-1800, Tue 1100-1300 and 1500-1900, rest of year ring T05 53 51 04 56). Some of Périgord's fortified churches show only a half-hearted *clocher-mur* (bell-wall) that wouldn't frighten anyone. This one is serious. Built in the 12th century and beefed up in the 14th when the English were on the prowl, it is one tough church, with walls 4 m thick, defensive parapets, a moat and concealed entrances.

For all that it is a work of considerable grace. The hard shell conceals the best Romanesque interior in Périgord. There's very little decoration (just one weird and wonderful capital, to the right of the altar, of serpents devouring sinners) but it is elegant and stately, more like the palatine chapel of some emperor than a church for rustic monks.

Terrasson-Lavilledieu

Far off on Périgord's border with Corrèze, Terrasson doesn't see a lot of tourists. In the 19th century coal mining and industry turned it from a small village to a big one. It's a rarity for the southwest today: a thriving, busy town with industrial suburbs that stretch 8 km down the Vézère. The centre though, up on its steep hill, remains a place of considerable charm.

Like St-Amand, Terrasson owes its birth to an abbey, founded by a very suspect holy man called St Sour, who washed up here in Merovingian times with his two pet doves. The city's landmark is the 12th-century **Pont Vieux** over the Vézère; the abbey's monks built it and grew fat off the tolls.

From here you can climb up by way of the 'hanging walkway', with great views over the town. At the top, little is left of St Sour's once flourishing abbey except the church, which was largely rebuilt in the 1880s, though it retains some medieval stained glass.

Jardins de l'Imaginaire

Place de Genouillac, T05 53 50 86 82, ot-terrasson.com.
Guided tours only, Apr and Sep-Oct Wed-Sun 1000-1130 and 1400-1700, May-Jun Wed-Sun 1000-1130 and 1400-1730, Jul-Aug daily 1000-1820. €7, €4 concession, under 10s free.

Two things make this garden special. It is completely modern in design and sentiment, and it was built not by a baron or a banker but as a project of the town's mayor, in 1990.

Jardins de l'Imaginaire.

Terrasson.

The gardens occupy a series of terraces with views over Terrasson, and there's a heavy dose of symbolism among the paths and hedges. The idea behind the design was an evocation of history in gardens; along the way are touches of the Middle Ages and (one of the loveliest corners) a slice of a classical French garden. As a centrepiece there's a grand cascade and fountain – an idea borrowed from Renaissance Italy – and, in a far corner, some 2000 roses in a special *roseraie* where new varieties are developed.

Musée du Chocolat

ZAES du Moulin Rouge, T05 53 51 57 36, bovetti.com.
Tue-Wed 1400-1800, Thu-Fri 1000-1200 and 1400-1800, Sat 1400-1800; in summer and school holidays Tue-Fri 1000-1200 and 1400-1800, Mon and Sat 1400-1800. €3.80, €3.10 child.

The Bovetti Company makes fine chocolates in this industrial zone and ships them all over the world. They have created a little museum devoted to the cocoa bean and its distinguished history; children get to mould a chocolate bunny of their own and take it home.

Go climb a tree

It's so new the French haven't found a name for it yet. You'll see it variously described as *accrobranche* (one firm has recently registered this as a trademark) or as an *airparc* or a *parc aventure* or *parcours aventure*. English-language lexicographers are wondering what to call this French invention, and so far they haven't come up with anything better than 'tree-climbing', which doesn't really describe it at all.

Whatever you call it, it's the hottest outdoor activity in France right now, with new centres opening all over the country. The idea is partly a good workout and a day in the fresh air, but it also has a touch of adventure. Actually, climbing trees isn't necessary – there's a ladder for that. But once you're up, you follow a trail through the forest, climbing up rope ladders and passing from tree to tree on Tarzan swings. Once you've reached some height you can enjoy the fun part: sliding down suspended from a wheel mounted on a long cable called a *tyrolienne*.

They *have* given this some thought. Participants are harnessed two different ways at all times, so there's no danger of falling. Before you start there's a briefing on rules and safety, and maybe a little test on the wires to see if you're up to it. All necessary equipment is provided.

Most facilities have several different *parcours* (runs) of varying difficulty. Some are designed specifically for small children (a few places admit kids as young as three), and they are graded up from there to runs that would tire out Tarzan himself. Since part of it involves dangling from ropes and pulling yourself across by hand, strong arms definitely help. Most places offer a day ticket for around €18-20 for adults, less for kids according to age, though if anyone lasted a whole day it would be quite a feat.

Parcs aventure tend to open from April through November, and are closed on days of heavy rain or wind. Reservations are recommended, especially in summer. In the Vézère Valley, **Appel de la Forêt** (Thenon, T05 53 46 35 06, appel-de-la-foret.com) has 10 different *parcours* and 25 *tyroliennes*. A few have popped up around Sarlat in the tourist zone of Périgord Noir: **Indian Forest** (Carsac, T05 53 31 22 22, indianforestperigord.com), with 17 *tyroliennes*, and nearby, **La Forêt des Ecureuils** (St-Vincent-le-Paluel, T05 53 29 84 54, laforetdesecureuils.com) – one of the *tyroliennes* there starts 40 m above the ground; they also do paintball if you ring ahead.

Airparc Périgord (St-Vincent-de-Cosse, T05 53 29 18 43, airparc-perigord.com) is located on an island in the Dordogne near Beynac. Part of it is over water, and there is a *tyrolienne* 180 m long. This park offers overnight camping in 'transparent bubbles' – clear plastic tents strung between the tree limbs that sleep up to three adults or four children, at €50 per night.

In the Lot, you can try out the trees at **Cap Nature** (Pradines, T05 65 22 25 12, capnature.eu), on the banks of the Lot just outside Cahors.

Sleeping

For all its hotels, the area around Sarlat (including the Vézère and Dordogne Valleys, Domme and Monpazier) can be completely overloaded in summer, and reservations are essential. If you can't get one, try contacting the **Club Hôtelier du Pays de Sarlat** (T05 53 30 20 87 or freephone from within France T0800-97 24 24, hotels-sarlat-perigord.com), a consortium of nearly 50 establishments in all price ranges: ring or book online.

Périgord Noir is gîte country par excellence; it's the most popular sort of holiday here and almost all of them are detailed on perigordnoir.com.

Sarlat

La Hoirie €€€

Rue Marcel Cerdan, T05 53 59 05 62, hotel-sarlat.fr.
Mar-Dec.
Map: Sarlat, p154.
In a lovely park on the southern edge of town, La Hoirie was a hunting lodge, and parts of the building date back to the 13th century. The rooms are luxurious, there's a pool and you can dine out (€€€) on a lovely terrace.

La Maison des Peyrat €€

Le Lac de la Plane, T05 53 59 00 32, maisondespeyrat.com.
Apr to mid-Nov.
Map: Sarlat, p154.
This is a quiet retreat, set in the hills above Sarlat but still within walking distance of the centre. The oldest part of the building goes back to the 14th century, and it previously served as a convent, a hospital and a hunting lodge. Rooms are big and cosy, and there's a large pool and a restaurant.

Le Jardin €€

14 rue du Jardin de Madame, T05 53 29 22 67, lejardin-sarlat.com.
Map: Sarlat, p154.
Comfortable, pleasant, English-run chambre d'hôte: four rooms, a pretty garden and small pool, a few minutes' walk from the historic centre.

La Couleuvrine €

1 place de la Bouquerie, T05 53 59 27 80, la-couleuvrine.com.
Map: Sarlat, p154.
There's a lot of history in this building. Its conspicuous tower was once part of the city wall. Some rooms fall in the inexpensive range; some of the spacious, beautifully decorated *chambres supérieures* are truly special and a good bargain. Half and full board are on offer and the restaurant (see page 186) is one of Sarlat's best.

Self-catering

In-Sarlat

16 rue Fénelon, T05 53 29 44 90, in-sarlat.fr.
In-Sarlat is an estate agency that has gone into running rooms, and they've done it in style. Accommodation is in five separate old buildings around the centre, each with a mix of high design and homely comforts; those in the 'Maison des Poètes' are equipped with wild Arabian Nights bathrooms. High-season rates range from €500-1000; see their website for special offers, including luxury theme breaks that include a cruise in a balloon or a helicopter.

Camping

La Ferme de la Croix d'Esteil

Ste-Nathalène, T05 53 59 15 81, camping-croixdesteil.com.
8 km east of Sarlat on D47.
Quiet and rural, this inexpensive family campsite offers a pool, bike rentals and activities for children (they have ponies). There are also two simple, good-value gîtes sleeping two to four people (€480) and six people (€540), and a mobile home that sleeps five (€480).

Carsac-Aillac

Le Relais du Touron €€

T05 53 28 16 70, lerelaisdutouron.com.
Late Mar to mid-Nov.
On D704.
Just outside the tourist vortex of Sarlat and the castles, things are a little cheaper and quieter. Carsac makes a good base, with this gracious budget establishment with a pool and forested park; there's an unpretentious restaurant.

Place du Marché aux Oies, Sarlat.

La Roque-Gageac

La Belle Etoile €
T05 53 29 51 44, belleetoile.fr.
Apr-Oct.
A very good-value choice in the village centre, with spacious rooms furnished with antiques and an excellent restaurant (see page 187). Rooms with a river view are €10 more.

Castelnaud-la-Chapelle

Les Jardin des Milandes €€
Parc Josephine Baker, T05 53 30 42 42, les-jardins-des-milandes.com.
May-Sep.
The lower parts of the Milandes estate, down by the river, are helping to pay for the château upkeep in a number of ways. The theatre Josephine built hosts summer cabarets and dances, and her Hollywood-style pool, tennis and mini-golf are open for visitors. There's a restaurant and these four simple chambres d'hôtes, one of them right on the Dordogne.

La Roque-Gageac.

Meyrals

La Rhonie €
Boyer, T05 53 29 29 07, coustaty.com.
Apr to mid-Nov.
3 km northeast of Meyrals.
Conveniently located off the D47 about halfway between Sarlat and Les Eyzies, this isolated country house has cosy rooms, a pigeonnier, a covered pool and great views over the hills. There is also one gîte in a separate building that sleeps up to five (€960 per week). La Rhonie is a *ferme-auberge*, with the best of duck and goose on menus of €19-33 (Mon-Sat evenings only), and they offer cookery courses for their guests.

Les Eyzies-de-Tayac

Les Glycines €€€
Rue du Laugerie, T05 53 06 97 07, les-glycines-dordogne.com.
Mar to mid-Oct.
Probably the best in town; the décor may be a little fussy but it's quite comfortable. The spacious gardens are wonderful, and there's a pool. See their website for special offers, cookery classes and activities. There's also an excellent restaurant (see page 188).

Le Ferme de Tayac €€
14 rue de Tayac, T05 53 06 04 61, fermedetayac.com.
The building, right next to Tayac's church, began as a 12th-century monastery, later converted into a simple farm. Now it's one of the better B&Bs in Périgord. The cosy rooms are decorated with personal care; there's a lovely garden and a pool, and bicycles are available. Minimum stay is two nights, three in high season.

Le Menestrel €€
1 rue de Laugerie, T05 53 04 58 94, menestrel-perigord.com.
Excellent value, big, well-appointed chambre d'hôte near the centre. There's a relaxing garden with a view and a big pool.

Moulin de la Beune €€
Rue du Moulin Bas, T05 53 06 94 33, moulindelabeune.com.
It's a genuine 16th-century mill, with its wooden mill wheel still in place, and the murmuring Beune flowing past helps make this a restful spot in the middle of the action. The rooms are an unpretentious good bargain, but the real attraction here is the restaurant (see page 188).

Montignac

Le Relais du Soleil d'Or €€€
16 rue du 4 Septembre, T05 53 51 80 22, le-soleil-dor.com.
Mar-Jan.

Montignac.

Centuries ago this was a post house, and in its current incarnation it is still a welcoming and refined establishment. The rooms are bright and modern, and each is different, hence a wide range of prices. It has a pool and extensive gardens, and one of the area's better restaurants (see page 188).

Auberge du Laurence €
Place du Forail, Auriac, T05 53 50 25 28, auberge-le-laurence.com.
6 km north of Montignac.
If Montignac is full of tourists, try this little hideaway, five minutes by fast mammoth from Lascaux. Good inexpensive rooms and a convivial restaurant with tables out on the village square.

St-Amand-de-Coly

Manoir d'Hautegente €€€
Coly, T05 53 51 68 03, manoir-hautegente.com.
3 km north of St-Amand-de-Coly.
The ultimate luxury hideaway, this ivy-covered manor has only 17 rooms, half of them directly overlooking the little River Chironde. The house has been in the same family for 300 years; they run it themselves, and they have exquisite taste. Large park and heated pool. There's a very recherché restaurant (€€€€), so posh there's foie gras on the children's menu.

Terrasson-Lavilledieu

Le Commanderie €€
Condat-sur-Vézère, T05 53 51 26 49, hotel-lacommanderie.com.
8 km south of Terrasson.
It began in the Middle Ages as an establishment of the Knights Hospitallers, was later reincarnated as a manor house, and now it's an elegant B&B with seven stylish rooms. The trees in the spacious gardens are centuries old too; there's a pool and a restaurant.

Eating & drinking

Sarlat

La Couleuvrine €€€

1 place de la Bouquerie, T05 53 59 27 80, la-couleuvrine.com.
Closed Jan to mid Feb and Mon lunch.
Part of the hotel (see page 182), this is an elegant, very Périgourdin room with a big fireplace for the winter. There's lots of beef and duck, but also some seafood. They do some traditional dishes you don't often see in restaurants, including stuffed duck's neck and even lamprey *à la Bordelaise*. In addition there's the adjacent Côté Bistrot, which offers the same cooking in inexpensive lunches (Mon-Sat); it also opens as a wine bar (Wed-Sat evenings), and occasionally puts on concerts – they even have their own jazz festival (Sep-Oct).

Le Présidial €€€

6 rue Landry, T05 53 28 92 47.
Closed Mon lunch and Sun.
Map: Sarlat, p154.
Without doubt this is the prettiest spot in Sarlat, especially on a fine day when you can sit out in the landscaped garden. The building is one of the city's landmarks, the home of the king's officials in the 17th century. The cooking is classic Périgord, though along with your duck there are some interesting seafood choices, even on the €19 weekday lunch menu.

Criquettamu's €€

5 rue des Armes, T05 53 59 48 10.
Closed Nov-Easter and Mon.
Map: Sarlat, p154.
For something a little different, head over to this little street west of the rue de la République. Criquettamu's is fun, with décor contributed by local artists and a menu that besides the usual Périgourdin cooking may include dishes from any part of the globe. There's a wide choice of *salades composées* and a special children's menu – something rare in these parts.

Le Bistro de l'Octroi €€

111 av de Selves, T05 53 30 83 40, lebistrodeloctroi.fr.
Daily.
This is the hot new address in Sarlat, a few streets outside the centre but well worth the walk. The setting is a building where townspeople had to come to pay their tax (*octroi*), but it has a pleasant terrace. It isn't quite a bistro, but it's friendly and informal and the cooking is innovative and refined; the afternoon €15 *formule* might include quail stuffed with chestnuts, vegetarian lasagne or venison steak. Don't feel constrained by the menu choices: you're encouraged to mix and match as you please.

Le Rossignol €€

15 rue Fénelon, T05 53 31 02 30.
Closed Mon.
Map: Sarlat, p154.
It's tucked away on the edge of the old town where few tourists find it. First impressions aren't the best either: a very plain room, no ambience and no fun, but some of the most refined cooking in town, on menus that offer good value. If you're into the wild side of southwest cuisine – *ris de veau* or *tête de veau* – this is definitely the place.

Créperie des Fontaines €

4 place des Fontaines, T05 53 30 27 38.
Closed Mon.
Map: Sarlat, p154.
Crêpes, salads and a glass of cider (strangely popular in Sarlat but nowhere else in the Dordogne). It's nothing out of the ordinary, but you can eat at shady outdoor tables on

Sarlat's prettiest and most peaceful square.

Paulin

La Meynardie €€
T05 53 28 85 98.
Closed Tue-Wed and Nov-Easter.
5 km north of Salignac-Eyvigues.
A long-time favourite, run by the same couple that recently opened L'Octroi in Sarlat (see above), and with the same informal, innovative cuisine, La Meynardie is a good pick for lunch after a visit to the Jardins d'Eyrignac. You dine in a pretty farmhouse, or in the courtyard in summer.

St-Génies

Le Château €€€€
T05 53 28 36 77, restaurantduchateau.com.
It's a château all right, a genuine medieval one, small but brave, watching over this village lost in the hills between the Jardins d'Eyrignac and Lascaux. The ambience is elegant and deadly serious, the candlelit terrace a dream date on a summer's night, and the kitchen insists that the truffles, lobster and such share pride of place with their bodacious locally grown vegetables. They encourage patrons to look around their huge cellar – an admirable custom.

Carlux

La Gabarre €€
Le Mondou, T05 53 29 61 43, restaurantlagabarre.com.
Closed Mon in summer, Sun evening and Mon-Tue lunch rest of the year.
South of the Dordogne, just east of St-Julien-de-Lampon.
This may be the most attractive terrace in Périgord, with a wonderful river view and a flowering albizia tree for shade. The cooking is quite sophisticated; the poached salmon with lemon grass and wasabi was a treat.

Domme

La Borie Blanche €€
Near Giverzac, T05 53 28 11 24.
Easter to mid-Sep daily.
5 km east of Domme.
Lost in the hills outside town, this *ferme-auberge* raises cattle, so you have a choice of beef as well as the usual duck and potatoes. It has a terrace with a view.

La Roque-Gageac

La Plume d'Oie €€€
Le Bourg, T05 53 29 57 05.
Closed Nov to mid-Dec and Jan to mid-Mar, and Mon and Tue lunch.
A beautiful setting by the river and first-rate cooking, lots of foie gras and usually at least one really tempting seafood choice. They're very good at the small

things here: well-considered *amuse-bouches*, an elderflower aperitif, artistically composed desserts. Menus change with the seasons.

La Belle Etoile €€
T05 53 29 51 44, belleetoile.fr.
Apr-Oct, closed all day Mon and Wed lunch.
You won't find many surprises on the menu here, but everything will be very well done and good value. The setting is a plush, old-fashioned salon, but come when the weather is good, as there's a delicious terrace overlooking the Dordogne.

Beynac

La Taverne des Remparts €
Place du Château, T05 53 29 57 76.
May-Oct, closed Sat-Sun evenings.
Located opposite the castle entrance, it seems to be only a café for tourists, but you can eat quite well here or just stop for a drink and enjoy the view.

Castelnaud-la-Chapelle

Le Tournepique €€
T05 53 29 51 07.
Closed late Feb and late Nov.
For years now, this place with the pretty view over the Dordogne has had a quirky Basque-Périgourdin split personality. Though there's still plenty of duck around, the tide seems to be turning Basquewards, with some interesting seafood and even an all-tapas menu.

Les Eyzies-de-Tayac

Les Glycines €€€€
Rue du Laugerie, T05 53 06 97 07, les-glycines-dordogne.com.
They set a very luxurious table here, with a style of cooking that is indefinable but usually hits the right notes. There are lots of truffles about if you're up for a splurge (with a special €95 all-truffle menu), and some inspired dishes like scallops with pumpkin and hazelnut cream or goose *magret* with caramelized figs.

Moulin de la Beune €€€
Rue du Moulin Bas, T05 53 06 94 33, moulindelabeune.com.
Easter-end Oct, closed Sat and Tue-Wed lunch.
Come on a fine afternoon to enjoy this place at its best, with its flower-strewn riverside terrace. However, the cooking's good any time of year: personal interpretations of the old favourites, with a good helping of wild mushrooms in season.

La Loulie €€
Mauzens-et-Miramont, T05 53 03 23 15, promenades-gourmandes.com/laloulie.htm.
8 km north of Les Eyzies off D47.
It's a bit out of the way, but locals come from all directions for good cooking and dishes not often seen around here, like the *civet de marcassin* (young boar stew). It's also a nice, inexpensive chambre d'hôte with five rooms, and art and cookery courses on offer in summer.

St-Léon-sur-Vézère

Auberge du Pont €€
T05 53 50 73 07.
Everything pleases here (no doubt the setting helps, as they have a great terrace by the bridge): cassoulet, coq au vin au Bergerac, *sandre* (pike perch) from the river.

Le Déjeuner sur l'Herbe €
T05 53 53 50 69 17.
In an idyllic setting by the river, this little shack serves up *tartines chauds* (toasted sandwiches) of all kinds, even vegetarian, along with more conventional sandwiches, salads, pastries, *assiettes* and a variety of local products to take away. Use their outdoor tables or assemble a picnic.

Montignac

Le Relais du Soleil d'Or €€€€-€€€
16 rue du 4 Septembre, T05 53 51 80 22, le-soleil-dor.com.
Mar-Jan, closed Sun evening and Mon lunch except Jul-Aug.
After a while in Périgord you may start to miss your seafood, but this old inn can remedy that with some ambitious dishes, such as lobster navarin with basil. They're also good with some of the less common traditional foods: venison, roast pigeon, pheasant and an unusual chestnut soup. There's a €12.50 lunch menu.

Terrasson-Lavilledieu

Hostellerie l'Imaginaire €€€€-€€€
Place du Foirail, T05 53 51 37 27, l-imaginaire.com.
Closed Mon, also Tue lunch and Sun evening outside high season.
Right next to the Jardins de l'Imaginaire, this 17th-century building has a terrace with great views over the old town, and some *soignée* cooking with hints of tropical flavours. They also offer seven rooms with a touch of luxury (€€).

The perfect Périgord picnic: start in Sarlat

The Kingdom of Duck is a land of the mandatory three-hour sit-down dinner, but if you want something a little less formal, Sarlat is at your service. Even if it's not a market day, it will take you less than half an hour to put together a picnic you'll never forget. Start at the deluxe Marché Couvert, where you can pick up most of what you need: fine cheeses, fruits, pâtés, and some special treats such as a crusty *feuilleté* stuffed with foie gras.

To really push your picnic over the top, head over to the Traverse: the Charcuterie Vaux (34 rue de la République, Mon-Sat 0800-1230 and 1500-1900) is a first-rate *traiteur* that can supply some exotic touches (the seafood terrine made from red mullet is excellent), along with ready-made main courses and *sarladaise* potatoes. To top it off, buy patisseries and *salamandre* chocolates from the award-winning L'Atelier du Gourmand at No 22, one of the finest pastry shops in France (Tue-Sun 0800-1930).

Entertainment

Sarlat

Bars & clubs

Le Bataclan
31 rue de la République, T05 53 28 54 34.
Right on the 'Traverse', Sarlat's rock bar is popular with a younger crowd and stays open until 0200.

Le Pub
1 passage Gérard du Barry, T05 53 59 57 98.
Yes, it is a bit English, but Duckville doesn't offer a lot of choices for a night out. It has more than 80 different kinds of beer and 30 whiskies, billiards, a calm and pleasant atmosphere, and occasional live music on weekend nights.

Shopping

Sarlat

Clothing

Locona
6 rue Fénelon, T05 53 59 60 90.
Tue-Sat 1030-1230 and 1430-1800.
This mother-daughter operation is quite a find for a small town: they design and produce women's and children's clothes under their own label – bright, colourful and truly original, especially the children's wear.

Food & drink

Distillerie la Salamandre
Temniac, T05 53 59 10 00, distillerie-salamandre.com.
Mon-Fri 0800-1200 and 1300-1830.
4 km north of Sarlat.
The Salamander wins lots of medals at the Paris Agricultural Show for its eaux-de-vie, made from plums (*vieille prune*), greengages and William pears. They also do fruit aperitifs, fruits in liqueurs and many other products, including some unusual bottles (how'd they get the pear inside?) that make great presents to take home. During office hours they also offer tours of the distillery.

Lagreze
Place du Peyrou, T05 53 28 50 18.
Tue-Sat 0830-1200 and 1330-1800.
You can buy foie gras and other duck products on every street corner in Sarlat. All the big names – Valette, Vidal, Rougie and the rest – have at least one boutique

Travelling distillery.

in town, and they're all good. We'll mention Lagreze, which wins medals at the Paris Salon d'Agriculture for their confits. Leave plenty of room in your bag, and take home all the foie and rillettes and *cou farci* and *gesiers confits* you can fit in

Jewellery

Les Perles à Bibi
Rue Jean Racine, T05 53 28 26 41.
Jun-Sep Mon-Thu 1030-1200 and 1400-1900, Mar-May and Oct-Nov Mon-Fri 1400-1900.
Wild, ethereal fantasy jewellery made from crystal beads and semi-precious stones, made on site.

Markets

The big markets in Sarlat take place in place de la Liberté, all day Saturday and Wednesday mornings. There is a flea market on the last Sunday of the month (all day), on place Marc Busson and avenue Gambetta.

Salignac

Ceramics

Annie Soret
20 av de Sarlat, T05 53 29 67 48.
Apr-Oct Mon-Tue and Fri 1300-1730.
Pretty things inspired by nature in faience and porcelain, terracotta and other materials, some for the kitchen and some merely decorative.

St-Cyprien

Art galleries

This fat village sits at the western limits of Périgord Noir, in the middle of some of the prettiest countryside in the department. There aren't any caves or churches to attract tourists, but quite a few artists have found a home here – so many, in fact, that you can make a car tour of studios and galleries around St-Cyprien and its neighbouring village of Meyrals almost as easily as you could walking around Paris's Left Bank. There are about a dozen altogether: get a list from the tourist office or go to stcyprien-perigord.com ('Nos artistes'), where there is a map and examples of their work.

Mortemart

Food & drink

Sangliers de Mortemart
T05 53 03 21 30.
Daily 1000-1900, guided tours daily in Jul-Aug at 1500. 12 km north of Le Bugue on D710.
This farm offers a unique meet-'em-and-eat-'em experience with the formidable, long-legged, chestnut-gobbling

Périgord boar. They have some 500 on hand, completely free range, and a lot of ducks too. After you've seen them, there's a shop full of quality foie gras and confits, boar charcuterie and stews, and fresh *marcassin* (baby boar) so you can cook your own.

Les Eyzies-de-Tayac

Arts & crafts

Palaïos/Atelier du Silex
45 av de la Préhistoire, T06 88 92 71 33, ginellames.fr.
Apr-Oct Sun-Fri 1000-1900.
Bernard Ginelli, through a lot of time and study, has recaptured some of the methods the Cro-Magnons used to chip and polish flint, and he makes fine reproductions of the tools and implements you saw in the museums.

Montignac

Arts & crafts

LA Boutique
Place des Armes.
Tue, Wed, Fri 1030-1220 and 1530-1915, Sat 1530-1830.
Intriguing trinkets from local artists and artisans: jewellery, paintings, clothing, clever fabric book covers.

Jewellery

Anne Caro de Lascaux
61 rue du 4 Septembre, T05 53 50 70 89.
Mon-Sat 1000-1200 and 1400-1700.
It's not unknown in this part of France to find that an internationally known designer has set up shop in a village. The world must come to Ms Caro, instead of the other way around, for bright, eye-catching bracelets and necklaces, with many pretty things under €100.

St-Amand-de-Coly

Metalwork

Alain Lagasse
T05 53 51 66 48.
Right opposite the church you can visit the workshop of a no-nonsense old-time *chaudronnier-dinandier* (copper- and tinsmith). M Lagasse has some articles for sale, and he can take your order for copper pots and pans and other kitchen needs, as well as everything from decorative vases to a complete still.

Activities & tours

Air trips

Air Châteaux
Aérodrome de Domme and La Cabane, Vezac, T06 89 78 53 07, airchateaux.com.
On offer are trips of varying length around the Domme-Beynac area in small planes and ULM (ultra-lights). From €30 per person.

Montgolfières du Périgord
La Roque-Gageac, T05 53 28 18 58, montgolfiere-du-perigord.com.
If you don't mind being caught in a balloon with a smiley face or a duck bill on it, flights of various lengths are available all year round in suitable weather; from €190 per person, €95 for children under 12.

Périgord Dordogne Montgolfières
La Balme, Beynac, T05 53 29 20 56 or 06 83 26 47 66, perigord-dordogne-montgolfieres.com.
They own the big blue balloon with the kingfisher on the side. Trips over the scenic centre of the Dordogne float over Castelnaud, Beynac and the other châteaux; €190 per person, €110 for under 12s.

Canoeing & kayaking

With so many castles creating picture-postcard backdrops, this is by far the most popular stretch of the Dordogne. On summer weekends, you can look down from the Castelnaud bridge and see the closest thing France has to a canoe traffic jam. Among the many rental places are **Couleurs Périgord** (Plage du Vézac, T05 53 30 37 61, couleurs-perigord.com), which will take you to destinations as far as Carsac and let you paddle downstream; they also arrange rock-climbing and spelunking expeditions. You'll get much the same deal from **Cénac-Périgord Loisirs** (Cénac, Domme, T05 53 29 99 69).

Paddling is just as popular on the Vézère; though there aren't as many castles to look at, it is still a scenic trip. **AVCK-Animation-Vézère** (T05 53 06 92 92, vezere-canoe.com) will bus you from the bridge at Les Eyzies up the river as far as Thonac. From St-Léon, you can do it with **Aventure Plein Air** (T05 53 50 67 71, canoevezere.com).

For any of these, it's a good idea to book ahead, especially in July and August.

Cycling

Bike Bus
T06 08 94 42 01, bike-bus.co.uk.
This convenient, British-run bike hire service has six bases around the area between Domme and Les Eyzies. They deliver within the area, offer a wide range of bikes and know all the good trails.

River cruises

If you don't care to paddle your own canoe, you can see the river

on an easy cruise in a *gabarre*, a modern re-creation of the old barges that used to carry the river trade. Take a 50-minute tour underneath the castles with **Gabarres de Beynac** (T05 53 28 51 15, gabarre-beynac.com; daily May-Sep 1000-1230 and 1400-1800, Apr and Oct 1100-1700; €7.50, €4 under 12s). Or you can go from La Roque-Gageac with **Gabarres Caminade** (T05 53 29 40 95, best-of-perigord.tm.fr; Easter-Oct daily 1000-1800; €8.50, €5 under 12s) or **Les Gabarres Norbert** (T05 53 29 40 44, norbert.fr; Apr-Nov daily 1000-1800, Oct-Nov afternoons only; €8.50, €6 under 13s). It's advisable to book in advance.

Northern Lot

Contents

Dordogne Valley near Souillac.

Introduction

The Northern Lot, or Dordogne Quercynois, is a world apart from the rest of the Lot, separated by expanses of empty *causse* where villages are few and far between. In fact this area has more in common with the Dordogne – for starters, it is that river that runs through it. This stretch of the Dordogne Valley isn't just an extension of its heartland in Périgord. It's wilder, more scenic – and emptier: there isn't a community in it with more than 4000 people. And while it can get busy in summer, the hordes that descend on Sarlat and La Roque-Gageac haven't really found this area yet.

After the heavier courses of tourism in this book, the northern Lot may seem like only a light dessert. Fittingly enough, this very rustic valley provides France with a lot of its walnuts and jam. Besides nut trees and berry patches, the looping course of the Dordogne between Souillac and St-Céré passes by some of France's most delicious little villages, a pair of exceptional Renaissance châteaux, a pair of Romanesque church portals that get into all the art history books, and a pair of spectacular stalactite caves.

To close this section, south of the river there is the utterly remarkable village of Rocamadour, glued to the side of a 160-m cliff. Rocamadour has monkeys, cockatoos, condors, toy trains and goats to show you; it has been an unabashed tourist trap for nearly 1000 years.

Clockface, Northern Lot.

What to see in...

...one day
A relatively small region, you could cruise through most of it in a day. But it isn't a place for hurrying. You might start in **Souillac**, with its church and the **Musée de l'Automate**, then leisurely drive up the Dordogne through **Martel** and **Carennac**. In the afternoon see the Renaissance fantasy château of **Montal**, or the **Gouffre de Padirac**, or head south to Rocamadour. If you're travelling with children, Rocamadour and its family-friendly attractions could occupy a whole day in itself.

...a weekend or more
You really can see it all. Linger around the lovely river, and take in beautiful villages such as **Creysse, Gluges** and **Autoire**. **Lacave** and the **Grotte de Presque** are not to be missed if you like sparkly stalactites, and the château at **Castelnau** contains a wealth of art.

Souillac & the Upper Dordogne

Souillac is no Sarlat; unlike its swanky neighbour, this is a well-worn working town, but likeable enough. Its population of 3970 leaves it slightly behind its sister city, the Souillac named for it on the island of Mauritius. But small though it is, this Souillac gets busy enough in summer to have its own tourist mini-train.

Heading east up the meandering Dordogne Valley, it would be hard to find any stretch of any river that would be closer to everyone's perfect fantasy of *la douce France*. Every village is gorgeous, the scenery is entrancing and the lunch on the terrace couldn't be better. If the atmosphere were any more relaxed here, no one would ever get out of bed.

How they manage to keep it so unspoilt and low key is something of a mystery, especially as there are quite a few interesting sights along the way: fine medieval art at Martel and Carennac, the refined châteaux of Montal and Castelnaud, and the magical underground cathedral at the Gouffre de Padirac.

Souillac

Like so many towns in this book, Souillac began with a monastery. Good St Eloi (or Eligius) founded it around 650; he is the jovial saint who gave up his blacksmith's job to be a bishop, according to legend, though the chroniclers say he was master of the mint to the Merovingian King Clotaire II. It isn't quite clear how, but Souillac grew quite rich and fat by the 11th century, controlling a monastic empire of some 150 priories between Limoges and Toulouse. The monks built their glorious Eglise Ste-Marie, and in its shadow a town grew up with a strong corporation of merchants. After that brilliant start came the usual calamities of the southwest: plague and loss of trade routes, a century of on-and-off occupation by the English, and finally a fire in 1570 that burned down almost everything but the church.

Essentials

Getting around You can walk around Souillac or take a one-hour tour aboard the Petit Train (T05 65 37 81 56, July-August daily 1000-1900, night tour at 2130; €5, €3 child).

Taxis Destrel, 36 rue des Ayrals, T05 65 37 80 31.

Train station Souillac station, on the northern edge of town, is on the SNCF Paris-Toulouse line; for details of regional train services see page 278.

Buses Services are extremely limited: see page 279.

Pharmacy 25 boulevard Louis-Jean Malvy, T05 65 32 79 48.

Hospital Brive-la-Gaillarde (40 km), T05 55 92 60 00.

Post office Boulevard Louis-Jean Malvy, T05 65 27 51 80, Monday-Friday 0830-1200 and 1330-1700, Saturday 0830-1200.

Tourist information In the old St-Martin church, boulevard Louis-Jean Malvy, T05 65 37 81 56, Monday-Saturday 1000-1200 and 1400-1800.

Eglise Abbatiale Ste-Marie belfry.

Eglise Abbatiale Ste-Marie

Like Périgueux and Cahors, Souillac topped its church with domes, and this is the perhaps the best of the three, the one where we can really feel the spirit of that very strange, very distant 12th century. Built sometime between 1075 and 1150, Ste-Marie definitely has an exotic air about it, as if it were some priceless bauble brought home from the Crusades.

The exterior is a reminder that, in the early Romanesque, what we think of as the back was architecturally often more important than the main entrance at the west front. The tremendous apse, with its ensemble of rounded chapels and double-arched windows, may have been intended to serve as an intimation of the Heavenly City.

Ste-Marie survived the English and the Protestants, but its worst enemies were the bewigged and powdered dandies of the age of Louis XIV. They trashed the medieval portal and its sculpture, put a wooden roof over the great domes, and turned the elegant interior into a plaster neoclassical pastiche. All that has been cleared away and, though a bit humbled and austere today, Ste-Marie has recovered something of its original effect.

Inside, bits of what must once have been one of the great portals of France were carelessly attached to the west wall. Above the door are lively reliefs that recount the legend of St Theophilus – how he sold his soul to the Devil, and how the Virgin Mary herself went down to Hell to snatch back the contract. Though a truly obscure saint, he is credited as one of the sources for the story of Faust.

The tall, monster-covered column to the right was originally one of the door jambs. And below Theophilus are two figures: a badly eroded Joseph and his companion – probably the most famous work of art in this book. Isaiah, often called the 'Dancing Isaiah', may be the most contagiously joyful figure in all of Christian art, and he has reason to be; the scroll in his hand is his prophecy, with the good news of a 'new heaven and a new earth'. The extreme stylization of the figure, exotic even by Romanesque standards, has led some scholars to conclude this is the work of the same hand that made southwest France's other sculptural masterpiece, the portal at Moissac in the Tarn-et-Garonne.

Sound as a bell

There's more art than you might think in Romanesque churches – and some science too. The simple constructive geometry behind the design creates some amazing acoustics. When there's nobody else inside, stand at the focal point, where the nave and crossing meet. Hum a low note and listen as the building around you rings like a bell.

Eglise Abbatiale Ste-Marie.

Musée de l'Automate

Place de l'Abbaye, T05 65 37 07 07,
musee-automate.fr.
Jan-Mar and Nov-Dec Wed-Sun 1430-1730, Apr-Jun and Sep-Oct Tue-Sun 1000-1200 and 1500-1800, Jul-Aug daily 1000-1900. €6, €4.50 concession, €3 child (5-12).

The Dancing Isaiah just might approve of this bit of whimsy directly outside his church. The *automates* to which the museum is devoted are mechanical dolls and entire moving tableaux from the 19th and early 20th centuries, many intended for shop window displays. The collection had its beginnings with Jean Roullet, who started making toys in Paris in 1855. His firm soon became the leading manufacturer of automata, surviving various changes and owners until 1995. The models were then acquired by the State and somehow ended up here in Souillac.

Most of the over 300 items are in perfect working order; there's a staff of clever technicians to keep them that way. It's all utterly charming, a trip back to the winsome, lost, long-ago France of pierrots and paper flowers. There are circus performers and Chinese jugglers, magicians performing tricks, snake charmers, family scenes, even an entire black American jazz band from the 1920s.

Viaduc Ferroviaire de Bramefond

Souillac has one more sight, startling in its way, though the Souillagais are so accustomed to it they pay it little mind. This magnificent viaduct at the entrance to the town, designed by Jean Vilette and finished in 1882, is 320 m long and 44 m high. Like the other works of the Chemin de Fer d'Orleans (now the Paris-Toulouse SNCF line) from this period, it is a monument of the heroic age of railway building; its slender arches and clean lines were a foretaste of the new age of modern architecture that was just around the corner.

Musée de l'Automate.

Dordogne Valley

Grottes de Lacave

T05 65 37 87 03, grottes-de-lacave.fr.
Guided tours daily mid-end Mar and Oct 1000-1200 and 1400-1700, Apr-Jun 0930-1200 and 1400-1800, Jul 0930-1230 and 1330-1800, Aug 0930-1800, Sep 0930-1200 and 1400-1730. €8.30, €5.50 child (5-14).
11 km south of Souillac on D43.

Like Rouffignac (see page 172), we get to see this cave the easy way, via a lift and an electric miners' train. It's easy on the brain too: no Palaeolithic art, no complex geology or dates to learn. Lacave is just for show, and it is truly beautiful. The exotic formations include some *excentriques* and some spectacular ones with properly romantic titles: the Milky Waterfall, the Elephant, the Tarasque (after the legendary turtle-backed monster of Tarascon in Provence) and, best of all, the *ville engloutie*, where the reflection of stalactites in a rock pool gives an uncanny impression of a 'drowned city'.

Tip...

You can now buy tickets in advance online, which may be helpful in the crush of August.

Grottes de Lecave.

Storybook villages: Meyronne, St-Sozy and Creysse

On this short stretch of the river beyond Lacave everything is exquisite and serene. First up is **Meyronne**, on a height overlooking the Dordogne. On the edge of town you can walk to the **Oratoire**, a lovely spot in the cliffs with a rock-cut chapel. If you like, you may ring the bell on the cliff face, as pilgrims did in the old days to announce their presence. Right across the river, **St-Sozy** makes its living mostly from foie gras. It has a charming market square and an air of sleepy contentment.

A small, neatly enamelled sign as you enter **Creysse** implores visitors to climb up and see the 'only twin-apsed church in France'. But the real attraction is the delightful village itself. Right on the edge of the stream that runs through it is a doll-sized stone **covered market**. Follow the winding lanes up to the **church**, and you will indeed see two apses (the key's in the Mairie across the lawn).

Gluges

Tiny Gluges seems a bit intimidated, sitting in the shadow of an enormous cliff. As in so many villages of the Dordogne, it grew out of cave habitations. Gérard de Mirandol, who owned it in the early 12th century, came home from the First Crusade with some holy relics and built the troglodytic **Eglise St-Pierre-es-Liens**, partially dug into the cliff face. It's currently closed and under restoration, though the exterior has some interesting carved corbels. The 19th-century church built to replace it was falling down too, when it found an angel in the form of Edith Piaf. The famous singer spent many holidays in nearby Cressensac, and when she saw the state of affairs here she financed some repairs and paid for new stained glass windows.

Just outside Gluges on the D840 there's a spot called the **Belvédère de Copeyre**, with spectacular views over the river valley.

Martel.

Martel

Seen from a distance, it could be a dream of the Middle Ages, the 'City of Seven Towers'. It was indeed a city once, back when 5000 people inside the walls was a lot. But since its heyday Martel has been only a brave village with the air of a city; its population of 1500 is barely enough to fill its few medieval streets.

Plan your picnic!

This delightful stretch of the Dordogne is ideal for picnics, but in the bitsy villages it may be hard to find everything you need. You can do so in Souillac or St-Céré easily enough, less easily in Vayrac or Bretenoux. There are good spots everywhere, such as under the abbey at Carennac, at the scenic Belvédère du Copeyre near Gluges, or among the Celtic ghosts of Uxellodunum high on the Puy d'Issolud.

The name is an old form of the word *marteau* (hammer). This and the three hammers on the city's coat-of-arms recall the legend that the town was founded by Charles Martel, the 'Hammer of the Saracens', who drove the Arab armies back over the Pyrenees in the 730s and founded the Carolingian dynasty.

The real history is a little more prosaic. Martel's fate was always bound up with that of the Vicomtes de Turenne. Among the most powerful nobles of France, they owned most of the northern Lot and the Corrèze. They seem to have founded the town sometime in the 11th century, and collected feudal dues from it until one of the last of their line sold it to Louis XV in 1738, to pay his gambling debts. In between, though, Martel enjoyed its time as a real city, ruled by its own consuls and making enough cash from the river trade to build its seven towers.

Musée de l'Uxellodunum

Place des Consuls, T05 65 37 30 03.
Jul-Aug Mon-Tue and Thu-Sat 1000-1200 and 1500-1800. €1.50.

One of those towers belongs to the stately **Palais de la Raymondie**, begun in 1280 by the Turennes. Now part of it serves as the town hall, the rest as home to this small museum, where Celtic and Roman items from the fabled Uxellodunum are on display.

Eglise St-Maur.

Opposite stands a rather elegant stone **market**, where you can still see the old grain measures bolted to a wall. Another medieval tower is built into the 15th-century **Hôtel Fabri**. Here, Henry Court-Mantel, son of Henry II and Eleanor of Aquitaine, died on his way home from sacking Rocamadour, leaving the throne of England open for Richard the Lionheart.

Eglise St-Maur

The tallest of Martel's seven towers is the steeple of the parish church, one of the few late-Gothic works you can see in this part of France. While most places were suffering in the Hundred Years' War, the English never took Martel by storm (though they did once briefly get it by treaty). The 12th-century **portal**, showing the *Last Judgment*, was recycled from an earlier church. It was worth keeping: most likely carved by the school of sculptors at Moissac, it has one of the great Romanesque tympanums of southern France. Though simple and small in scale, it gains an electric immediacy from the twisting forms of the four angels that surround Christ, playing the trumpets that symbolize divine justice at the end of days.

Inside, behind the altar, St-Maur has another treasure, some rare **stained glass** dating from 1531, believed to be the work of students of the greatest Renaissance glass painter, Arnaud de Moles.

St-Maur was originally a fortified church, built right into the city walls like that of Cahors. Those walls are gone, though another of the defence towers remains nearby, the **Tour Tournemire**.

Where's Uxellodunum?

It is one of the most important places in the history of France – but the French had to spend centuries looking for it. Uxellodunum was the last stronghold of the Gauls in 52 BC. While the Romans were besieging it, Julius Caesar came in person to finish his conquest. He drove the defenders to despair by cutting off their water supply, and when they surrendered he cut a hand off each and sent them to every corner of Gaul *pour encourager les autres*.

Unfortunately, the accounts of Caesar and other historians weren't clear enough for anyone to tell where Uxellodunum was. Even 15 years ago, several villages around France disputed the honour, including Luzech and Capdenac in the Lot. The arguments could get pretty fierce, until archaeologists in the 1990s found proof that the famous fortress-town was in fact on the **Puy d'Issolud**, a rough plateau 10 km from Martel near the village of Vayrac. There isn't much to see but some fragments and foundations, but the views over the valley are wonderful.

Carennac

All the villages are beautiful in this charmed corner, but Carennac is special. It was photogenic enough to attract the famous photographer Robert Doisneau, who spent a lot of time here and incorporated the village and its people in many of his shots.

Before Doisneau, there was Fénelon (see page 158), who loved spending his summers here, where his uncle was in charge of the priory. He later succeeded him as prior and may have written his *Aventures de Télémaque* here. Carennac was a wealthy, rarefied place then, but a long decline and the Revolution brought it back to earth. The priory, with its treasures of medieval art, the château and the village huddle together so closely that under the skyline of steep roofs it seems like a single building – a rugged, crumbling form with a turret or a finely carved Renaissance window here and there as a reminder of its long-ago glory.

After you've seen the sights, take the rocky path by the bridge that leads past a picturesquely ruined Renaissance tower down to the river. The grassy riverfront promenade is a beautiful spot and a great place for a picnic, though you'll need a canoe to visit the island opposite. This was a magical place for young Fénelon, who called it the **Ile de Calypso**.

Prieuré St-Pierre

T05 65 10 97 01.
Cloister and chapter house Jul-Aug daily 1000-1300 and 1400-1800, rest of year Mon-Sat 1000-1200 and 1400-1830. €2.50.

You can see it peeking out at you through the little archway at the entrance to the village: a Romanesque **tympanum** as good as Martel's and in much better shape. Christ appears in a mandorla, surrounded by the twelve Apostles, with an intricate border of folded ribbons and tiny animals beneath. Inside, there is some more good sculpture on the capitals (though they are hard to see in the gloom), and in the **cloister**, which has only one surviving Romanesque gallery; the other three are Flamboyant Gothic.

It's lucky there's anything left at all, as for a while after the Revolution this cloister was used as a pigsty. All of the priory's other works of art disappeared in those years, except for one lovely, solemn 15th-century *Mise au Tombeau (Deposition of Christ)* in the chapter house; the villagers thought it too beautiful to sell.

Espace Patrimoine

T05 65 33 81 36.
Apr-Jun and Oct Tue-Fri 1000-1200 and 1400-1800, Jul-Sep Tue-Sun 1000-1200 and 1400-1800. Free.

Right next to the church, Carennac's lovely castle, the 16th-century **Château des Doyens**, has been pressed into service as a heritage centre, with exhibits on the history, art and culture of the area, including an animated model of the entire upper Dordogne valley.

Castelnau-Bretenoux

This is one of France's many two-headed villages, created when tiny places are merged into larger ones for efficiency's sake. The destinies of these two have always been intertwined; the larger is **Bretenoux**, a bastide of half-timbered buildings founded in 1277 by the lord of the tiny one – the medieval village and Renaissance château of **Castelnau**. Bretenoux is an up-and-coming place, with a crack basketball team and a crack rugby team; thanks to the presence of 'Bonne Maman' company Andros and other firms, it's also the 'European Capital of Jam'.

Carennac.

Tip...

Castelnau, up on its hill, is a pedestrian village, and there's really no room for cars; to see the château you'll have to park at the bottom and make the 10-minute climb.

Castelnau.

Château de Castelnau

T05 65 10 98 00, castelnau-bretenoux.monuments-nationaux.fr. Apr and Sep daily 1000-1230 and 1400-1730, May-Jun daily 1000-1230 and 1400-1830, Jul-Aug daily 1000-1900, Oct-Mar Tue-Sun 1030-1230 and 1400-1730. €7, €4.50 concessions, under 18s free; joint ticket with Château de Montal €10, €7 concessions.

The castle was begun around 1000, and gradually evolved into the tawny-coloured Renaissance palace that makes such a grand sight from the surrounding plains. If you take a guided tour they'll tell you the story of how in 1184 its proud barons were forced to swear fealty to the Turennes, and as tribute sent them every year a single egg, delivered in a grand procession nestled in a coach behind four horses.

After falling into ruin, Castelnau got its break in 1851 when it was purchased by a local boy who had gone to Paris and become wealthy as an operatic tenor. Jean Mouliérat restored the château and filled it with the collection that is still on display today. This is mostly late-medieval religious art, including two large Spanish retables.

The impressive **Grande Salle** once hosted meetings of the Estates of Quercy (on those rare occasions when the king allowed them to meet). There are oubliettes where some forgotten skeletons were recently discovered, and you can climb up the main tower, the **Tour de l'Artillerie**, for views over the valley.

The barons of Castelnau built the equally elegant **Collégiale St-Louis,** down below the château in the village of Prudhomat. This is one of the rare churches spared by the Revolution, and still has its original ensemble of artworks, including some good stained glass.

St-Céré

St-Céré is by far the biggest town in this corner of the Lot, and its suburbs sprawl over the hills around the little River Bave (babbler). Though a busy, workaday town, St-Céré has a bit of quirky character. Once it was the 'Venice of the Lot', laced with canals, though all but one – near the tourist office – have been filled in. The striking medieval castle of **St-Laurent-les-Tours**, on a lofty conical perch just outside town, peeks over the rooftops, while every square is decorated with a bronze statue of some local worthy. In the central **place de la République** there's the ferocious-looking François Certain Canrobert, who led French armies from Algeria to the Crimea, and a few streets away stands the more serene Charles Bourseul, who invented a working telephone 20 years before Bell.

The two most interesting corners of St-Céré are the **place du Mercadial**, the picturesque old market square surrounded by half-timbered buildings, and the streets along the Bave, embellished with an old mill wheel and the 18th-century **Chapelle des Recollets**.

Market in St-Céré.

Lurçat and his cockerel

Jean Lurçat (1892-1966) grew up around St-Céré. After establishing himself as a painter he spent the Occupation years working for the Resistance as a clandestine radio operator. When the war was over he resumed his career as an artist, working in ceramics, furniture and, most importantly, in a brave attempt to revive the art of tapestry in France in a modern style. One of his favourite images – and something you'll see reproduced all over the Lot – was a brightly coloured *coq*, that eternal symbol of Gaul, designed to cheer up his countrymen after the grim years of the war. If you like Lurçat there are more of his works in the exhibition space called the **Casino** in St-Céré.

St-Laurent-les-Tours

T05 65 38 28 21.
Mid-Jul to Sep daily 0930-1230 and 1430-1830.
€2.50.

This prominent hill was called *Mons Serenus* in ancient times, and it was the site of the martyrdom in 794 of St-Céré's protectress, Ste Spérie (if the legends are true, it's interesting to hear there were still pagans causing trouble in this part of the Lot in Charlemagne's time). The castle, with its two skyscraper-like keeps, grew up after that; for most of its life it belonged to the Turennes. In the 1950s Jean Lurçat, a local artist of considerable renown (see above), purchased the castle and began restorations. Some of his works are on display here.

Château de Montal

St-Jean-Lespinasse, T05 65 38 13 72, montal.monuments-nationaux.fr.
May-Aug daily 1000-1230 and 1400-1830,
Apr and Sep daily 1000-1230 and 1400-1730,
Oct-Mar Wed-Sun 1000-1230 and 1400-1730.
€7, €4.50 concessions, under 18s free;
joint ticket with Château de Castelnau-Bretenoux €10, €7 concessions.
3 km west of St-Céré.

Like Bourdeilles in Périgord (see page 126), this is a castle with a woman's touch – and a tragic story. The widow Jeanne de Balzac d'Entraygues began building it in 1523, for her son Robert who would soon come of age and inherit it. Jeanne had been to Italy with her soldier husband, and she must have brought back some Italian ideas – and probably Italian artists. She had just finished when they brought Robert's body back from the wars.

Today the château rather haughtily turns its back on the golf course below, but once you climb up you're confronted with a courtyard that is one of the masterpieces of Renaissance art in France. The gables, dormers and windows may be French, but the sculpted *grottesca* panels and reliefs in between are pure Italian. The busts in the stately niches represent Jeanne and the other members of her family, and each is a carefully considered portrait.

Inside there is a magnificent Italianate grand staircase in creamy stone with a wealth of sculpture, and rooms with a museum's worth of period furnishings, all furnished by Montal's angel, Maurice Fenaille, who bought the château in 1908 after some scurrilous operators had stripped and sold all the sculpture you see now. Fenaille spent decades tracking down every bit in America and Europe, and exhausted his fortune paying over-the-top prices to bring it back.

Grottes de Presque

T05 65 40 32 01, grottesdepresque.com.
Daily mid-Feb to Jun and Sep 0930-1200 and 1400-1800, Jul-Aug 0930-1830, Oct 1000-1200 and 1400-1700. €7, €4.50 concessions, €3.50 child (6-11).
2 km south of Montal on D80.

The entrance is right on the roadside, stuck into the side of a cliff, and you enter as if into a theatre. And theatrical it is, with colourful Gaudiesque chambers, fairy columns, stone waterfalls and celestial castles made of cauliflower. Along with Proumeyssac in Périgord (see page 170), it's one of the best stalactite caves you'll see.

Gouffre de Padirac

Padirac, T05 65 33 64 56, gouffre-de-padirac.com.
Daily Apr-Jun 0930-1700, Jul 0930-1800, Aug 0830-1830, Sep-Oct 1000-1700.
€9, €5.70 child (4-12).
9 km north of Gramat on D14.

There are no paintings, and stalactites are few, but this may be the most memorable of all the Lot's many caves. The entrance is through the *gouffre*, an immense underground cave formed by water erosion. It's over 100 m straight down, with a small round entrance at ground level where the roof collapsed long ago. Local people considered it the entrance to Hell, and there is a legend that the Devil himself made it, during a dispute with St Martin over a sackful of souls on a stormy night; with a little imagination you can see the hoof print of the saint's mule where he jumped over the abyss.

The trip begins with the descent into the chasm by a glass lift. From there you pass through a long corridor to where boatmen with gondola-like craft are waiting to punt you down an underground river. You may feel as if Charon is ferrying you into the underworld of Greek mythology, passing huge columns, lagoons formed by natural limestone dams and narrow defiles, all discreetly lit. The climax of the trip is another cave called the **Salle du Grand Dôme**. This one, 93 m in height, still has its roof, and is a tremendous and solemn space unlike anything you have ever seen. Taking photos inside is prohibited (but they'll catch *you* by surprise while you're in the boat and sell you the photo at the exit).

Gouffre de Padirac.

Rocamadour & around

We wouldn't want to discourage anyone from visiting Rocamadour. This nearly vertical village, draped on its cliffside, enjoys an incredible setting. The first sight of it, coming up the gorge of the Alzou on the D32 *route touristique*, is unforgettable. (This is the only way to approach Rocamadour properly, otherwise you'll miss the famous view and wonder what all the fuss is about.) And a visit here is guaranteed fun, especially if you have children.

But ever since it became a pilgrimage site in the 12th century, this village of some 250 souls has been so thickly larded with fakery it's hard not to laugh. Quite shamelessly, they claim it's the second most visited site in France. In the Middle Ages they were showing pilgrims Durendal, the sword of the legendary hero Roland, stuck in the stone where the archangel Michael had thrown it all the way from the Pyrenees, after Roland was ambushed by the Saracens at Roncesvalles; today they'll show you monkeys and eagles and model trains, and the crowds are bigger than ever.

Rocamadour.

Village & shrines

Guided tours Mon, Wed, Fri 1030, 1600 and 1800; much more frequently in summer. €5. Details from tourist office.

In the old days pilgrims made the climb from the bottom of the gorge up to the few alleyways of the medieval village around place de la Caretta. (The **Hôtel de Ville** nearby has two colourful tapestries by Jean Lurçat.) The climb continued up the **Grand Escalier** to the 'Holy City' with its chapels and shrines; now there's a **lift** (€4 round trip).

Today, the main entrance to Rocamadour is from the other direction, where the lifts are, leading directly to the **Parvis de St-Amadour**, the small square at the centre of the Holy City. Around this are seven churches and chapels, which mirror the 'Seven Churches' of Rome, making Rocamadour a kind of substitute for a lengthier pilgrimage there. None is particularly compelling; the Protestant wreckers did a very thorough job, and the 19th-century restorations are uniformly grim.

The biggest is the **Basilique St-Sauveur**, where pilgrims would hear Mass. Adjacent to it, you can

Essentials

Getting around The D32 is a narrow, twisting road, and in July and August when it gets very crowded you might want to give it a miss. However you arrive, follow the signs to the upper town (**l'Hospitalet**), where most of the attractions are and where there's plenty of parking. The old town is completely pedestrianized (unless you're booked into a hotel with a garage). Take the **lift** down from the top (€3 round trip, runs only until 2200). There's also a **tourist train** (April-September) that runs between the village and l'Hospitalet.

Tourist information L'Hospitalet, T05 65 33 22 00; there's also a branch in the lower town, in the Hôtel de Ville.

Tip...

Only two of the churches are generally open: St-Sauveur and Chapelle Nôtre-Dame. To see the rest, you'll have to take the tour. For pilgrimage information and schedule of masses, see notredame-de-recomadour.com.

Rocamadour.

Le Grand Escalier.

see **Roland's sword** stuck high in the wall at the entrance to the 1479 **Chapelle Nôtre-Dame**, the holy of holies of Rocamadour, partially built into the cliff. Inside are fragments of medieval frescoes and the 'Black Virgin', claimed to be the work of St Amadour himself (though it's really 11th century); the blackness comes from the tarnishing of the silver coating. The church is full of votive offerings, many of them left by Breton sailors, who always held the Virgin of Rocamadour in particular reverence.

The **Chapelle St-Michel** retains some frescoes from the 14th century: a giant one of *St Christopher*, patron of travellers and pilgrims, at the entrance, and inside, a better-preserved one of *Christ in Majesty*. Behind this is the **Musée d'Art Sacré** (T05 65 33 23 30, daily 1000-1200 and 1330-1730, Jul-Aug 1000-1900; €4.70, €2.60 child) with a grab bag of religious art and exhibits on the history of Rocamadour and the pilgrimage.

L'Hospitalet

Up above Rocamadour, at the top of the cliffs, medieval pilgrims would stay at the Hôpital de St-Jean. Today the area is called l'Hospitalet and it's full of hotels, as well as the car parks and attractions that have grown up since the 1970s and now attract as many visitors as the shrine itself.

Rocher des Aigles

T05 65 33 65 45, rocherdesaigles.com.
Displays Apr-May Tue-Sun 1430 and 1700, Jun Tue-Sun 1330, 1500 and 1630, 1-14 Jul daily 1330, 1500, 1630 and 1745, 15 Jul-Aug daily 1130, 1330, 1500, 1630 and 1745, Sep Tue-Sun 1430 and 1600. €8, €5 child (4-13). You can come at any time before the shows to look at the birds.

On the edge of the cliffs near Rocamadour's château, watch them let loose not only eagles, but hawks, owls, kites, giant condors, parrots and cockatoos, over 60 species in all, soaring over the village and diving for food. Parrots will eat out of your hand and buzzards will walk over your head. It's an impressive show, and intelligently presented, with a strong environmental message. This isn't a circus, but an institution dedicated to raising and caring for the birds, especially endangered species (you'll probably see some babies in the nursery on the way in). The show enables them to pay the bills.

Forêt des Singes

T05 65 33 62 72, la-foret-des-singes.com.
Apr and 1-15 Sep daily 1000-1200 and 1300-1730, May-Jun daily 1000-1200 and 1300-1800, Jul-Aug daily 0930-1830, 16-30 Sep Mon-Fri 1300-1730, Sat-Sun 1000-1200 and 1300-1730, Oct Mon-Fri 1300-1700, Sat-Sun 1000-1200 and 1300-1700, Nov Sat-Sun 1000-1200 and 1300-1700. €8.50, €4.50 child (5-14).

Like the Rocher des Aigles, this is a research centre as well as a spectacle. Some 130 free-range Barbary apes have been living here since 1974 (they're really Barbary macaques, and some of them did come from Gibraltar). You can watch them live in the almost-wild, learn about their habits and feed them popcorn.

La Féerie Autour du Rail

T05 65 33 71 06, la-feerie.com.
Apr-Oct, schedule of performances changes frequently: ring ahead for times. €8.50, €5.50 child (4-11).

For some, Robert Mousseau's little toy train set might be the highlight of Rocamadour. The trains, 60 of them, run past an entire city, with some 600 hand-made buildings and 200 animated scenes; it took M Mousseau nine years to build. The show begins with miners trudging off to the mountain in the morning light, and follows a whole day in the life of the town below. High-wire acts are performed in the miniature circus, trams and cars cruise the streets, firefighters put out a burning building. It's endlessly clever and utterly charming – and so big that Mousseau has built a moving grandstand so you can watch it all happen.

Grotte Préhistoriques des Merveilles

T05 65 33 67 92, grotte-des-merveilles.com.
Daily Apr-Jun and Sep 1000-1200 and 1400-1800, Jul-Aug 0930-1900. €6, €4 child (5-11).

This cave was only discovered in 1920, just in time to join the ranks of roadside attractions in l'Hospitalet. It has plenty of glistening stalactites, a small underground lake and some fragments of 20,000-year-old drawings.

La Borie d'Imbert

Route de Lacave, T05 65 33 20 37, rocamadourlaboriedimbert.com.
Easter-Oct daily 0900-1900. €5, €3 child.

This is a working family farm, with plenty of goats cranking out Rocamadour's famous Cabécou cheese. You can learn how it's made and visit the goats, pigs, donkeys, geese, an old-time garden and much more. There's a house fitted out as it was a century ago, and farm products on sale.

Gramat

The biggest village in this part of the Lot, Gramat is a dour-looking place at first glance. The name is derived from the Celtic for 'mound', and besides its popular zoo, it is known for the many Neolithic tumuli and dolmens in the area. They include one misshapen tumulus on the D15 at the edge of town, covered in wild flowers in the spring and one of many sights in France called the **Etron de Gargantua** (Gargantua's turd).

Parc Animalier de Gramat

Route de Cajarc, T05 65 38 81 22, gramat-parc-animalier.com.
Mid-Jan to Easter daily 1400-1800, Easter-Sep daily 0930-1900, Oct Sun and school holidays 0930-1800. €9, €5 child.

This is one of the biggest zoos in France, with over 1000 animals, and besides some of the usual zoo favourites it specializes in raising such endangered species as the European bison, Przewalski horse and European otter. There are plenty of bears and four noisy wolves, who seem to think they are a barbershop quartet. The zoo also raises threatened barnyard animals: obscure races of horses, goats, sheep, pigs and most of all chickens. The collection of these is one of the biggest anywhere, each patrolling rather self importantly in front of its little house, with the medals it has won in competitions tacked to the façade.

Gramat.

Sleeping

Souillac

La Vieille Auberge €€
1 rue de la Recège, T05 65 32 79 43, la-vieille-auberge.com.
Mid-Feb to mid-Nov.
By the river on the edge of town, seven attractive rooms attached to one of the best restaurants in the area (see page 220). They pamper guests here, with a heated pool, sauna, jacuzzi and massage available; they also have bikes to rent.

Pavillon St-Martin €€
5 place St-Martin, T05 65 32 63 45, hotel-saint-martin-souillac.com.
Souillac's centre is full of hotels, but this one, in the shadow of St-Martin's outlandish bell tower, is one of the better ones. It's a restored 16th-century building, with brightly furnished rooms, broadband and parking.

Lacave

Le Pont de l'Ouysse €€€
T05 65 37 87 04, lepontdelouysse.fr.
Closed mid-Nov to Feb.
The setting is tremendous, between white cliffs and the little River Ouysse, and the house has been run by the same family for five generations. It's luxury without pretensions: 12 rooms decorated in country style, with a/c, most with great views. There's a pool and one of the Lot's finest restaurants (see page 220). Check their website for special offers and theme weekends.

Meyronne

La Terrasse €€€-€€
T05 65 32 21 60, hotel-la-terrasse.com.
The château goes back in parts to the 11th century; it has been a hotel since the 1920s. They take great pride in the exquisitely decorated rooms here. There's a good restaurant too (€€€€) with tables out on the wonderful, trellis-covered terrace that gives the establishment its name.

St-Sozy

Grangier €
T05 65 32 20 14, hotelgrangier.free.fr.
Pleasant, rooms for *trois fois rien* (next to nothing), as the French would say, in an inn with an equally unpretentious a/c restaurant and a pool, all entirely within the relaxed spirit of lazy St-Sozy.

Creysse

Auberge de l'Ile €€-€
T05 65 32 22 01, auberge-de-lile.com.
A friendly and very charming inn, right next to the little brook that runs through this village. There's a pool and a quite good traditional restaurant, with plenty of duck and big 'Gargantua' salads.

Self-catering

Les Bouyssières
T06 32 12 36 27, thehouseatcreysse.com.
A delightful cottage in a very peaceful spot. It sleeps up to 5 people, with a/c, broadband and a large garden. €790 per week.

Gluges

La Tuilerie €€
T05 65 27 04 47, latuilerie.akoonet.com.
Stylish chambres d'hôtes in a 19th-century mini-château, set in a spacious park in this scenic corner of the valley. For a special touch, there's an amazing garden pavilion with a billiards table.

Les Falaises €€-€
T05 65 27 18 44, les-falaises.com.
An impossibly picturesque old inn right under the cliffs, with good simple rooms, a heated pool and restaurant. Special fishing and nature holidays are on offer.

Martel

La Maison du Sonneur €
Place de l'Eglise, T05 65 37 38 30.
Jul-Aug only.
Staying in this urbane little city can be a kick, especially in this charming spot, the 'bell-ringer's house', with only two B&B rooms and a garden tucked right up against the church.

Carennac

Fénelon €€
T05 65 10 96 46,
hotel-fenelon.com.
Mid Mar to Dec.
Ask for a room overlooking the river and the little island the great Fénelon liked to call 'l'Ile de Calypso'. Rooms are simple and there's a pool. The restaurant (€€, closed Fri-Sat and Mon lunch except in summer) is a cut above the others.

Autoire

Auberge de la Fontaine €
T05 65 10 85 40,
auberge-de-la-fontaine.com.
A very modest Logis de France inn, but one where you can enjoy some peace and quiet in this lovely village. Try to get a room with a view. The restaurant (€€) is popular with locals and serves authentic country cooking, with home-made terrines and pâtés.

Montal (St-Jean-L'Espinasse)

Les Trois Soleils €€€-€€
T05 65 10 16 16,
lestroissoleils.fr.st.
Mid-Feb to Dec.
Right across from the Château de Montal and the nine-hole golf course that surrounds it, the 'Three Suns' is a modern but gracious hotel set in a 6-ha forested park. The rooms are well decorated in warm colours; all have air conditioning and some have balconies. There's a pool, tennis and a fine restaurant (see page 221).

Rocamadour

Grand Hôtel Beau Site €€
L'Hospitalet, T05 65 33 63 08,
bestwestern-beausite.com.
Spacious, well-appointed rooms in a building that dates back in part to the 15th century. Rooms with a view cost a little more; there's also one with a jacuzzi. This long-established, family-run hotel has a pool and garden; it can also supply bikes and picnic lunches. It includes one of Rocamadour's best restaurants, Jehan de Valon (see page 221) and also a brasserie.

Le Troubadour €€
Belveyre, T05 65 33 70 27,
hotel-troubadour.com.
Mid-Feb to mid-Nov.
An alternative to the difficult logistics of staying in Rocamadour itself, this is one of the better places out in the countryside nearby. It has a pool and extensive gardens, and a restaurant (€€). There is also a gîte on site, a charming cottage that sleeps up to five (€950 per week).

Hôtel du Roc €
Le Bourg, T05 65 33 62 43,
hotelduroc.com.
Apr-Oct, booking essential.
A rugged stone building just inside the eastern gate houses this welcoming establishment: basic accommodation, good breakfast, some rooms with valley views and, perhaps most importantly, a car park.

Eating & drinking

Souillac

Le Redouillé €€€€-€€€

28 av de Toulouse, T05 65 37 8725.
Wed-Sun.

It's an unassuming little house on the edge of town, but inside it's quite elegant; the chef mixes his take on the traditional, like duck confit in a little tart (*pastilla*), with more exotic touches, such as pork loin with kumquats.

La Vieille Auberge €€€

1 rue de la Recège, T05 65 32 79 43, la-vieille-auberge.com.
Mid-Feb to mid-Nov, closed Sun evenings and Mon out of season.

This restaurant is an institution in the northern Lot, thanks to award-winning chef Robert Véril. They take their foie gras and duck seriously here, and they also like *cèpe* and truffle omelettes and game dishes. For all that, many people come for the exceptional seafood dishes, rare in this region; there's also a very tempting vegetarian menu.

L'Imprevu €€€-€€

1 allée Verninac, T05 65 32 78 30, grandhotel-souillac.com.
Apr-Oct.

Part of the Grand Hotel, a simple but gratifying restaurant. Try a little vol au vent with snails and *cèpes*, grilled tuna in a cream tarragon sauce and desserts warmed up with a touch of Souillac's famous *vieille prune*.

Cabécou with cabbage leaves and honey, Le Pont de l'Ouysse.

Lacave

Le Pont de l'Ouysse €€€€

T05 65 37 87 04, lepontdelouysse.fr.
Closed mid-Nov to Feb.

On this stunning terrace by the river you can't go wrong, and the kitchen has been getting rave reviews from the French critics. The approach is nothing too complex, but they do wonders with game dishes, including venison in a very popular *civet de chevreuil*, as well as some traditional fare.

Calvel €€-€

Le Bougayrou, T05 65 37 87 20.
Jul to mid-Sep Tue-Sun lunch, Jan-Jun and Nov-Dec weekends only.
North of Lacave on D23.

A welcoming, popular duck palace; one of the best dishes at this *ferme-auberge* is a savoury *pastis* (millefeuille tart) with chicken and salsify.

Montvalent

Le Vieux Chêne €€

T05 65 37 40 15.
May-Oct Sat-Sun, Jul-Aug daily.

The pretty village of Montvalent, across the river from Creysse, is home to this revamped version of an old-time *guinguette*. There's a café with a terrace, a restaurant, lots of countryside to wander in, and music once or twice a week in summer, which might be anything from reggae to country.

Martel

Le Patio St Anne €€€€-€€€
Rue du Pourtanel, T05 65 37 19 10, patiosainteanne.com.
A new address with an atmosphere of unabashed luxury, where the dishes are presented with the sensibility of an artist. You can go broke happily here on the *menus dégustation*, or have a wonderful €25 lunch menu with perhaps a dish of boar with chestnuts and wild mushrooms. Bring the kids and educate their palates with the special *petit gastronome* children's menu.

Floirac

Le Pourquoi Pas? €
T05 65 32 46 79, lepourquoipas.fr.
Between Martel and Carennac on D43.
Once you start letting the Belgians in, good beer can't be far behind. This jolly bar-crêperie has a huge selection, along with sweet or savoury crêpes, some other choices, the occasional darts tournament and mussels-and-chips nights. Book ahead.

Montal (St-Jean-L'Espinasse)

Les Trois Soleils €€€€
T05 65 10 16 16, lestroissoleils.fr.st.
Mid Feb to Dec, closed Sun evening and Mon lunch out of season.
After a visit to the Château de Montal across the way, this restaurant completes the aristocratic experience. Chef Frédéric Bizat offers not just the traditional dishes but a real *cuisine d'auteur*: the €30 lunch menu makes a good introduction to it.

Rocamadour

Jehan de Valon €€€€
Grand Hôtel Beau Site, L'Hospitalet, T05 65 33 63 08, bestwestern-beausite.com.
Jehan's not the chef; he's the Knight of Malta who built this manor long ago. Both the room and the terrace have panoramic views over Rocamadour, but the cooking takes top billing: most of the usual Quercy favourites, but also dishes with an Asian or Italian touch; the desserts are beautiful compositions.

Sainte-Marie €€
Place des Senhals, T05 65 33 63 07, hotel-sainte-marie.fr.
Easter-Nov.
If you're looking for lunch in the middle of the old town, you won't do better than this long-established hotel-restaurant. The lunch menu may have confits, cassoulet, roast lamb, even a duck shepherd's pie, on a terrace with a view.

Gramat

Relais des Gourmands €€
2 av de la Gare, T05 65 38 83 92, relais-des-gourmands.com.
Closed Sun evening and Mon except in summer.
No pretentions at all here, just extremely good traditional cooking at this local favourite: duck of course, but also Quercy lamb and grandmotherly recipes like *tête de veau* and a *cassolette* of duck hearts. And a very good bargain too. It's also a hotel (€).

Pick of the picnic spots

Buy your picnic at the market in St-Céré and head west beyond the Château de Montal for the heights above the Bave. It's a gorgeous area, and you can lunch while enjoying the view at the **Cirque d'Autoire**, on the D38 just south of Autoire. Autoire and nearby **Loubressac** are two more *plus beaux villages de France* to visit, and if you need a good long walk there's a particularly attractive stretch of the GR352 that runs through both. It's steep in parts, but along it you'll find a ruined castle and a tall waterfall, the **Cascade d'Autoire**.

Shopping

Ceramics

Poterie de Cressensac
Cressensac, T05 65 37 72 50. Daily 0900-1900.
17 km north of Souillac on N20.
This is the showroom for over 80 potters from around the area, so there's a little bit of everything in every style and price range.

Clothes

La Ferme de Siran
Loubressac, T05 65 38 74 40, aux2pigeonniers.net/siran.
Apr-Jun and Sep-Oct Wed-Sun 1500-1830, Jul-Aug Sun-Fri 1500-1830, Nov-Mar Wed-Sun 1400-1730.
4 km southwest of Autoire off D673.
There's nothing quite as fond and silly as an angora goat, and you can visit some very pampered and happy ones at the farm of Gaëlle and Julien Taillefer, which also includes a shop selling fine scarves, gloves, shawls, socks and much else made from the mohair they provide (we didn't know it, but mohair comes from angora goats; angora wool comes from angora rabbits).

They also offer guided tours of the farm (€3) at 1530 and 1700.

Food & drink

Distillerie Louis Roque
41 av Jean-Jaurès, Souillac, T05 65 32 78 16, lavieilleprune.com.
Mon-Fri 0900-1200 and 1400-1700.
You'll have seen those dark bottles of *La Vieille Prune* all over; their plum brandy is as much a part of the Lot mystique as the Pont Valentré. It's excellent stuff, one of the great liqueurs of France. Louis Roque has been run by the same family for generations, and they have created a small museum to go with their sales room here. Beside the 'old plum' they make flavoured wine aperitifs and pear, juniper and walnut *eaux-de-vie*; also *vielle prune*-laced chocolates. Whee!

Distillerie Louis Roque.

Markets

Souillac has the biggest market in the area, on Fri; there's also a farmers' market on Wed afternoons in summer, and a *foire* selling clothes and a little bit of everything else on the first and third Saturday of each month.

Some of the other good markets: Tuesday: Carennac (summer afternoons only), Bretenoux, Gramat; Wednesday: Martel; Friday: Gramat; Saturday: Martel (also a truffle market, December-January only), Bretenoux, St-Céré.

Toys

Clepsydra
Place de l'Abbaye, Souillac, T05 05 65 37 86 91.
Same hours as Musée de l'Automate (see page 201).
The museum gift shop is run by the same people that maintain the Musée de l'Automate, and it's always full of fascinating toys and trinkets. If you want to commission an automaton of your own they'd be glad to do it.

Activities & tours

Adventure sports

Port Loisirs-Compagnie Sports Nature
Creysse, T05 65 32 27 59, portloisirs.com.
This firm can set you up with just about any activity that can be done here: canoeing and kayaking, canoeing on the Dordogne between Pinsac and St-Sozy, potholing, mountain bikes, canyoning and rock climbing. They train novices and organize trips of a half day or up to several days at reasonable rates, or you can just rent one of their boats or mountain bikes.

Children

Quercyland
Les Ondines, Souillac, T05 65 32 72 61, copeyre.com.
May-Sep daily 1100-2000.
€7 (some activities cost extra).
Sooner or later, everyone with kids gets dragged to this aqua-park. It has a sweet, somewhat amateurish air that parents may find more appealing than the big-time attractions. But there are some major water slides, mini-golf, trampolines, go-karts, canoes and kayaks to rent, bouncy castles and more.

Excursions

Train du Haut Quercy
Gare de Martel, T05 65 37 35 81, trainduhautquercy.info.
Apr-Sep (see website for timetable), steam trains €9.50, €5.50 child (4-11), diesel trains €7/4.

Train du Haut Quercy.

Local rail fans have revived a bit of nostalgia for visitors, on a train that used to carry truffles from Martel's market. They offer a one-hour scenic trip from the town station along the river and back, with both steam and diesel engines.

Golf

Souillac Golf & Country Club
Lacapelle-Auzac, T05 65 27 56 00, souillaccountryclub.com.
Open all year round.
6 km north of Souillac.
This is the Lot's only 18-hole course. Our golfing friends confirm it is a beautiful and challenging one, a little short at par 67, 4465 m, but with plenty of water to wash your balls in. Green fees, depending on season, €35-50 for an individual, €60-80 for a couple. The course also offers accommodation in bungalows; see their website for details and special offers.

Hang-gliding

Parapente Valley
Foussac, T06 08 58 07 75, parapente-valley.com.
2 km southwest of Floirac.
There are good updraughts around Martel and Floirac; Hervé Delaunay offers complete training, or just initiation flights with an instructor from €50.

Lot Valley

Contents

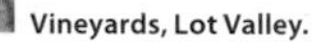

Vineyards, Lot Valley.

Introduction

The Lot is a lazy, meandering river, one that never really seems to make up its mind where it wants to go. You won't be here long before you sense that it is inviting you to be a little lazy too; the temptation to kick back and dream along with the river on its winding mazy way can be strong.

It's not a place for great art and big museums. Nothing much has disturbed its dreams since the 16th century, and the main sights are medieval time capsules, which range from city-sized – Cahors and Figeac – down to little villages like St-Cirq-Lapopie and Puy-l'Evêque.

It *is* a place for good wine, seriously good traditional cooking, and messing about on the river in boats. The Lot itself is always the main attraction here, and the pretty villages hang on it like pearls on a string. Cahors, the capital since Roman times, sits in the centre. To the west the valley is open and smiling and mostly covered in vines. East of Cahors rugged cliffs close in, providing some of the best scenery this book can offer. This is the big tourist area in summer, not just along the Lot but also in the narrow valley of its delightful little sister, the Célé.

Lot Valley between Figeac and Cahors.

What to see in...

...one day
Start off in **Cahors**: take a look at the Pont Valentré, then walk through the old town to the market and the cathedral. In the afternoon, if wine tops your list of interests, you might head westwards down the valley into the **Vin de Cahors area** to visit an estate or two. But most people will head in the other direction for the scenery around **St-Cirq-Lapopie**; there'll be time to fit in a visit to the great painted cave of **Pech Merle**.

...a weekend or more
Again, the attractions are in the valleys of the Lot and the Célé east of Cahors. Beside the capital itself and St-Cirq, you'll have time to explore a little; take in the castles at **Cénevières** and **Laroque-Toirac**, enjoy a cruise or canoe trip on the river, have a laugh at the wonderful **Musée de l'Insolite**, and take a walk through old **Figeac**.

Cahors

Long before Caesar and his legions tramped through Gaul, a town grew up around the sacred Celtic spring of Divona. Despite its unpromising setting, deep in a bowl of scrubby hills, Cahors grew up to be a city of distinction. The Romans made it a rich and lavish *municipium*, and when they passed from the scene the city's powerful bishops picked up the pieces and ruled much of the valley for centuries. The medieval Cahors they built is an introspective place, one that doesn't give up its secrets lightly. But give it some time and you'll get to know one of the most evocative cities in France.

Boulevard Léon Gambetta

Cahors' main drag is a beautiful boulevard lined with tall plane trees and crowded cafés. Until the 19th century, this was the route of the city wall; everything east of the Gambetta is the medieval centre, while the train station and some quiet residential neighbourhoods lie to the west. As the boulevard passes the Mairie it opens into the **allées Fénelon**, with a colossal and dramatic statue of Cahors' local hero, Léon Gambetta (see below, page 234). The building of the big underground car park here, completed in 2009, uncovered a section of the **Roman Amphitheatre**. The find delayed construction a year, but you can go down to the first level of the car park in the lifts behind Gambetta's statue and have a look at it.

Cathédrale St-Etienne

Bd Léon Gambetta.
Daily 0900-1900, Nov-Apr closed Sun afternoon.

There isn't another cathedral in France quite like this incomparable mongrel – Gothic at both ends and Romanesque in the middle, with medieval France's two largest domes piled on top and its front portal tacked on to the side. The powerful bishops of Cahors (who were also secular counts by virtue of their office), needed an impressive home, and the current version was begun in 1112.

In 1316, the very year that Cahors' own Jacques Duèze was elected Pope John XXII, work began to completely modernize the cathedral in the Gothic style. A tall new façade was built, in the familiar Quercy style of the *clocher-mur* (bell-wall).

The **north portal**, one of Quercy's greatest artistic treasures, originally stood at the main entrance. It survived only because the builders of the new façade simply walled it up. Rediscovered by accident in 1840, it was moved and reassembled in its current position. With its bulbous stone rosettes and grey and white parfait stripes, this portal shows just how florid the Romanesque in these parts could be. On the tympanum, *Christ in Majesty* appears inside his mandorla, over scenes

Essentials

Getting around There is no public transportation around the centre except the **Petit Train** (July-August, buy tickets at the Pont Valentré). It's not much fun on a bike either: the streets are narrow and jammed with parked cars. But Cahors is small enough to explore on foot, and it's a pleasure to do so. Parking is always a problem in the centre, but the new underground garage under the allées Fénelon (entrance on boulevard Léon Gambetta) is helping a lot.

Taxis The main stand is on boulevard Gambetta in front of the tourist office. Two 24-hour services are **Allo Taxi** (T06 75 54 21 70), and **Cahors Union** (T05 65 22 60 60).

Trains The train station is on avenue Charles de Freycinet, a 15-minute walk west of the centre. For details of regional train services see page 278.

Buses SNCF buses leave from in front of the train station. For regional services see page 279.

Hospital **Centre Hospitalier de Cahors**, 335 rue Président Wilson, T05 65 20 50 50, between boulevard Gambetta and the Pont Valentré.

Post office 257 rue Président Wilson, T05 65 20 61 00, Monday-Friday 0815-1800, Sat 0830-1200.

Tourist information Place François Mitterrand (facing boulevard Gambetta), T05 65 53 20 65, tourisme-cahors.com, Monday-Saturday 0900-1230 and 1330-1800, also July-August Sunday 1000-1300; also 107 quai Cavaignac, near Pont Valentré (summer only).

Stonework in the Cathedral.

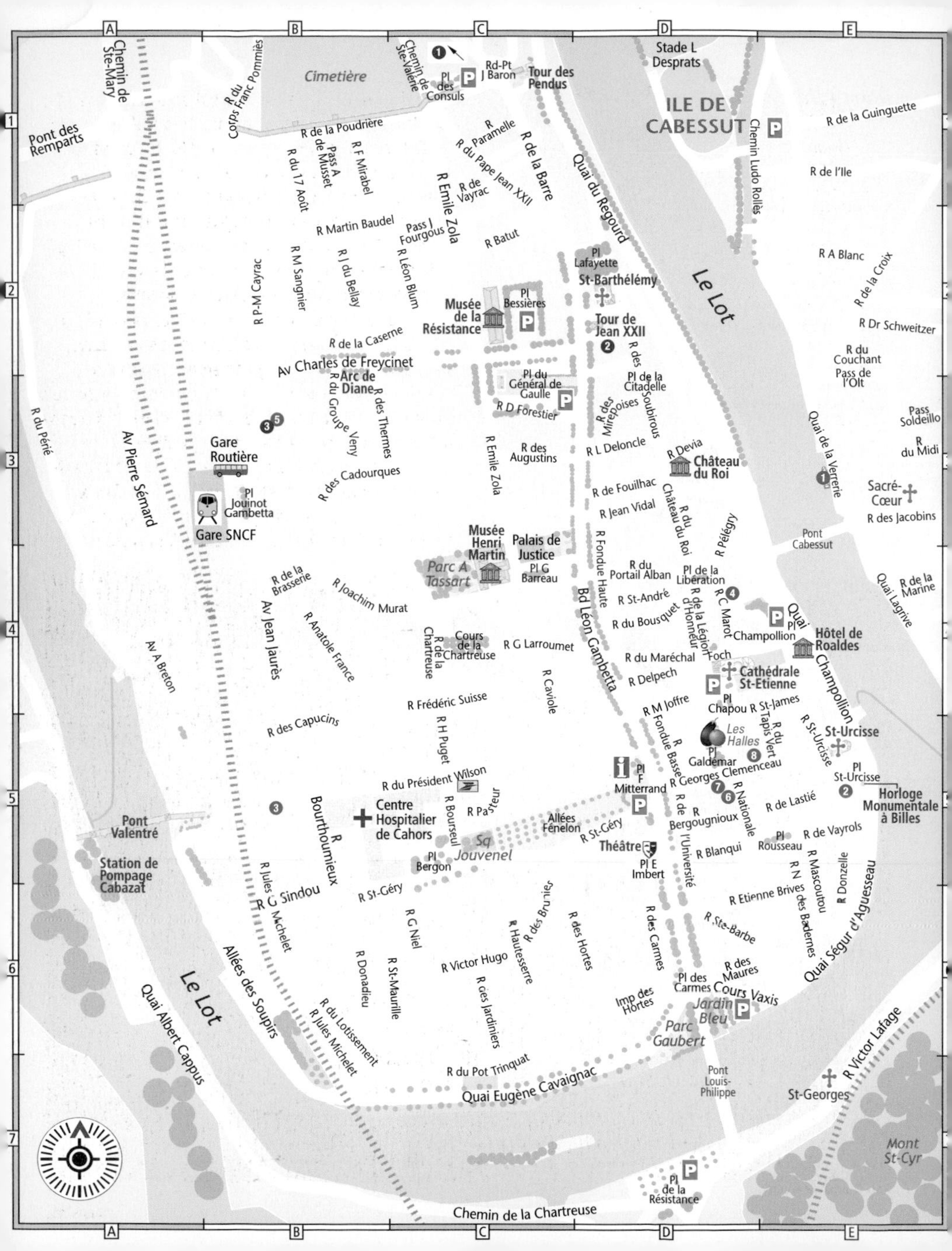

A
B
C
D
E
1
2
3
4
5
6
7
Chemin de Ste-Mary
R du Corps Franc Pommiès
Cimetière
Chemin de Ste-Valérie
Pl des Consuls
Rd-Pt J Baron
Tour des Pendus
Stade L Desprats
ILE DE CABESSUT
Pont des Remparts
R de la Poudrière
R du 17 Août
Pass A de Musset
R F Mirabel
R Paramelle
R du Pape Jean XXII
R de la Barre
Quai du Regourd
Chemin Ludo Rollès
R de la Guinguette
R de l'Ile
R Emile Zola
R de Vayrac
R Martin Baudel
Pass J Fourgous
R Batut
R M Sangnier
R J du Bellay
R Léon Blum
R P-M Cayrac
Pl Lafayette
St-Barthélémy
Le Lot
R A Blanc
R de la Croix
Musée de la Résistance
Pl Bessières
Tour de Jean XXII
R Dr Schweitzer
R de la Caserne
Av Charles de Freycinet
Arc de Diane
R du Groupe Veny
R des Thermes
Pl du Général de Gaulle
R D Forestier
R des Soubirous
Pl de la Citadelle
R des Mirepoises
R du Couchant
Pass de l'Olt
Pass Soldeillo
R du Midi
Quai de la Verrerie
R du Périé
Av Pierre Sémard
Gare Routière
R des Cadourques
R Emile Zola
R des Augustins
R L Deloncle
R Devia
Château du Roi
Sacré-Cœur
R des Jacobins
Pl Jouinot Gambetta
Gare SNCF
R de Fouilhac
R Jean Vidal
R du Château du Roi
R Pélégry
Pont Cabessut
Musée Henri Martin
Palais de Justice
Pl G Barreau
Parc A Tassart
R de la Brasserie
R Joachim Murat
R Fondue Haute
R du Portail Alban
Pl de la Libération
R St-André
R C Marot
R de la Marine
Quai Lagrive
Av Jean Jaurès
R Anatole France
Bd Léon Gambetta
R du Bousquet
R de la Légion d'Honneur
Quai Champollion
Pl Champollion
Hôtel de Roaldes
Av A Breton
R de la Chartreuse
Cours de la Chartreuse
R G Larroumet
R du Maréchal Foch
Cathédrale St-Etienne
R Delpech
R Caviole
R Frédéric Suisse
R M Joffre
Pl Chapou
R St-James
R des Capucins
R H Puget
R Fondue Basse
Les Halles
R du Tapis Vert
R St-Urcisse
St-Urcisse
Pl Galdemar
Pl F Mitterrand
R Georges Clemenceau
Pl St-Urcisse
R du Président Wilson
R Nationale
Horloge Monumentale à Billes
R Bourthoumieux
Centre Hospitalier de Cahors
R Bourseul
R Pasteur
Allées Fénelon
R St-Géry
R de Bergougnioux
R de Lastié
Pont Valentré
Sq Jouvenel
Théâtre
Pl E Imbert
R de l'Université
R Blanqui
Pl Rousseau
R de Vayrols
Station de Pompage Cabazat
Pl Bergon
R Jules Michelet
R G Sindou
R St-Géry
R G Niel
R des Brunies
R Hautesserre
R des Hortes
R des Carmes
R Etienne Brives
R Mascoutou
R N des Badernes
R Donzelle
Quai Ségur d'Aguesseau
R Ste-Barbe
R Donadieu
R St-Maurille
R Victor Hugo
R des Jardiniers
Pl des Carmes
R des Maures
Cours Vaxis
Le Lot
Allées des Soupirs
Quai Albert Cappus
R du Lotissement
R Jules Michelet
Imp des Hortes
Jardin Bleu
Parc Gaubert
R du Pot Trinquat
Quai Eugène Cavaignac
Pont Louis-Philippe
St-Georges
R Victor Lafage
Mont St-Cyr
Pl de la Résistance
Chemin de la Chartreuse

Cahors listings

Sleeping

1 Château de Mercuès *rue du Château de Mercuès* C1
2 Hôtel Jean XXII *2 rue Edmond Albe* D2
3 Hôtel Terminus *5 av Charles de Freycinet* B3

Eating & drinking

1 Au Fil des Douceurs *90 quai de la Verrerie* E3
2 L'O à la Bouche *134 rue St-Urcisse* E5
3 Lagarrigue *543 rue Président Wilson* B5
4 Le Baladin *57 rue Clément Marot* D4
5 Le Balandre *5 av Charles de Freycinet* B3
6 Le Dousil *124 rue Nationale* D5
7 Le Lamparo *76 rue Georges Clémenceau* D5
8 Marie Colline *173 rue Georges Clémenceau* D5

from the life of St Stephen, the first Christian martyr (on the right, he is being stoned to death).

Entering the church, turn and look up to see some rare **frescoes** from the 1290s, portraying Adam and Eve and other figures from Genesis. There are more original frescoes on one of the domes: eight giant prophets and another stoning of St Stephen. The rest of the interior is a 19th-century restoration in the style of Viollet-le-Duc – not genuine medieval, more a Victorian parlour.

The **cloister** was built around the same time, and despite the thorough trashing it got from Henri IV's Protestants in the Wars of Religion, there's still enough of the sculpted detail left to appreciate what a sumptuous work this originally was.

Behind the cathedral by the river, don't miss the delightful **Parc Olivier de Magny**, one of Cahors' secret gardens, overlooked by the city's grandest palace, the 15th-century **Hôtel de Roaldès**.

Parc Olivier de Magny.

Pont Valentré

Anyone in Cahors will tell you that the Pont Valentre (pontvalentre.com) is the most beautiful bridge in France. It's the city's symbol, and appears on its coat of arms. You could say it is also a symbol of Cahors' medieval golden age, and perhaps of some broken dreams too.

It was an ambitious and immensely expensive project. Cahors was fortunate to have local boy John XXII on the papal throne to help with the financing, though with all the interruptions caused by the Hundred Years' War it still took 70 years (1308-1378) to get the bridge finished. Unusually, it was sited about 1 km from the town: in its glory years Cahors thought it would soon expand that far westwards, but the endless wars with the English put a stop to that too. In those difficult times, it was prudent to fortify the bridge, hence the three tall towers that give it its distinctive silhouette. Ironically, no one ever attacked it.

One of the best ways to get a feel for Cahors is to take a boat tour around the Lot from the Pont Valentré: **Bateaux Safaraid** (T05 65 35 98 98) run 75-minute trips all year round daily 1100, 1500, 1630 and 1800; €8.50, €4.50 child (over 3). In July and August there is also the **Fénelon** (T05 65 30 16 55; Mon, Thu, Sat and Sun, 1200, 1430, 1600 and 1730; same fare). In summer, both companies also run river cruises up to St-Cirq-Lapopie or Douelle.

The Devil on the Pont Valentré

Legends about devils and bridges are common from Wales to Romania. The seemingly impossible feat of making stone hang in the air by means of an arch made a strong impression on the medieval imagination.

Cahors' tale relates how the architect sold his soul in return for Old Nick bringing him all the materials he needed. Fortunately, the Devil isn't as smart as he thinks he is, for in these stories he always gets tricked. When the bridge was almost finished, the architect ordered him to bring him some water in a sieve. That foiled him, but the Devil got his revenge by pulling out one stone; no matter how many times the builders replaced it, it would be gone again by morning. To commemorate the story, the men who restored the bridge in 1879 added the little grimacing devil high up on the middle tower, with his fingertips trapped forever in the mortar between the stones.

Pont Valentré.

Five of the best

Fêtes

❶ **Fête du Vin de Cahors**, Albas, May. Best party of the year. See page 55.

❷ **Puy-l'Evêque** village fête, August. The fête with the fireworks. See page 57.

❸ **Africajarc**, Cajarc, July. African drums on the Lot. See page 56.

❹ **Anglars-Juillac** village fête (near Prayssac), early August. Finishes with a giant confetti battle. See page 56.

❺ **Luzech** village fête, August. The end-of-silly-season bash. See page 240.

Léon Gambetta

The French aren't very sentimental about old advertising signs, but you'll see one lovingly preserved on a building on place Chapou across from the cathedral: *Bazar Genois: Gambetta Jeune et Cie*. This was the grocer's shop of an Italian immigrant from Genoa whose son moved up to Paris to become one of France's great heroes, Léon Gambetta.

This radical firebrand lawyer made a name for himself in the 1860s, in the last days of the corrupt and decadent Second Empire. Although only in his 20s, Gambetta became a leader of France's republicans, and the Franco–Prussian War of 1870 brought him to national prominence. After the French army was destroyed at Sedan, Gambetta proclaimed the deposition of Napoleon III, and when the Prussians surrounded and besieged Paris he made a sensational escape from the city in a hot-air balloon to organize resistance in the provinces.

Gambetta was lucky: in those days there was no way of controlling the balloon (another man who tried to escape Paris in one ended up atop a mountain in Norway). He reached Tours and raised a new army there, unfortunately too late to change the course of the war.

As France got back on its feet, Gambetta helped found the Third Republic, and fought for fair elections and free universal education. He served briefly as prime minister, and might well have become president of France, had he not shot himself while cleaning a gun in 1882, at the age of only 44. Some murmured that it was really his mistress who pulled the trigger; history isn't telling.

Station de Pompage Cabazat

Quai Albert Cappus, T05 65 53 04 99.
Fri-Sun 1400-1830, Jul-Aug daily 1000-1300 and 1500-1900. Free.

Once you've crossed the Pont Valentré, turn left and in a minute you'll come to the **Fontaine des Chartreux**, the spring from which Cahors was born. It still pours out of the cliffs as it did in prehistoric times. The Celts worshipped their goddess Divona here, though in modern times the spring has had the more prosaic job of providing the city's water supply. The elegant stone **waterworks**, no longer in use, was built in 1854; recently restored, it now contains exhibits on the history of the site, as well as the original machinery and explanations of how it worked.

Musée de la Résistance

Place Charles de Gaulle, T05 65 22 14 25.
Daily 1400-1800. Free.

Even if you can manage only a little French, this small museum will be a fascinating trip back to a dark time that still means a lot to people here. Photos, documents and memorabilia recount the story of the German occupation, the mass deportations, the beginnings of the Resistance in the southwest and the brutal tour of the SS *Das Reich* that was sent down to terrorize its people.

Musée Henri Martin

792 rue Emile Zola, T05 65 20 88 66, mairie-cahors.fr/musee.
Mon, Wed-Sat 1100-1800, Sun 1400-1800. €3, €1.50 concessions, €0.50 child (6-18).

This little museum, named for the Lot's best-known painter, finds room for much more than just art – fortunately, since the art collections have been closed for restoration for years. Right now, you can see prehistoric relics, including a chubby Neolithic goddess, collections of Egyptian, Etruscan, Roman, early-Christian and medieval finds, and objects from the South Seas brought back by missionaries. When they've finished the works, you'll be able to see a lot of Henri Martin, a painter who hovered between Impressionism and Pointillism, and is best known for his landscapes.

Painting by Henri Martin.

Walking old Cahors

After the cathedral and the Pont Valentré, Cahors' greatest attraction is the city itself: a unique, intact, slightly Italian-influenced medieval centre built of grey Quercy limestone, with half-timbering and brick the colour of a properly grilled *magret de canard*. A walk around will give you a sense of just how important Cahors was before 1500 – and just how sleepy it became afterwards.

Packed into the narrow space between the walls (where boulevard Gambetta runs today) and the river, there was nowhere to build but up. Old Cahors is a city of tiny alleys, some lined with tall old tenements, which give it the air of a miniature Naples. Keep an eye out for details, like the occasional ornately carved wooden door or a Renaissance window surround carved with patterns of parallel lines called *batons écotés*. Some of the oldest alleys are partially covered with vaulting; these are called *botes*, a word unique to Cahors. One very attractive feature you'll see on some of the buildings is an arcaded top-floor sun porch, called a *soleilho*.

Place Chapou, with the cathedral and the market, has of course always been the centre of town. From there you have a choice of two main routes, north or south. To the north, the quarter called the **Soubirous** was the aristocratic side of town. Take little rue Clément Marot from the north side of the cathedral, passing place de la Libération and continuing up **rue du Château du Roi**. This was the elegant street of the bankers and merchants, and their palaces line both sides. The big Gothic arches on their fronts are another distinctive feature of Cahors architecture, though they would look more at home in Tuscany. In fact, the lower end of rue du Château du Roi could be a street in medieval Siena.

That's no surprise, since a whole thriving colony of Italian bankers once lived here. Medieval Cahors first grew rich through native efforts, as the Caorsins, local bankers and traders, created a commercial network that spread from Italy to England. They were famous – or infamous – everywhere for sharp dealing; Dante mentioned them in the *Inferno*, and placed them firmly in one of the lower circles of Hell. But Quercy, with little but wine and sheep, was never a rich province and couldn't provide its clever capitalists with much capital. Bigger fish from Italy, then Europe's banking headquarters, had gobbled up most of their business by 1300.

One of the most impressive surviving Italian palaces is the crumbling **Hôpital de Grossia** at No 102. The **Château du Roi**, just across the street, was Cahors' castle. The government turned it into a grim-looking prison in the 19th century, but you can still see the top of its medieval *donjon* (keep)

Soubirous.

Horloge monumentale à billes.

sticking up over the walls. Some of the oldest and most picturesque alleys are here; take the one that runs right under the Hôpital de Grossia and you'll find another **secret garden** hidden in a charming courtyard painted with scenes of a fantasy carnival.

Cahors' secret gardens

One of the delights of walking in old Cahors is discovering these pocket-sized gardens. There are 28 in all, tucked into odd corners of the city. Some recall the past, like the medieval herb garden at St-Barthélemy and another close by, just inside the walls, containing plants introduced to France during the Crusades. There is a herb garden next to the cathedral, near a separate one that provides flowers for the high altar. Some are purely decorative, like the tiny, charming Moorish garden tucked away on rue du Petit-Mot near St-Urcisse. At the Pont Valentré, they've planted a little patch of Vin de Cahors vines. The tourist office can give you a complete list.

Continue to the top of rue du Château du Roi and the complex of buildings left to Cahors by its most famous son, Jacques Duèze, the shoemaker's son who in 1316 became Pope John XXII. There are the remains of the Palais Duèze, the wonderfully urbane **Tour de Jean XXII** and the adjacent **Eglise St-Barthélemy**, which he rebuilt.

South of the cathedral, the main street changes its name to rue Nationale as it runs through the **Badernes**, the working people's quarter in the Middle Ages. There aren't many palaces on this side of town, but a lot of interesting buildings, including the 13th-century **Eglise St-Urcisse** on rue Clémenceau. Pick your way through the alleys to the **riverfront** at place St-Urcisse, and you'll find one of Cahors' typically modest but delightful surprises, the **Horloge monumentale à billes**. Created by Michel Zachariou in 1997, this crazy clockwork mechanism under glass works by shooting steel bearings through a Heath-Robinson array of slides and swings.

Vin de Cahors: Lower Lot Valley

It's all vines, as far as the eye can see. Well, they plant some corn too, to feed the ducks, and some sunflowers (for the colour, we suspect), but beyond these almost every available square metre of the valley between Cahors and Fumel goes to producing the dark nectar that washes down the *confits de canard* and keeps the Lotois warm in the winter.

This is the busiest, most densely populated part of the Lot, but you still wouldn't really call it busy or dense. Amid the vines you'll find a smattering of medieval and modern art, a castle Hollywood would die for, sweet riverside villages such as Puy-l'Evêque, Luzech and Albas, and about 200 family-run vineyards, where you can sample a glass of AOC Cahors in a cool cellar and talk about the weather and the grapes.

Duravel.

Douelle

This village was once a major river port, where barrels of Cahors wine would be loaded on *gabarres* to make the long meandering voyage down to Bordeaux. Today it's a centre for pleasure boating, and also boasts a hang-gliding school (see page 273). It claims to have the largest mural painting in the world – 122 m of it, along the embankment on the quay. It's the work of Didier Chamizo, and depicts the history of wine, all the way from Noah and Dionysos to the present. When he painted the wall, in 1992, Chamizo was on conditional leave after nine years in prison for gun running, bank robbery and other politically motivated indelicacies. Now he's famous, and his works sell for serious money in Paris and New York.

Chamizo mural, Douelle.

Queen of Denmark weathervane.

Château de Caïx

On your way through Caïx, just upstream from Luzech, you'll see the château of wine grower and diplomat Henri de Montpezat dominating the little village from the hill above. If the Danish flag is flying, Henri is in residence with his wife – Denmark's Queen Margrethe II. The royal couple have been spending relaxed summers here since the 1970s, and you might catch a glimpse of the queen out painting a watercolour or carrying her basket through Cahors market.

Luzech

This lovely village of peculiar geography sits on a narrow neck of land where the looping Lot almost doubles back on itself; its short main street used to be a canal, cutting off the loop for the convenience of the *gabarres*. Right behind the old town's medieval streets is a rather elegant art deco hydroelectric plant bored into the cliffside; once a day sirens blow and it releases a flood around the river loop, sending fishermen scurrying up the grassy banks and into the cafés.

Luzech used to be a busy place; on the hilltop above the hydro plant you can see scanty ruins of a Celtic *oppidum* that became a Roman settlement. In the Middle Ages the bishops of Cahors built a castle here, strong enough to repel the Arabs in 732 and the Vikings a century later, but not quite good enough to keep out Richard the Lionheart or Simon de Montfort.

All that's left of the castle today is the imposing white **Tour de l'Impernal**, the village's landmark. Underneath it, the 13th-century **Maison des Consuls** was Luzech's old town hall; it now houses the tourist office and the **Musée Municipal Armand Viré** (T05 65 20 17 27, Jun and Sep Mon-Fri 1000-1300 and 1400-1700, Jul-Aug Mon-Sat 1000-1300 and 1400-1800; €3, under 12s free), really three small museums in one, with finds from Celtic and Roman times, dinosaur fossils and working models of old-fashioned wind- and watermills.

Albas

Perched gorgeously on a cliff high over the river, this village gives the Lot Valley its most picturesque postcard shot. Like Douelle and Puy-l'Evêque, Albas was a big wine port; you can still see the old cellars lining the street that runs down to the river dock. These come alive again once a year in May (on the Saturday nearest Ascension Day) for the valley's best festival, the **Fête du Vin de Cahors**. There's a beach on the river here that is a popular spot for swimming or just sitting; you'll see it from the bridge at the bottom of the village, on the opposite bank.

Castelfranc

If someone were to draw a model bastide for a schoolbook illustration it would look just like Castelfranc. Little changed since the Middle Ages, the village has a 14th-century church with a *clocher-mur*, a newly built timber market in the square opposite, and a pretty garden down by the river called the **Jardin des Sens**.

La Masse

North of Castelfranc on the D37, the hamlet of La Masse grew up around a priory in the Middle Ages; on one old building you can still see a slender, carved Gothic *lanterne des morts* (see page 153). The priory's little church survives (the neighbours have the key), and inside it some 15th-century rustic painter covered the walls with charming allegories of the *Seven Deadly Sins*, each being led down the road to perdition by a grinning demon.

Prayssac

Prayssac started out as a bastide – one of the few round ones ever built. Around the church in the centre is a circular, tree-lined boulevard, where you can see the marble statue of the town's famous son Jean-Baptiste Bessières, born in 1768, Marshal of France and briefly Duke of Istria. Bessières followed Napoleon from Spain to Italy to Egypt to Russia and back; after distinguished service on the desperate retreat from Moscow he became head of all the Emperor's cavalry – and soon afterwards took a cannonball right in the chest.

Prayssac is the main shopping town for the valley, and it's especially busy during the Friday morning market around the church.

Circuit des Dolmens

The route runs through an important though surprisingly little-known Neolithic site, dating from around 1500 BC. Even the Prayssac tourist office (bd de la Paix, T05 65 22 40 57, Mon 0900-1230, Tue-Sat 0900-1230 and 1400-1730) doesn't know all of what's up there, but they'll give you information on the marked trails through the area, and you can be an explorer in a truly fascinating place.

The Circuit occupies a long, forested ridge between Prayssac and Castelfranc. If you're hiking, the GR36 conveniently takes you up from the centre of Prayssac. If you want to drive up and walk from the top, start from Castelfranc (going west on D811, take the first right), or take a signposted road at the northern edge of Niaudon just north of Prayssac. A rough and rocky road it is, but passable if your car has an average clearance.

Iron bridges

Until the late 19th century, if you wanted to get across the Lot anywhere outside Cahors you'd have to get some local farmer to punt you over in his flat-bottomed barge. Villages and local families eventually raised money to build bridges, collecting tolls to pay themselves back.

Today, these rustic bridges are one of the delights of touring the river. They're only single-lane, so you have to be careful crossing and pay attention to the priority signs. But some are strikingly beautiful and built to last, tributes to the days when French engineers began to rival Britain's as the best in the world. Some are graceful suspension bridges – miniature Golden Gates hidden among the vineyards and walnut groves. The best are at Douelle, Albas, Castelfranc, Anglars-Juillac, Vire and Touzac, and east of Cahors, there's a fine one at Cajarc.

Vin de Cahors

If Vin de Cahors didn't exist they would have had to invent it, for nothing goes so well with the noble duck and the other stout protagonists of Quercy cooking. Fortunately, it has been around almost as long as the quackers. When Caesar invaded, the local Gauls were already making wine good enough to send back to Rome. Later Roman emperors issued edicts to root up the vines, as they were driving Italian wines out of the market.

Vin de Cahors was prized across Europe – especially after Cahors' Pope John XXII made it his official communion wine. Every year, hundreds of barges carried it down the Lot to send it on its way to the thirsty English. The dastardly wine men of Bordeaux put a stop to that after the Hundred Years' War; they simply refused to allow the boats through, so that their own wine would have the monopoly.

Cahors wine had become little more than high-octane *pipi du chat* (as wine critics gracefully put it) by the 1950s, when a few vintners began to bring it back. AOC status came in 1971. Cahors isn't to everyone's taste. The 'black wine' is heavy with tannin and has a high alcoholic content. It perfectly matches Quercy cooking and the Quercy temperament, but to appreciate it fully you'll have to spend a dismal, drizzly winter in the Lot, and carry your 11-litre container up to your favourite estate every week for a refill of the stuff that keeps everyone going.

The sights are strung out along the ridge, and most are marked. Coming from Niaudon the first is the **Dolmen des Trois Pierres**, and then the **Bertrandoune Dolmen**; from here a die-straight walled avenue follows the modern road to what seems to have been a kind of sanctuary at the very top of the ridge. It's a jumble of stones set around three mighty menhirs: the locals call it **Chaos**.

Farther along is an odd well and a seat cut out of the rock, called the **Fauteuil de César** (Caesar's armchair), and finally a more modern creation, the Lot's only double *garriote*, or shepherd's stone hut, with twin corbelled domes. Best of all, though, is an unmarked feature that hardly anyone here knows about. Just before the Bertrandoune dolmen, a path to the left leads to a small clearing on its left. Head into the trees from here and you'll find what the archaeologists who passed through in 1978 called the **Solar Temple**. This is a huge irregular heap of small stones, from which radiate two long walls, one running east–west and one along the solstice line. Between them runs a row of giant menhirs. The archaeologists, who didn't stay long, suggested this construction was some kind of astronomical calendar or calculator, like Stonehenge, but no one has yet guessed how it might have worked. There's nothing else like it in Europe.

Puy-l'Evêque

Prayssac may have all the shops and the bustle, but its neighbour Puy-l'Evêque ('bishop's hill', for the bishop of Cahors of course) is the valley's historic centre. The famous view of it is the one from the bridge over the Lot. Medieval buildings in warm, tan-coloured stone spill down the hill; in early August they provide the backdrop for one of the region's most spectacular fireworks displays.

It's small, but well worth a walk around. Start at the Cale, where the wine barges once docked. **Rue de la Cale** was the medieval main drag; side streets off it bear the names of the trades once practised there: rue des Teinturiers (dyers), rue des Ferroniers (ironworkers). The two round stone towers that poke up above the rooftops once served as lookouts for anyone trying to sneak past Puy-L'Evêque without paying the bishop's tolls.

On the way up, **rue du Bovila** was the wealthy heights, with a small row of mansions showing carved Renaissance details (note the river boat from Puy-l'Evêque's coat of arms carved over the door of No 6). On the next level up is the elegant 13th-century **Palais des Consuls**, the old seat of government. At the top of the town, the **donjon** attached to the Mairie is the only part of the castle that survives. As so often in Quercy, the church was built right into the town wall: **St-Sauveur**, at the highest point, completes the medieval skyline with a Flamboyant Gothic tower and some fine carved details.

If you missed the *Seven Deadly Sins* in La Masse, there's another set, more skilfully painted, in **Martignac**'s little church (daily 1000-1800), in the hills just north of Puy-l'Evêque.

Duravel

This village grew up around a monastery, and its **Eglise St-Hilarion** (begun 1055) is one of the best Romanesque works on the Lot. Inside, some of the finely carved capitals still have some of their original colour. That's rare, though in early medieval churches, as in classical Greek temples, the carved reliefs were usually brightly painted.

Underneath is an interesting **crypt** that goes back to an earlier church from Merovingian times. This contains the relics of three of the mustiest, dustiest saints of France: Hilarion, Poémon and Agathon, hermits from the beginnings of Christian monasticism in fourth and fifth century Egypt, are allowed out only once every five years, when their bones are paraded through the village (next appearance is the last Sunday in October 2010). The relics are said to have been a gift from Charlemagne.

Montcabrier & Pestillac

These two towns on opposite hills fought like the Kilkenny cats. Pestillac was the seat of the powerful barons who owned Duravel. They were good pals with the English, so in 1298 the French King Philip the Fair founded the bastide of Montcabrier almost within spitting distance. And spit they did, all through the Hundred Years War, until the Montcabrier men and some royal troops bushwhacked the hated Amalvin de Pestillac, scourge of the neighbourhood, and burned his castle and town to the ground.

Today **Montcabrier** is a sweet, sleepy little place, with its grid of streets and a 14th-century Gothic church that houses a relic of Philip the Fair's grandfather, St Louis (left of the altar); once it was a pilgrimage for victims of scrofula.

The ruins of **Pestillac** lie on the round-topped hill just across the D673 (signposted). Introduce yourself to the lady who lives there (she's the owner and she won't mind) and ask if you can see the ruins; the path leads up the hill from behind her house. Covered in trees, it's an utterly magical spot. The best part is the Romanesque church: a beautiful, roofless ruin with a big oak tree growing through the window. If you have time to explore, there are bits of walls and towers and other ruins spread all over the area.

Inside Montcabrier church.

Château de Bonaguil

Bonaguil, T05 53 71 90 33, bonaguil.org.
Daily Feb-May and Oct 1030-1230 and 1400-1700, Jun and Sep 1030-1200 and 1400-1800, Jul-Aug 1000-1700, Nov Sun 1030-1230 and 1400-1700. €6, €3.50 child (7-16).

Some of the Lot's most polished landscapes surround this fairytale castle, lost in the hills above the steelmaking town of Fumel, and it is a tremendous sight when it first appears around a corner. The oldest parts date back to 1259, but most of what you see today is the work of Jean de Roquefeuil and his son Bérenger in the late 15th century.

The Roquefeuils were the richest of barons, with lands all over southern France, but they didn't have many friends. Jean once joined in a rebellion against his king, and Bérenger (1448-1530) was a miserly hunchback who spent most of his revenues building Bonaguil into a castle so strong that it would defend him even against the king himself. Unfortunately, by Bérenger's time medieval-style castles like this one were not just obsolete but downright silly. Bérenger's engineers tried every trick to make Bonaguil cannon-proof, but had anyone ever really wanted to take it, the gigantic walls and towers would have been good for nothing but target practice.

Bonaguil was little more than a curiosity from the day it was built. Soon forgotten and neglected, one owner in the 18th century sold it for 100 francs and a bag of walnuts. The castle's charms are best seen from a distance. Inside there's nothing but stone – no floors or roofs, only carved windows and fireplaces hanging in the air. Confiscated in the Revolution, the château was given to a zealous bourgeois official to liquidate, and he ripped out everything that could be sold or burnt for firewood.

Quercy Blanc

'White Quercy', south of the Lot, takes its name from the chalky stone under its rolling meadows. It's a sparsely inhabited region, where the cows are so bored they look up expectantly as you drive by. There are pretty landscapes and a few sights, notably Montcuq, where the white stone surfaces to make a gleaming and gracious village.

Montcuq

The best guess is that its name comes from the Latin *mons cuculi*, 'mount cuckoo'. Once there was an impressive castle here, but Simon de Montfort seized it and St Louis levelled it, leaving only the **Tour Comtale** (tours Jul-Aug Mon-Fri 1500-1900, otherwise ask at the tourist office), a landmark visible for miles around.

Montcuq has two broad *plans d'eau* for swimming, one to the north on the St-Matré road, with a little beach and canoe rentals in summer, and the other just to the south. Near the latter is the medieval **Eglise St-Pierre de Rouilhac**, with bits of medieval frescoes that have been connected with the Cathars; it's hard to tell, since the local priest destroyed the best of them in the 1980s, thinking them heretical.

Une histoire de Montcuq

If you've spent much time in the southwest, you'll know to pronounce the final consonant in names like 'Montcuq'. Otherwise you'll make the locals fall about laughing when you call the village something that sounds rudely like 'my posterior' –'*Excusez-moi, madame*, I'm trying to find *mon cul*.'

Georges Brassens helped make the place famous by mentioning it in a song ('The Ballad of Those Who Are Born Someplace'). Recently, the firm that makes the French version of Monopoly held a nationwide contest to rename the squares on the board, with towns instead of street names. Montcuq won the top spot in a landslide, and the embarrassed company had to cancel the promotion.

Castelnau-Montratier

East of Montcuq, this bastide has an unusual triangular arcaded *place*. It's famous for its windmills – there are three of them, on the hills above the village, the only survivors among the hundreds that once punctuated the hilltops of Quercy. One, just north of Castelnau, can be visited by appointment: the **Moulin à Vent de Boisse** (Ste-Alauzie, T05 63 21 84 56; donation €1.50). For the others, you'll have to come back on National Windmill Day (no kidding – it's the Sunday closest to mid-June, and every last windmill in France is open for tours).

There's also a watermill nearby. Parts of the **Moulin de Brousse** (just west of Castelnau on D4; visit by appointment, T05 65 81 95 81) date back to the 13th century; it's owned by a family of millers and is still in use.

Montpezat-de-Quercy

Quercy Blanc extends beyond the boundaries of the Lot department; in fact the whole Tarn-et-Garonne was once Quercy too, and was governed from Cahors until the city fathers of Montauban talked Napoleon into letting it have a department of its own. South of Castelnau, it's worth sneaking across the border to see Montpezat-de-Quercy.

For centuries, Montpezat belonged body and soul to a single family, and the **Collégiale de St-Martin** on the edge of town is their monument. The des Près were the counts of Montpezat, while their younger sons ran a little ecclesiastical dynasty on the side. Some of them served the King of France at the same time. Cardinal Pierre des Près, who built this church, was a friend and confidant of the Cahors Pope John XXII. The smiling effigy on his Carrara marble tomb is one of the sights of the church.

About 1520, another des Près commissioned the wonderful set of brightly colourful **Flemish tapestries** from Tournai that line the walls of the choir. Recently restored, they chronicle the life of St Martin of Tours. The familiar episodes of his life – cutting his cloak in two to share with a beggar, casting out idols and wrecking pagan temples, fighting with the Devil – are portrayed with verve and a kind of comic-book realism.

Les pigeonniers

As every French schoolchild used to learn, before the Revolution only nobles had the right to keep pigeons. The peasants weren't allowed to molest them, even when they were feasting on their grain. The pigeons would fly home and poop all over their noble *pigeonniers*, and then the nobles would sell the guano back to the peasants as fertilizer. That would make anyone start a revolution, *non*?

It isn't entirely true, especially in the south, where old Roman common law still spread guano rights a little more widely. But there's no denying that pigeons were often better housed than people. Big, elegant pigeonniers are a part of the architectural heritage here, and every corner of the southwest has its own distinctive style: round ones, square and hexagonal ones, some set up on columns to foil the rats, some proper little pigeon châteaux with carved stone fenestration and cornices.

Not many are still in use. The French much prefer chicken for their Sunday dinners now, and no one wants to scrape up pigeon poo when you can buy fertilizer in a bag. That leaves owners with the task of finding new uses for their pigeonniers. They might put *you* in one: some of them, with a good scrubbing, have been turned into holiday accommodation.

The Bouriane

North of the Lot is some real backwoods country, the kind of place where nearly everyone drives a little van known as a *fourgonnette* – great for carrying firewood, or game during hunting season. The Bouriane is a maze of hills covered in thick groves of chestnuts and oaks, with the occasional clearing for pasture or a duck farm. Ducks are definitely the stars here; the Bouriane is an excellent place for getting lost in a leisurely way, only to turn up for a memorable all-duck repast at a rustic *ferme-auberge*.

Start from Cahors on the D811 east, then north on the D6 to **Catus**. Catus grew up around a medieval priory, where the chapter house still has some finely carved capitals. Just to the west, the **Lac Vert** is a great spot for a swim; there's a café and restaurant, and pedal boats and canoes to rent.

Carry on into the heart of the Bouriane, north towards **Les Arques**, a tiny village full of surprises. There's a famous restaurant (see page 267) and the fascinating early-Romanesque **Eglise St-Laurent**, with a mystic spiral carved over one of its portals and 'horseshoe' Mozarabic arches inside in the style of Moorish Spain. Its restoration was begun by the celebrated Russian-Scottish modernist sculptor Ossip Zadkine, who spent a lot of time in Les Arques and left some of his works to the **Musée Zadkine** (T05 65 22 83 37, Tue-Sat Jul-Sep 1000-1300 and 1500-1900, rest of the year 1400-1800; €3, €1.50 child). Just outside Les Arques, the pretty **Eglise St-André-des-Arques** has some 15th-century frescoes (pick up the key at the Musée Zadkine).

Cazals, just to the north, has a popular *plan d'eau* along the D673 if you want another swim. Further up that road, **Salviac** is another little market town, where the church still has some of its original medieval stained glass. The road then passes an impressive ruined Cistercian monastery, **L'Abbaye Nouvelle**, before reaching the third-largest town in the Lot department, **Gourdon**.

Gourdon is a handsome town, with a tree-lined circle of boulevards around its ancient centre. Its lords once ruled much of the region, until that churlish medieval troublemaker Richard the Lionheart wiped them out – all except one, who later avenged the family by killing Richard with an arrow during a siege. There's surprisingly little art and culture to detain you (the Protestants thoroughly wrecked the place in the Wars of Religion), but just north of town on the D704 you can see needle-like stalactites, colourful limestone formations and prehistoric paintings of deer, mammoths and human figures at the **Grottes de Cougnac** (T05 65 41 47 54, grottesdecougnac.com; Apr-Jun and Sep daily 1000-1130 and 1430-1700, Jul-Aug daily 1000-1800, Oct Mon-Sat 1400-1600; €6.50, €4.50 child (5-12); no disabled access).

Les Arques.

East of Cahors: Upper Lot Valley

You'd think it was two different rivers. West of Cahors the Lot passes through smiling open country carpeted in vines. On this side, long ruddy cliffs crowd up to the water's edge. The roads that follow the valley sometimes have to pass through ancient tunnels, made for the mules that once pulled river barges upstream. It's green and beautiful and peaceful here, a world apart.

Villages of more than 400 people are rare, but the upper valley can get a little crowded in summer. It has two of the Lot's biggest attractions – the Palaeolithic painted cave of Pech Merle and the stunning village of St-Cirq-Lapopie, as well as a sprinkling of châteaux and medieval relics, and one rather incredible surprise, the Musée de l'Insolite. There are really two valleys here, the Lot and the little Célé that runs parallel to it; in both, the relaxed atmosphere is much the same. Follow either of them to the eastern end of the department and you'll find Figeac, a town of distinction and fine architecture where time stopped back in the 14th century.

St-Cirq-Lapopie & around

Spilling gorgeously down its rugged cliff, this village combines its most improbable setting with a wealth of architecture. Today it's one of the most visited sites in southwest France, but what you think of it may well depend on when you come. In summer it's a jolly but merciless tourist trap, packed with galleries and souvenir shops. The rest of the year, St-Cirq's population of 207 has the place pretty much to itself.

St-Cirq's history is as improbable as its site. It started as a Roman villa, and grew into a town in the Middle Ages. The expensive carved stone details on the mansions show there was a fair amount of wealth around. And it lived under a political arrangement that was absolutely unique. Four of the most powerful noble families shared control of the town, and each built a separate castle on top of the cliffs.

Tip...

There are car parks at either end of this vertical, pedestrianized village. The upper one is closer to the centre, but trying to reach it via the single narrow street can be nightmarish on busy summer days. If it looks too crowded, use the lower car park and make the climb first – after that, it'll all be downhill.

As you can imagine, this set-up didn't always work. When Simon de Montfort came through, two of the families supported him while the others were for the heretics and the Counts of Toulouse. In the Hundred Years' War some supported the French, some the English. In the Wars of Religion one was conspicuously Catholic, another among the leaders of the Protestants. Castles got wrecked (and not a single one is left today).

Politics and money gradually left St-Cirq behind, but its charm and beautiful setting

St-Cirq-Lapopie.

couldn't go unnoticed forever. The Impressionist painter Henri Martin was perhaps the first of many artists to move in, and when the slightly burnt-out old Surrealist André Breton fell in love with the place in 1950 its fortune was made. More Surrealists turned up (including briefly Man Ray) and St-Cirq began to attract not only artists but buyers, establishing the role as an artsy tourist destination it enjoys today.

For all the art, St-Cirq's greatest attraction is the village itself, with its lovely half-timbered buildings, arcaded passageways, carved stone windows and balconies. Watch out for chunks of Gothic carved stone built randomly into old walls; they're probably recycled bits of all those demolished castles, whose ruins you can see at the top of the town. Nearby is the **church**, built in the 1520s; note the old grain measures carved into the façade, and the baptismal font carved from a Roman capital. From the church, the most picturesque (and narrowest) street, **ruelle de la Fourdonne**, leads into the heart of the village.

Maison de la Fourdonne

T05 65 31 21 51.
Apr to mid-Nov Tue-Sun 1430-1900. €1.50.

This 17th-century mansion is one of the architectural stars of St-Cirq; it contains the **Musée du Patrimoine**, with archaeological finds and exhibits on the village's history, as well as woodworking: a century ago St-Cirq made its living from carving boxwood taps for barrels.

Musée Rignault

T05 65 31 23 22.
Mar-Oct Tue-Sun 1000-1230 and 1430-1800 (Jul-Aug 1900). €3 in summer, free in spring.

Collector and friend of artists, including Henri Martin, Emile-Joseph Rignault moved to St-Cirq in the 1920s. He left some of his collection for this museum, which also stages regular exhibitions: drawings in the spring and contemporary sculpture in summer.

St-Cirq-Lapopie.

Tip...

Away from the towns, most of the Lot is fine for swimming. Some of the most popular spots are monitored daily in summer, and a few even have lifeguards. In summer you can get daily water quality (and weather) reports at T08 05 46 46 00, or lot.fr/infoloisirs.

Maisons Daura

T05 65 40 78 19, magp.fr.
Jul-Aug daily 1500-1900. Free.

A project of the Maison des Arts Pompidou in Cajarc, which grants a residence in the Maisons Daura to a select few artists from around the world each year. You can see what they're up to on summer afternoons when they have open house.

Fun on the river

St-Cirq is hardly just about art. Most people come for the scenery, for walks in the countryside and for paddling around in boats. There's a lot to do on the river. St-Cirq itself has a 'beach', with a boat dock, picnic area and canoe rentals, but **Bouziès**, 4 km to the west, is the main base for pleasure boating on this stretch of the Lot. As well as canoes, kayaks and other boats you can hire (see page 273), there are river tours under the cliffs: **Safaraid Croisières** (T05 65 35 98 88, sud-croisieres.com, Apr-Oct 1100-1630, Jul-Aug 1100-1800) operate continuous tours lasting 45 minutes (€6) or 75 minutes (€9).

Also from Bouziès, you can take an interesting shady walk along the **Chemin de halage de Ganil**, a 1-km stretch of towpath carved out of the cliffs for the mules that pulled the *gabarres* upstream.

Memorail-Quercy Vapeur

St-Géry, T05 65 35 46 91, memorail.quercylot.com.
Jun and Sep Sun and holidays 1430-1830,
Jul-Aug Sun-Fri 1430-1830. €3.
13 km west of St-Cirq.

The rail line that used to connect Cahors with Capdenac down the valley is long gone, but the old St-Géry depot and its track have fallen into the hands of the local rail nuts: it now contains an H0-gauge set with 100 m of track and a Quercy village, with a *petit train* outside for the children to ride and lots of models and memorabilia.

An Englishman's castle

Some peoples are plagued with locusts, some with bedbugs. In old Quercy, it was the English. During the Hundred Years' War (and in some areas, before and after it) bands of mercenaries, freebooters and deserters turned bandits ranged over the province. In this part of the Lot Valley, they often holed up in caves in the river cliffs: hence the mocking nickname *châteaux des Anglais*.

During the French Revolution in 1792, a mob of peasants came to burn the château, but a clever servant welcomed them all in and let them have a go at the Marquis' wine cellar instead. Blessed with a spectacular site, you'll see a few of these caves on the narrow stretch of river where the roads on the banks began as towpaths. Here the cliffs bore in so closely on the Lot that the boatmen had tunnels dug through them. (Driving along them today can be exciting; they're only one lane wide, so slow down!) At one of the tunnels, near Bouziès downstream from St-Cirq, you can see a *château des Anglais* right next to it, with a stone façade and fake crenellations that really do make it look like a castle.

Château de Cenevières

T05 65 31 27 33, chateau-cenevieres.com.
Apr-Sep daily 1000-1200 and 1400-1800, Oct-Nov daily 1400-1700. €6.
8 km east of St-Cirq.

It's a wonder the *Da Vinci Code* crowd hasn't found Cenevières yet, for one of the last surviving Merovingians, Duke Waiofar of Aquitaine, was run to ground here by Pepin the Short (Charlemagne's dad) back in 767. Politics has mostly left the place in peace ever since, though the old castle was revamped into a proper Renaissance château by a lord named Flottard de Gourdon, who made his fortune as Francis I's top artilleryman through that king's many campaigns in Italy.

During the French Revolution in 1792, a mob of peasants came to burn the château, but a clever servant welcomed them all in and let them have a go at the Marquis' wine cellar instead. Blessed with a spectacular site on the edge of the cliffs over the river, it's a charming château in its way, one that for all its frills still has a faint air of Quercy farmhouse to it. The most interesting parts are the secret Protestant chapel, added during the Wars of Religion (Henri IV stayed here while plotting his attack on Cahors) and a real mystery, the room called the **Cabinet d'Alchemie**, painted with allegorical pictures of gods and mythological heroes – Artemis, Orpheus, Atlas, Achilles, Jason, Hercules, Phaeton (who fell off his father Apollo's chariot) and Numa Pompilius, an early priest-king of Rome. As with the similar room at the Château de Puymartin near Sarlat (see page 156), its meaning has never been explained.

Cajarc & around

It's a charmer: a small medieval centre cradled in a curving tree-lined boulevard where its walls once stood. Cajarc's population of only 1200 makes it the mighty metropolis of this stretch of the Lot, and it has seen some trouble in its day. Cardinal Richelieu knocked those walls down in 1623, as Cajarc had been a stronghold of the Protestants.

More recently, Cajarc has had a reputation as a retreat for the famous. Novelist Françoise Sagan was born here, and from the 1960s until his death President Georges Pompidou made it his summer home, while the comedian Coluche – who facetiously ran for the presidency once himself – was holding forth at the Café Moulino.

Like St-Cirq, Cajarc today gets more than a little overrun in the summer, thanks to a big dam on the river that has given it an artificial lake perfect for water sports. In summer, this little Lot village startles its guests with France's biggest festival of African music and dance, called 'Africajarc'.

Maison des Arts Georges Pompidou

Route de Gréalou, T05 65 40 78 19, magp.fr.
Jul-Sep daily 1300-1900, rest of year hours vary. Free.

Something just as unexpected as Africajarc is this polished palace of the arts, a tribute to the president who was always one of the biggest boosters for the avant-garde in every field (one of his biggest personal accomplishments was the building of the Centre Pompidou in Paris). Each year brings a full schedule of temporary exhibitions. The art you'll see is generally dry, academic and excruciatingly Parisian, but occasionally the Maison gets lucky.

Château de Laroque-Toirac

Laroque-Toirac, T06 12 37 48 39, chateautoirac.com.
Guided tours daily May-Jun and Oct 1430-1730, Jul-Sep 1030-1200 and 1400-1800. €6.
13 km east of Cajarc.

This dramatically sited castle attracted a lot of attention in the Hundred Years' War. Besieged and taken repeatedly, it was finally chopped down to size by the English in 1372 (the keep was originally, and quite eccentrically, some 30 m taller). The tour will show you some fine period furnishings and paintings, medieval kitchens never remodelled, and a garden with exotic plants. It's lucky anything's left at all; in the 19th century an impoverished owner sold off the castle by lottery, one room at a time.

St-Pierre-Toirac

This village's stoutly fortified 11th-century **church** (Easter-Oct 0800-2000; if it's closed, get the key from the Mairie) has some remarkable carvings in a vigorous, naive early medieval style: dozens of capitals and some reliefs built into the walls – note the tympanum with a scene of Samson felling his lion, with a nosy angel standing by apparently giving the strongman some advice. Outside, you can see the Merovingian-era sarcophagi that have recently been excavated.

St-Pierre is as rustic and unchanged as a village could be, and it makes a fitting home for the **Musée Rurale Quercynois** (route de la Gare, T05 65 34 26 07; Jul-Aug Sun-Fri 1430-1800, rest of year by request; €2), a rather charming local effort in which 60 *mouniques* (mannequins in costume) demonstrate the various occupations of rural life. There are exhibits on old-time folklore, medicines and superstitions, and gardens maintained the old-fashioned way.

Cajarc.

Valley of the Célé

If you liked the Lot Valley, you'll probably want to put the Célé in your pocket and take it home as a souvenir. In every way, it's the upper Lot in miniature. The sparkling river itself meanders around dreamily just like its bigger sister; the cliffs that hem it in are just a little lower than those on the Lot. The road underneath them is narrower and quieter, and the few tiny villages along it make the rustic toy-town atmosphere complete.

The Célé is all too perfect to be left in peace, and if you come in July or August you'll be joining the annual flood of tourists looking for tranquillity and pretending they've found it. Better to visit in the spring, when it's at its comeliest, or really any other time, and you'll get all the tranquillity you can stand.

There is everything the heart could desire; old, sometimes rather ruined, and small; tall poplars by the fishy stream, a Renaissance castle standing in the fields…

Freda White, Three Rivers of France (1953)

Valley of the Célé.

Grotte de Pech Merle

Cabrerets, T05 65 31 27 05, quercy.net/pechmerle. Apr-Oct daily 0930-1200 and 1330-1700. €8, €4.50 child (5-14). Numbers limited to 700 a day so advance booking is recommended (by phone or online). Guided tours in French: ask at the booking office for a written explanation in English.

We can't see the original paintings at Lascaux any more, which leaves this and Font-de-Gaume (see page 172) as the greatest prehistoric painted caves open to the public. Two teenagers, André David and Henri Dutertre, discovered the paintings in 1922. By happy chance, their parish priest at Cabrerets happened to be Amédée Lemozi, a scholarly man who had spent much of his life exploring caves and carrying out archaeological digs around the Lot. Lemozi did the studies and documentation, and got the place opened to the public in 1926.

While you're waiting for the tour to start, you can have a look through the adjacent **Musée Amédée Lemozi** (same hours and ticket), which has some of the spear points, carved bones and other items Lemozi discovered, as well as a film and exhibits on Palaeolithic society.

There's a lot to see on the tour. Right inside the entrance, the **Black Frieze** is a circle of mammoths in black outline surrounding a horse. A herd of dappled horses follows, and then more animals, including a bison cleverly positioned over a bulge in the rock that makes it appear to be carved in relief.

Not all Pech Merle's wonders are made by human hands. The next chamber is called the **Hall of the Discs**, from the unusual circular formations caused by capillary action. After that, in a section that was sealed off at the end of the last Ice Age and only recently reopened, the guide will show you bear scratches (and fossilized bear turds) along with something simple but strange and wonderful – a footprint of an adolescent boy, 10,000 years old.

A corridor with more bear remains – and a skilfully executed drawing of a bear – leads to the climax of the tour, the **Hall of Paintings**, with more spotted horses, a provocative 'wounded man' with a spear in his back, apparently being attacked by something that looks a little like a bat and a little like a spaceship. There is a stencilled human hand, more deer, bison, mammoths and horses, and yet more natural curiosities: the 'cave pearls' and a bizarre, perfectly formed 'spinning top', all formed naturally by thousands of years of calcite accretion and erosion.

Pescalerie Fountain, Valley of the Célé.

Tip...

The cave is not accessible by wheelchair, though the museum is. The tour takes about an hour and involves lots of stairs and uneven ground; anyone who might have a hard time should mention it to the guide at the beginning.

Cabrerets

The village closest to the caves, Cabrerets sits under the bluff, no-nonsense **Château de Gontaut Biron** (not open), built in the 14th-15th centuries. Outside the village along the Célé you'll see a very impressive *château des Anglais*, like a castle wall built right into the cliff face; see box page 252. This one is also sometimes called the 'Château du Diable' (devils, English ... same thing!), but it was really built by the local gentry, the Barasc family, and they lived in it before they built the château.

Musée de l'Insolite

Liauzu, T05 65 30 21 01, museedelinsolite.com.
Apr-Sep daily 0900-1300 and 1400-2000.
Small donation requested.
East of Cabrerets along the Célé.

What at first glance appears to be a scrapyard, piled between the river and the cliffs, is in fact just that, though a merry scrapyard it is. Surrealism is alive and well and residing in the Célé Valley, thanks to artist Bertrand Chenu and his 'museum of the unusual'.

It's all crammed in a narrow space beneath menacingly overhanging cliffs, bits of which occasionally come down (most recently on Remembrance Day, falling smack on to the Tomb of the Unknown Deserter). Chenu isn't quite as highfalutin' as Dalí, but he does have the firm intention of making us laugh. Amid the painting, sculpture, ironwork and literally tons of *objets trouvés,* a tour bus full of leering pigs glides along, past the tail of an army helicopter trapped in the cliff and a Brobdingnagian motorcycle made of junk, while zombies pedal furiously up and down the cliffside. There is also a small, rusty zoo, a Quercynois pagoda, France's only iron dolmen, and lots, *lots* more. All the clutter can't quite conceal the presence of a quite talented artist, doing what he damn well pleases.

Musée Departmentale de Cuzals

Sauliac-sur-Célé, T05 65 31 36 43.
May-Jun and Sep Wed-Sun 1400-1800, Jul-Aug daily 1000-1900. €4, €2.50 concessions, under 12s free.
8 km east of Cabrerets.

Up in the hills above Sauliac, this 'open-air museum' does its best to bring the rural Quercy of the old days back to life. In part it's a working farm, where the costumed staff take care of the seasonal chores. City folk can learn the difference between

hay and straw, while the kids get to meet horses and donkeys. It isn't just farming; you can learn about steam engines, printing and furniture making or watch a weaver at work or a craftsman fashioning *sabots* (wooden clogs). Plenty of home-made snacks on hand.

Abbaye de St-Pierre

Marcilhac-sur-Célé, T05 65 40 65 52.
Church (with best parts) open normal hours; rest of abbey open Jul to mid-Sep Mon, Wed and Fri at 1700, other times by appointment. €3, €2 child (under 16).

The pretty, comfortably down-at-heel village of Marcilhac-sur-Célé grew up around what was once the most important monastery on the Lot. Most of the monastic establishments in Quercy owed their start to the great mother house at Moissac, in the Tarn-et-Garonne west of Montauban. In the ninth century, when Moissac was under constant menace from the Vikings, some of the monks fled to this remote spot for safety. The new house rapidly became a power in its own right, controlling Rocamadour and scores of other monasteries. Marcilhac's downfall came with those troublesome English in the Hundred Years' War, and what they didn't wreck was finished off by the Protestants in the Wars of Religion.

Still, what survived is a marvel, all the more so in this out-of-the-way location. The tympanum over the church's main door, with *Christ in Majesty* between a sun and moon, may well be the oldest one in France. The church and chapter house have some carved capitals in a unique pre-Romanesque style, and there are rare traces of early-medieval paintings, including scenes from the life of St James – advertising for the pilgrimage to his shrine at Compostela.

Marcilhac in summer has the air of a holiday village, when its empty houses fill up with interesting families from Britain and elsewhere, with lots of children, lounging on the grassy beach on the riverbank by day and igniting barbecues around the monastic ruins by night.

Espagnac.

Espagnac

This genteelly shambolic little village is one of the places where saffron is grown in Quercy. This exotic crop, brought to France by the Arabs, was once important for food, medicine and also for dyeing cloth. As Quercy grew poor after the Hundred Years' War the culture gradually died out, only to be revived in the last two decades. You might see fields of the little purple saffron crocuses before the harvest in late autumn. That's hard work – it takes over 200,000 of them to make a kilo of saffron.

Espagnac's landmark is its **Eglise Notre-Dame du Val Paradis**, with a unique, impossibly picturesque half-timbered steeple and an outsized Gothic choir; inside are medieval tombs from two great houses, Cardaillac and Hébrard, who between them owned almost everything in the valley.

Figeac

The Lot's second city seems a long way from anywhere. Cahors lies a twisty 60 km to the west, and in every other direction there is nothing but scrubby causse and increasingly rugged hills all the way to the Massif Central and the Rhone. So it's all the more surprising to find this rather refined little city among the solemn hills and quiet valleys.

Like Cahors, Figeac had a medieval golden moment. It grew up around a monastery on the major pilgrimage route to Compostela in Spain, and then clever merchants made it briefly and spectacularly rich. The Hundred Years' War put an end to its trading career, and the terrible plague of 1361 killed off most of the population, but this left Figeac with a truly impressive historic centre full of half-timbered and stone palaces.

Place des Ecritures.

A walk through old Figeac

On some streets you'd swear you were in Tuscany. As in Cahors, Figeac's merchants were well connected with Italy, and the architecture shows a strong Italian influence. The churches aren't much to look at, because the Protestants destroyed everything they could when they took over Figeac in 1576. But a collection of medieval civic architecture like Figeac's is truly rare – even Paris can't show you as much.

The tourist office hands out a very useful leaflet called *Les clefs de Figeac*, detailing an hour's walking tour that passes most of the best buildings. Along the way, the highlights will include **rue Gambetta**, with two of the most splendid palaces at Nos 41 and 43, both with interesting sculptural details. At the end there's **place Carnot** with its iron market *halle*, a popular gathering spot for the Figeacois when the market's not on.

Place Champollion, as the grand buildings around it attest, was the real city centre, while just a block away on rue Emile-Zola is the grandest palace of all, the **Château du Viguier du Roi**, now the city's top hotel.

You may feel there's something strangely modern about medieval Figeac, especially around rue Gambetta: all those big, blocky grey forms casting the streets into shadow are just like the concrete canyons of a modern business centre. Some of the old palaces even look like banks, not surprisingly since that's just what some of them were. They follow the same form as in Florence and other Italian cities. The ground floor behind those big Gothic arches was a great open space where goods were stored and business transacted. The boss's family lived on the upper floor behind the delicate traceried windows, while the top floor was for storage and the servants.

As in Cahors, look out for the wonderful top-floor galleries called *soleihos*. It's fun to imagine the tycoons sitting up there with a glass of wine, enjoying the view, but the truth is the *soleihos* were mostly used for hanging out the laundry.

Musée du Vieux Figeac

Place Vival, T05 65 34 06 25.
May-Jun and Sep Mon-Sat 1000-1230 and 1430-1800, Sun 1000-1300, Jul-Aug daily 1000-1900, Oct-Apr Mon-Sat 1000-1230 and 1430-1800. €2, €1 child.

The 13th century **Hôtel de la Monnaie** is a fine introduction to Figeac's medieval architecture. Built as the home of a wealthy merchant, it was later used as a mint. Today it houses the **tourist office** and, upstairs, this odd little museum, a kind of rummage through the city's attic: there are costumes, folk art, furniture, axes, a pair of elephant tusks – and some aeroplane parts, a reminder that this town of barely 15,000 used to craft all France's propellers. Thanks to the huge Ratier works west of town, it still makes its living largely from aerospace.

Musée Champollion/Les Ecritures du Monde

Place Champollion, T05 65 31 50 08, ville-figeac.fr.
Jan-Mar Tue-Sat 1400-1730, Apr-Jun and Sep Tue-Sat 1030-1230 and 1400-1800, Jul-Aug daily 1030-1800. €4, €2 concessions, under 12s free.

Behind a façade covered with ideograms from a score of languages, this tribute to Jean-François Champollion offers some items from the Louvre's enormous Egyptian collection, exhibits dedicated to the great scholar's life and works, and a new section on the history of writing, with artefacts from all over the world. The building that houses the museum is the 12th-century **Maison de Griffon**. Out at the back, the pavement of the old courtyard, now called the **place des Ecritures**, is covered by a giant copy of the Rosetta Stone, which you can walk across.

Espace Patrimoine

Mairie, 5 rue du Colomb, T05 65 50 05 40, ville-figeac.fr.
Apr-9 Jul and 20 Sep-Oct Tue-Sat 1400-1800, 10 Jul-19 Sep daily 1000-1230 and 1500-1900, rest of year on request. Free.

This small exhibit tells the story of Figeac, with photos, models and written explanations. It provides a good capsule history of the city and its architecture – but only in French.

The lover & the linguist

Some Figeacois would say their most famous son is Charles Boyer, the slow-walkin', trash-talkin' romantic star of over 80 films in Hollywood and Europe (and the model for Looney Toons' amorous cartoon skunk Pepé le Pew). Boyer may never really have said "Come vis me to ze casbah" in *Algiers*, but he showed that a clever boy from the Lot with big brown eyes could go a long way.

But for most, the real hometown hero is Jean-François Champollion (born 1790), a boy from a poor family who never had much formal schooling but nevertheless mastered some two dozen languages while still in his teens, including Amharic, Syriac and Persian. The government allowed him to avoid conscription so he could finish his Coptic dictionary, while Napoleon's men on their Egyptian campaign in 1799 had done him the further service of finding the **Rosetta Stone**, a decree of Ptolemy V from 196 BC that carried the same inscription in Greek, demotic Egyptian and Egyptian hieroglyphs. No one had yet taken even a baby step toward understanding hieroglyphics; many experts still believed they were nothing more than decoration.

The British had nabbed the Rosetta Stone after they chased Napoleon out of Egypt, and much of the early work of deciphering the hieroglyphics was done by an Englishman, Thomas Young, who would become Champollion's bitter rival. But the French had taken a plaster cast, and Champollion got the last word with his comprehensive *Précis du système hiéroglyphique*, published in 1824. That got him a post as curator of the new Egyptian collection at the Louvre and, in 1828, the chance to lead an expedition to Egypt himself. But too much time staring at dusty old books gave him a bad case of nerves, and he died four years later, only 42 years old.

Abbatiale St-Sauveur

Place de la Raison.
Daily (except Sun in winter) 0900-1900.

Figeac grew up around this great abbey church; the abbots themselves ruled the city until the merchants snatched control in 1302. Today, a gosh-awful post-Protestant era façade conceals it, but there's an impressive Gothic interior, and an acre or two of 19th-century stained glass brightens it up considerably.

In the right aisle, don't miss the 13th-century chapel of **Notre-Dame de Pitié**. This sophisticated chamber, with its intricate rib vaulting, was originally the chapter house of the abbey. After the Protestant interlude it was turned into a chapel, newly embellished with naive polychrome wood reliefs of the Passion.

Notre-Dame-du-Puy

Place du Foirail.

Even before the monks founded their abbey of St-Sauveur, there was some sort of church up on the steep hill that overlooks the town from the north. The medieval version was apparently almost as grand as St-Sauveur, but when the Protestants controlled Figeac (1576-1622) they trashed it and turned the ruins into a fortress. This 17th-century rebuilding has a light and gracious interior, which nicely balances the heavy and ornate wooden altarpiece. What makes the climb up the Puy worthwhile though, is not the church so much as the wonderful view over the towers and gables of old Figeac.

Les Aiguilles

The 'needles' are Figeac's modest medieval mystery: two slender and graceful stone towers with pointed tips, believed to have been constructed in the 11th century. The **Aiguille de**

Notre-Dame-du-Puy.

Lissac, just west of the town on the road to Lissac, is the taller of the two at 14.5 m. Across the Célé on the Colline du Cingle, the big hill that dominates Figeac from the south, the **Aiguille du Cingle** (or 'du Pressoir') measures 13.5 m. Guesses abound as to their purpose: some say they were a local version of the *lanternes des morts* (see page 153), or monuments along the pilgrim route to Compostela; others are convinced there were originally two more, and the four marked the cardinal points and the limits of the right of asylum enjoyed by Figeac's abbey.

Around Figeac: Capdenac

It's two towns in one, and they couldn't have less in common. **Capdenac-Gare**, an industrial town that grew up around the railway in the 19th century, has all the people. Up above, high on its hill, **Capdenac-le-Haut** seems lost in a medieval daydream. Despite the recent excavations at Martel (see page 205) the Capdenacois still like to believe their village was the ancient Celtic Uxellodunum, and no one's going to convince them otherwise.

Since all the people decamped to Capdenac-Gare, the old town has been almost perfectly preserved, with crooked streets of half-timbered houses. Some of the medieval walls and gates survive, while the 14th-century keep now houses the **Musée de Capdenac** (place Lucter, T05 65 38 32 26; Apr-Jun and Sep-Oct Thu-Tue except Sun morning 1030-1130 and 1430-1700, Jul-Aug daily except Sun morning 0930-1230 and 1430-1830; €2.50, €2 child), with finds from Gallo-Roman times and earlier, though the best of it was taken to Cahors.

Sleeping

Cahors

Château de Mercuès €€€€
Mercuès, T05 65 20 00 01, chateaudemercues.com.
8 km west of Cahors.
Map: Cahors, C1, p230.
This glorious 13th-century castle, a conspicuous landmark on its hilltop, was for centuries the home of Cahors' powerful bishops. Charles de Gaulle wrote parts of his memoirs here in 1951. Long neglected, the castle was completely restored and turned into a hotel by local wine baron Georges Vigouroux (his friend Tony Blair sometimes comes to visit). There are great views (de Gaulle wrote that from the walls you 'could see history climbing towards you'), a pool, tennis and a pricey restaurant.

Hôtel Jean XXII €€
2 rue Edmond Albe, at bd Gambetta, T05 65 35 07 66, hotel-jeanxxii.com.
Map: Cahors, D2, p230.
Cosy modern rooms in what was part of the 13th-century Palace Duèze. Air conditioning is available for a small supplement; free Wi-Fi, but no pets.

Château de Mercuès.

Hôtel Terminus €€
5 av Charles de Freycinet, T05 65 53 32 00, balandre.com.
Map: Cahors, B3, p230.
The top choice in Cahors for over a century, the elegant Terminus has a touch of art nouveau and a location across from the train station that's convenient but quiet; parking is provided. The rooms are good value, though not so grand as the public areas. Downstairs is one of the department's best restaurants, Le Balandre (see page 265).

Albas

Self-catering

La Carrière
T05 65 36 74 98, lotfrance.com.
Three well-appointed gîtes on descending terraces in the centre of a very bijou village – it could be a film set. Each sleeps four people, and costs €800 per week in high season. There's a nice pool and plenty to do in the area, but if you stay here you might be tempted just to sit and enjoy the wonderful views over the valley.

Duravel

Domaine du Haut Baran €€€€-€€€
T05 65 24 63 24, hautbaran.com.
William and Rosalie Haas are complete perfectionists, which shows in their devotion to doing whatever it takes to make your stay enjoyable. They run the

finest luxury chambre d'hôte in the Lot, in a gracious rambling house set in an extensive, beautifully landscaped park with a large pool. The real story, though, is the unique special tours and themed visits they organize: horseback and cycling tours, cookery lessons with Jacques Ratier of the celebrated La Récréation in Les Arques (see page 267), special wine and art tours. Meals are on offer too; the cooking is exceptional.

Montcabrier

Atelier de la Rose €
T05 65 24 66 36, french-rose.com.
It's simple accommodation in a lovely setting in the village centre, with a big plus: Sally Gaucheron knows everything there is to know about the region, and she arranges guided tours of the sights and walking tours in the country. Meals are on offer, and there's also an artist's studio available at attractive daily or weekly rates.

Mauroux

Self-catering

Les Places
Sérignac, T05 65 36 42 17, lesplaces.com.
Steve Collier is a property restorer; Tessa's an artist. Between them they've made their secluded farm into a unique property, where the highlights are an infinity pool beside a field of lavender, and a Minoan-frescoed bathroom. Rates for their gîte are €328-415 per week for two people, depending on season. They'll also let the entire property in July to August, an ideal place if you have a crowd: it sleeps 14 (€1900-2295 per week). Sérignac is up in the hills south of Puy-l'Evêque.

Montcuq

La Grange de Marcillac €
St-Cyprien, T05 65 22 90 73, grangedemarcillac.free.fr.
Southeast of Montcuq.
Chambres d'hôtes and apartments; dinner is available, also cookery courses – learn how to make foie gras – and music courses in summer.

Montpezat-de-Quercy

Domaine de Lafon €€
Pech de Lafon, T05 63 02 05 09, domainedelafon.com.
In a farmhouse 4 km from Montpezat, gorgeous rooms are decorated with a personal touch by Mme Micheline Perrone. A table d'hôte, art courses and gastronomic weekends are also available.

Vers

Camping

La Chêneraie
Le Cuzoul, T05 65 31 40 29, cheneraie.com.
Apr-Nov.
This family-run campsite between Cahors and St-Cirq specializes in nature activities and fun on the water, canoeing, horses, even ultra-light aircraft classes; also pool, tennis, evening entertainments and many activities for children. There's a restaurant and snack bar. In high season pitches are €17-22 per day for two people; bungalows €360-690 per week depending on size.

St-Cirq-Lapopie

Auberge du Sombral €€
T05 65 31 26 08, lesombral.com.
Apr-Oct.
A slightly less expensive choice than the Pelissaria, the Sombral is another deliciously restored village house, covered with wisteria. Rooms are modern but comfortable, and there's a fine restaurant downstairs (see page 267), and a pool.

Cabrerets

Hôtel-Restaurant des Grottes €
T05 65 31 27 02.
Apr-Oct.
A simple, good bargain choice for visiting the cave of Pech Merle. There's a big pool and an inexpensive restaurant on a shady terrace overlooking the river.

Château du Viguier du Roi.

St-Pierre-Toirac

Self-catering

La Clôterie
T05 65 34 64 61.
Arlette and Paul Adam de Villiers, who run Le Soleilho in Figeac (see below), have five lovely gîtes in the village, sleeping two to eight, furnished partly with antiques, some with gardens; €360-820 depending on size.

Figeac

Château du Viguier du Roi €€€€
52 rue Emile-Zola, T05 65 50 05 05, chateau-viguier-figeac.fr.
It's hard to believe that only 20 years ago this château was an abandoned ruin. The building itself is an important part of Figeac's past, built in the 14th century for the judge sent here by Philip the Fair to oversee the king's justice. Now meticulously restored, along with its spectacular garden courtyard, it is the most luxurious hotel this end of the Lot has to offer. There's an elegant restaurant, a pool and a solarium.

Hôtel des Bains €€-€
1 rue du Griffoul, T05 65 34 10 89, hoteldesbains.fr.
A lovely old establishment on the Célé, with a breakfast terrace (and some rooms) overlooking the river, this simple, good-value hotel has Wi-Fi in every room, and some have air conditioning. There are tennis courts, and they'll be happy to set you up with water sports and other activities in the vicinity.

Le Soleilho €€
8 rue Prat, T05 65 34 64 41, chambres-hotes-figeac.com.
Excellent chambres d'hôtes with a personal touch, off a real *soleilho* with views over Figeac's medieval centre. The owners are friendly and helpful, and the breakfasts good.

Capdenac-le-Haut

Relais de la Tour €€-€
Place Lucter, T05 65 11 06 99, lerelaisdelatour.fr.
In the centre of the old town, an elegant 15th-century building houses this hotel of character. The rooms may be completely modern, but they're light and airy, and some have great views over the valley below. The hotel also includes a good simple restaurant (closed Sun night, Mon and in winter) with traditional Lotois cuisine.

Eating & drinking

Cahors

Le Balandre €€€€
5 av Charles de Freycinet, T05 65 53 32 00, balandre.com.
Tue-Sat.
Map: Cahors, B3, p230.
The restaurant of the Hôtel Terminus (see page 262) is a place that has been able to maintain its reputation for decades. It has a wonderful old-time ambience inside with a touch of belle époque style, and a pleasant terrace in summer. The kitchen is best for seafood and creative starter combinations with foie gras, though the *carte* is a little short. €17 and €31 lunch menus.

Au Fil des Douceurs €€€
90 quai de la Verrerie, T05 65 22 13 04.
Tue-Sat, closed 2 weeks in mid-Jun.
Map: Cahors, E3, p230.
It's a restored old river barge, moored in a perfect spot where you can contemplate Cahors' medieval skyline while you enjoy traditional Quercy cooking, with lots of duck and Vin de Cahors. €13 weekday lunch menu.

L'O à la Bouche €€€
Place St-Urcisse, T05 65 35 65 69.
Tue-Sat.
Map: Cahors, E5, p230.
A relatively new arrival to the conservative Cahors restaurant scene, the place with the punning name has quickly become the most acclaimed restaurant in town. The welcome is friendly and informal and so is the cuisine, where everything is designed to delight: little *tourtes* and tajines, hints of the Mediterranean and irresistible desserts. Lunch menus from €19.

Lagarrigue €€-€
543 rue Président Wilson, T05 65 34 01 12.
Closed Sat evening and Sun.
Map: Cahors, B5, p230.
To get away from the tourist crowds at the Pont Valentré all you need do is sneak through the little tunnel under the rail tracks. On the other side you'll find the real Cahors, and this very pleasant and popular spot; solid home cooking on a €13 lunch menu.

Le Baladin €€-€
57 rue Clément-Marot, T05 65 22 36 52.
Closed Sun, and Mon in winter.
Map: Cahors, D4, p230.
With outside tables on a little side street next to the cathedral, this is a good spot for crêpes, salads and light lunches.

Picnic with a view

Cahors market and the shops around it can supply all your needs for a picnic. If it's not a windy day, carry your lunch over the Pont Louis-Philippe and follow the signs to the top of Mont-St-Cyr, from where you look straight down into the medieval city. There are other spots like this on the hills above the Pont Valentré.

Le Lamparo €€-€
76 rue Georges Clémenceau, T05 65 35 25 93, lelamparo.com/lamparo.
Mon-Sat.
Map: Cahors, D5, p230.
It's right across from the covered market, but if you don't look closely you'll never see it. Inside,

this hole-in-the-wall opens up to a huge room that's packed every day with Cadurciens, who enjoy its dependable cooking and wide choice; the enormous menu offers pizza, pastas, salads, grills, seafood and lots more.

Marie Colline €€-€
173 rue Georges Clémenceau, T05 65 35 59 96.
Mon-Fri lunch only.
Map: Cahors, D5, p230.

In the Kingdom of Duck, many people aren't even sure what a vegetarian *is*, and vegetarian restaurants are rare as alligator restaurants. This may be the only one in the department, but its creative cooking has made it extremely popular; you'll have to book to get a seat.

Le Dousil €
124 rue Nationale, T05 65 53 19 67, ledousil.free.fr.
Wed-Sun.
Map: Cahors, D5, p230.

Just around the corner from the Lamparo, this relaxed wine bar offers charcuterie, cheeses and pâtés, salads, and a few entrées (cassoulet, duck with *cèpes*), plus a wide range of Cahors wines and many others.

Douelle

La Marine €€€
On D8 in village centre, T05 65 20 02 06.
Closed Sun evening and Mon.
This quiet village might seem an unlikely setting for a fine restaurant that specializes in seafood, but La Marine has been cooking up tasty *bouillabaisses* beside the Lot for a long time. The fresh fish comes straight from the Atlantic; the mixed grill is a treat. Menus €25 and up.

St-Médard

Le Gindreau €€€€
T05 65 36 22 27, pagesperso-orange.fr/le.gindreau.
Wed-Sun, closed mid-Oct to mid-Nov.
It's an old village school, the centrepiece of this attractive hamlet between Cahors and Prayssac, but for some three decades now chef Alexis Pelissou has kept up its reputation as perhaps the best restaurant in the Lot. Come for the €37 lunch menu or go for a splurge, preferably on a sunny day when lunch on the gorgeous terrace makes life seem blissfully perfect.

The cooking is classic southwest fare, though in a moment of madness you might go for the all-truffle menu.

Prayssac

La Vénus €€
Square de la Vénus (on D811), T05 65 22 47 10, restaurant-la-venus.com.
Jul-Aug Tue-Sun, rest of year Wed-Sun (Nov-Mar closed Sun evening).
Right on Venus Square, in front of the bodacious nude statue of the goddess (which usually has a bikini or sunglasses painted on it by the local kids), this popular restaurant does the usual Quercy favourites, but complements them with some well-crafted Italian treats: a range of fresh pasta dishes and veal *scallopine* in several forms, including with morel mushrooms when they can get them.

Goujounac

La Poule au Pot €€
T05 65 36 65 48.
Closed 1st 3 weeks of Jan.
Just west of village; signposted.
There are two great *fermes-auberges* hidden away in the woods north of Puy-l'Evêque, and both draw crowds from all over for their massive duck dinners, including home-made pâté with foie gras. The Poule au Pot is famous for its *pommes de terre sarladaise* (see page 156), by general acclaim the best potatoes on the planet.

Frayssinet-le-Gélat

La Serpt €€
La Thèze, T05 65 36 66 15. Tue-Sun.
Between Puy-l'Evêque and Villefranche-du-Périgord on D28: follow hand-painted yellow signs.
The other *ferme-auberge* in the neighbourhood is really, truly in the middle of nowhere. La Serpt's ducky potatoes aren't quite up to the standard of the *poule au pot*, but the soup (a memorable *tourin à l'aoucou*) and the pâté are to die for. Take your choice.

Les Arques

La Récréation €€€
T05 65 22 88 08.
Mar-Oct Fri-Tue.
The menu never changes but the people keep on coming. Lobster ravioli and codfish in a nutty crust are perfect for an evening out in what used to be the yard of this former village school (*récréation* means 'playtime'). The restaurant was locally famous even before it was featured in a popular book published a few years ago, Michael Sanders' *From Here You Can't See Paris*.

Puy-L'Evêque

La Terrasse €€
Grézels, T05 65 21 34 03.
Lunch only, closed Mon and mid-Sep to mid-Oct.
6 km south of Puy l'Evêque on D44.
This is a mom-and-pop operation where there's no choice – one set menu every day, and you must ring ahead. But it's six or seven courses of wonderful home cooking for €23 (€27 on Sun, with an extra main course), wine included.

Montcuq

Café de France €€
Place de la République, T05 65 22 90 29.
Daily in summer, rest of year Tue-Sat.
This pleasant village has no less than three excellent, inexpensive restaurants, neighbours with adjoining tables on shady place de la République. You can choose which one you fancy from the daily specials chalked up on the boards out front, but the Café de France, with some rather refined cooking, is usually our pick.

St-Cirq-Lapopie

Auberge du Sombral €€
T05 65 31 26 08, lesombral.com.
Apr-Oct daily for lunch (closed Thu out of season), dinner Fri-Sat only.

Though the *escargots* of the Lot rampage through everyone's garden, they've never figured prominently on local menus. The Sombral, part of the hotel listed above, remedies this with a nice little snail *cassolette*, in addition to Quercy lamb roasted with figs, poached trout, and duck of course. Honest €15 lunch menu.

Le Gourmet Quercynois €€
Rue de la Peyrolerie, T05 65 31 21 20, restaurant-legourmetquercynois.com.
At the top of the village.
Who says you can't eat well in a tourist trap? Here there's plenty of foie gras prepared in inviting ways, a hint of truffle and *cèpes*, a humble cassoulet raised to star status. All this in a 17th-century building covered in flowers, with a lovely terrace for the summer. Rare for this village, it's open all year round. There's also a shop with some fine Vins de Cahors and other local products.

Boussac

Le Relais Creusois €€€€
Route de la Châtre, T05 55 65 02 20, restaurant-traiteur-creuse.com.
Mid-Mar to Dec, closed Tue evenings all year and Wed outside summer.
Boussac is on the Célé, 12 km west of Figeac, an unlikely setting for a quite sophisticated restaurant. Roast pigeon and a surprising *salade composée* with quail share the menu with more exotic dishes and some seafood. Desserts are good.

Figeac

La Cuisine du Marché €€€
15 rue Clermont, T05 65 50 18 55, lacuisinedumarchefigeac.com.
Tue-Sat.
Chef Santiago Navazo-Centeno hails from Spain, and not surprisingly the emphasis here is on seafood, including a memorable *parillada* (mixed grill), though he has a way with Quercy lamb and other local dishes too. All this in a restored former wine cellar with an open kitchen, so you can watch Santiago at work.

La Puce à l'Oreille €€
7 rue St-Thomas, T05 65 34 33 08.
Tue-Sat and Sun lunch, also Mon in summer.
Anyone can cook a *magret de canard*; here they do it in a sauce with chestnut blossom honey and ground pepper. Figeac's bright and fashionable restaurant devotes itself to taking the Quercy essentials – duck and foie gras – and doing them as they've never been done before.

Restaurant Pizzeria Del Portel €€-€
11 rue Orthabadial, T05 65 34 53 60.
Tue-Sun.
If you don't know what you want for lunch, this is the place to go (near the tourist office). They do pizza, pasta, Greek salad, mussels and chips, sandwiches, followed by banana splits and other fancy ice cream desserts. Outdoor seating is in a pleasant courtyard across the way.

Entertainment

Cahors

They roll up the sidewalks early in this narcoleptic town, and nightlife is generally limited to a drink in the cafés along the boulevard Gambetta.

Le Duplex
16 rue Gustave-Larroumet, T05 65 22 14 56, leduplex.free.fr.
One of the few bars with live music, it draws a younger crowd; it also does theme nights, and tapas on Saturday afternoons.

Le Goût des Arts
292 quai de Regourd, T05 65 35 75 47, scapin.fr/legoutdesarts.
Cahors' smorgasbord of the arts is the exception to the rule. No telling what will turn up next: on alternate nights there may be jazz or music from around the world (even France!), comedy, cabaret, or some sort of exhibition. Some nights they put on workshops, such as painting or drawing, in which you can participate.

Les Docks
430 allées des Soupirs, T05 65 22 36 38.
Cahors' big concert venue, in the old wine warehouses near the Pont Valentré, includes a cybercafé.

Puy l'Evêque

La Batelière
1 rue de la Cale, T05 65 36 95 31.
Tue-Sun.
Right on the riverfront in a medieval building, this is the liveliest bar in the lower Lot Valley; it often has live music at weekends.

Lherm

Le Bar à Trucs
T05 65 22 84 66, gaia-coop.fr/baratrucs.aspx.
Mon-Tue and Thu 1030-1430 and 1630-1900, Fri-Sat 1100-1430 and 1630-2100, Sun 1100-1430.
25 km northwest of Cahors.
An interesting project in a lovely village of 200 that previously had no businesses at all, this is an experiment in sustainable development that right now consists of a bar and bio food co-op. The bar does snacks and meals (book ahead) to eat in or take away; they also have computers with internet, bikes and DVDs to rent and a room for children, and there is some good music and other entertainment at weekends.

Shopping

Cahors

Antiques

Passé & Présent
33 place Claude Rousseau, T05 65 23 03 31.
Tue-Sat 0900-1200 and 1400-1830.
There's a touch of whimsy in the owners' tastes that makes coming here fun. Prices are entirely reasonable, and there's always a wide choice of odd old trinkets that will fit in your bag.

Arts & crafts

Atelier Cibèle Alegretti
117 rue Georges Clémenceau, T05 65 36 96 45, bijoux-alegretti. over-blog.com.
Tue-Sat 0900-1300 and 1400-1930.
When the sun hits it, this glass studio lights up the whole street with colourful fused glass jewellery, tableware and trinkets.

Carré d'Art
46 rue Pelegry, T06 77 81 99 97, carre-dart.fr.
Tue-Sat 1000-1900.
Lost in its medieval slumbers, Cahors hardly notices this sharp and subversive oasis of art tucked down on a back street by the river. Do drop in – it's a delightful place, no matter what the exhibition. You'll meet some interesting people, or maybe catch one of the occasional concerts.

Food & drink

Bière d'Olt
Arcambal, T05 65 53 05 63.
Fri 1400-1800, Sat 1000-1200 and 1400-1800, in summer

Mon-Sat 1000-1200 and 1600-1800.
7 km east of Cahors, by the castle.
In Cahors wine country the last thing you'd expect is a microbrewery, but local boy Christophe Ratz went to Belgium to learn his trade, and now his Bière d'Olt wins prizes. It's excellent stuff, particularly the *ambrée*. There's a bar, and a tour of the brewery with the enthusiastic staff.

Sudreau
91 bd Gambetta, T05 65 35 26 06.
Tue-Sat 0930-1215 and 1415-1900.
Sudreau has long been known as one of the major outlets for the Lot's good foie gras. The Cahors shop can also supply wines, eau-de-vie, conserves and all the other culinary souvenirs you can fit in your bag.

Gifts

Limitroff
125 rue du Maréchal Foch, T05 65 22 01 02.
Tue-Sat 0900-1200 and 1400-1830.
A very clever shop guaranteed to have something to make you laugh; also some wild jewellery.

Markets

Cahors on Saturday mornings holds the biggest market in the Lot, with over 200 stalls selling everything from ducks to dishpans, and lots of good food to try. There's a smaller outdoor market on Wednesdays, and the *halle* has excellent seafood and cheeses, local specialities and some exotic Moroccan snacks.

Porcelaine Virebent.

Puy-L'Evêque

Ceramics

Porcelaine Virebent
Rue de l'Usine, T05 65 36 46 31, virebent.com.
Daily 1000-1200 and 1400-1900, closed Sun in winter.
One of the last surviving artisan porcelain makers in France, founded in 1924, Virebent supplies some of Europe's fine restaurants and also sells its clean, modern decorative pieces in its Paris showroom and in its workshop here.

Montcuq

Arts & crafts

El Colibri
Rue du Faubourg St-Privat, T06 33 51 00 33.
Tue-Sat 1000-1330 and 1500-1900.
Just what you came to Montcuq for – ceramics, textiles and whatnots from Mexico in wild

Village markets

Libos, just outside Fumel, is the place to be for everyone in the Lot Valley on Thursdays. The market's enormous, filling up most of the village, and it's a genuine people's market, where tourists are few and the area's diverse population is reflected in the Moroccan, Spanish and Portuguese foods and other items on offer.

Other good village markets: Tuesday: Puy-l'Evêque; Wednesday: St-Cirq-Lapopie (afternoons in Jul-Aug only); Friday: Prayssac, Montpezat-de-Quercy; Saturday: Lalbenque, Cajarc (afternoon); Sunday: Montcuq (farmers' market Thu morning in Jul-Aug), Castelnau-Montratier, St-Géry, Limogne-en-Quercy.

Frida Kahlo colours. You won't leave empty handed.

Books

Librairie Chimera
Rue du Faubourg St-Privat, T05 65 22 97 01.
Tue-Sun 1000-1200, Tue, Thu and Fri 1500-1630.
A godsend if you live here, and interesting even if you're just passing through: an English-French bookshop that, despite its small size, always seems to have something you've been looking for.

St-Cirq-Lapopie

Food & drink

Quercy Terre d'Arômes
Les Bories, Crégols, T05 65 24 79 32, quercy-terre-arome.com.
Jul-Aug daily 1030-1900, rest of year ring ahead.
Saffron was one of the traditional crops in Quercy, and its revival is being effected by dedicated producers like Catherine Calvet, on her farm up in the hills 7 km above St-Cirq. In summer she welcomes visitors to learn everything about this modest little flower, its medicinal uses and what to do with it in the kitchen. Besides selling saffron as is, she also makes it into some interesting products of her own invention: saffron-flavoured oils and vinegars, and a saffron syrup that does amazing things for crêpes and even *magrets de canard.*

Figeac

Bric-a-brac

Cour des Miracles
47 rue Gambetta, T06 14 85 86 58.
Tue-Sat 1030-1200 and 1500-1900.
Figeac isn't much of a shopping town, but you ought to have a look in this shop, which occupies one of the town's most interesting medieval courtyards and its surroundings: it sells books, prints, trinkets and a little bit of everything else.

Activities & tours

Adventure sports

Bureau des Sports-Nature
Conduché, T05 65 24 21 01, pagesperso-orange.fr/bureau-sports-nature.
Near Bouziès, 5 km downstream from St-Cirq.
Canoeing and kayaking on the Lot and the Célé; they also offer canyoning, rock-climbing, potholing and more.

Kalapca
St-Cirq-Lapopie, T05 65 30 29 51, kalapca.net.
From the *plage* below the village, you can rent canoes for an hour or a day. They also organize excursions and adventure trips of up to a week, including river tours, hiking or mountain bikes, camping and tours with guides schooled in the nature and history of the area.

Passion Aventure
Pont de Marcilhac, Marcilhac-sur-Céle, T06 10 73 73 12.
Canoe and kayak tours on the Célé, from 90 minutes to a whole day, plus rock-climbing, abseiling and other sports.

Balloon rides

Air Libre Montgolfières
Les Génevriers, Carnac-Rouffiac, T05 65 30 03 83, air-libre-montgolfieres.com.
Balloon excursions are becoming an increasingly popular way to see the Lot. Air Libre offers tours over Quercy Blanc from this village near Montcuq (€200-220 per person).

Donkey tours

If you've got the time to do it the slow, old-fashioned way, you can hire a placid beast for an increasingly popular way of seeing the countryside around St-Cirq. An interesting website, hikingwithdonkey.com, will tell you everything you want to know about it. You can get one short-term or from about €200-250 a week; just make sure you book ahead. Combine a donkey trip with a visit to the saffron farm **Quercy Terre d'Arômes** (see opposite page, T05 65 24 79 32, ane-et-rando.com), or arrange a tour with **Les Cadichons** (Les-Bouygues-Hautes, Sauliac-sur-Célé, T05 65 30 91 56, pagesperso-orange.fr/les-cadichons), where you can also stay in a *roulotte* (an old-fashioned horse-drawn caravan) or a Mongolian yurt.

Hang-gliding

Parapente Max/Ecole de Parapente du Lot
Place de l'Ormeau, Douelle, T06 81 88 03 98, parapente-max.fr.
The high cliffs above this old river port west of Cahors are perfect for updraughts, and squadrons of brightly coloured gliders have become a familiar sight on this stretch of the Lot. Your 'aerial baptism' (with an instructor) will cost only €50. Go on.

River trips

The regional government is working on plans to make the entire river navigable. Right now a score of weirs are in the way, but the old locks around them are being refurbished and new ones built. Meanwhile, you can rent a two- to 10-berth boat for a river cruise at **Le Boat** (Douelle, T05 65 20 08 79, leboat.fr/bases/france/lot/douelle). Also at Douelle, **Antinéa Loisirs** (T05 65 30 95 79, pagesperso-orange.fr/antinea.loisirs) rents canoes, kayaks, pedalos and mountain bikes. In summer, you can rent canoes from the Cale in Puy l'Evêque for a two- or three-hour excursion on one of the prettiest stretches of the river.

Lot Navigation
Port de Bouziès, T05 65 24 32 20, lot-navigation.com.
Apr-Sep.
Houseboats for hire by the week as well as smaller boats for day cruises; no licence required.

LETTRE

Practicalities

Contents

Practicalities

Getting there

Air

The only international airports in the Dordogne and Lot are those in Bergerac and the new one between Soulliac and Brive, which is scheduled to open in June 2010, with flights planned from London and Paris. Toulouse (1½ hours south of Cahors) and Bordeaux (one hour west of Bergerac) offer many more options, on both regular and discount carriers.

From UK & Ireland

Bergerac is well served from spring to autumn by **Ryanair** from Bristol, East Midlands, Liverpool, and Stansted (year round); Ryanair also fly to Rodez (convenient for Figeac and eastern Lot) from Dublin and Stansted, and to Bordeaux from Edinburgh. **Flybe** fly to Bergerac (mainly in season) from Birmingham, Edinburgh, Exeter, Gatwick, Manchester and Southampton; also to Toulouse from Birmingham. **Jet2** fly to Bergerac and Toulouse from Leeds-Bradford and to Toulouse from Belfast International.

Other services include **Easyjet** to Bordeaux from Luton, Bristol and Liverpool, and to Toulouse from Bristol and Gatwick. **Aer Lingus** fly to Bordeaux and Toulouse from Dublin. **BMIBaby** fly to Toulouse and Bordeaux from Manchester, and **British Airways** fly from Heathrow to Toulouse and from Gatwick to Bordeaux. **Air France** fly to Toulouse from Cardiff, Leeds, Bradford, Liverpool and Norwich and to Bordeaux from Cardiff, Glasgow, Humberside, Norwich and Liverpool.

From North America

There are no direct flights to the Dordogne and Lot, and trying to connect to Bergerac isn't always easy (although there are possibilities with the new **Delta** flights from New York to Gatwick, followed by **Flybe** to Bergerac, or **KLM** to Amsterdam and **Transvia** to Bergerac). **Air France**, **Air Canada**, **Delta**, **British Airways** and **United** fly into Charles de Gaulle Paris, where you can pick up direct **Air France** flights to Toulouse or Bordeaux, but also

Airport information

Aéroport de Bergerac (T05 53 22 25 25, bergerac.aeroport.fr) is a few minutes south of Bergerac. There are plenty of car hire counters and taxis, but no shuttles.
Aéroport Périgueux-Bassillac (T08 92 70 77 37, aeroport-perigueux.com).
Aéroport de Bordeaux-Mérignac (T05 56 34 50 50, bordeaux.aeroport.fr) is 12 km from the centre of Bordeaux and linked every 45 minutes to the train station by Jet'Bus (from Hall B, €7, €12 return).
Aéroport de Brive-Soulliac (aeroport-brive-souillac.com).
Aéroport Toulouse-Blagnac (T08 25 38 00 00, toulouse.aeroport.fr) has shuttle connections (navette-tisseo-aeroport.com, €4) every 20-40 minutes to the centre of Toulouse and train station, from where frequent trains on the Paris line go to Cahors, Agen and Bordeaux.

Bergerac Airport.

Going green

Flights are faster and nearly always cheaper than the train – at least at first glance. That said, trains do have advantages beyond saving on your carbon footprint. You don't have to be at the airport hours in advance and pay airport parking fees; you can take your luggage for free; and as a travel experience French trains are 100 times more pleasant than an airborne cattle truck. You can also find significant discounts if you book rail tickets well in advance and are travelling as a couple or family; under 26s and seniors are eligible for discounts, too.

look into flights via Amsterdam, Munich or Frankfurt on **KLM** or **Lufthansa**.

From the rest of Europe

There are numerous flights from all over Europe to Bordeaux and Toulouse, but only a few to the Dordogne. **Ryanair** fly from Brussels (Charleroi) to Bergerac. There are two direct flights each weekday from Paris Orly on **Twin Jet** to Périgueux and Bergerac. **Transvia** fly to Bergerac from Amsterdam and Rotterdam.

Rail

London to Périgueux, via **Eurostar** (T08705-186186, eurostar.com) and the **TGV** (tgv-europe.com) from Paris to Bordeaux, takes just over seven hours if the timing is right. In Paris you have to transfer from the Gare de Nord to Gare de Montparnasse (a direct metro route on M5). For the Lot Valley, the nearest TGV station is in Montauban, but it's easier to take the **Corail** train from Paris's Gare Austerlitz (also on the M5 metro line) direct to Cahors (5-6 hrs). See Eurostar and TGV or **SNCF** (voyages-sncf.com) websites for more information or to arrange the journey on your own, or contact **European Rail** (T020-7619 1083, europeanrail.com) and let them do all the arranging for you. Note that with 'Prems' fares available on both kinds of trains you can get big discounts by booking up to 90 days before you travel.

Road

Bus/coach

Eurolines (T08717-818181, eurolines.co.uk) run from London Victoria to Soulliac and Cahors several times a week. There are often special offers, and discounts for over 65s, under 26s and children. Journey time is 18 hours.

Car

London to Périgueux is 700 km and can be done in a day with an early start. Once you get to Paris from the ferry ports of Calais or Boulogne, take the A10 as far as Vierzon, where you can pick up the A20 to the Dordogne and Lot. Tolls are €36.50 from Calais to Périgueux.

To bring a GB-registered car into France, you need your vehicle registration document, full driving licence and insurance papers (or Green Card), which must be carried at all times when driving, along with your passport. You'll need to adjust or tape the headlamps, and carry a warning triangle and safety vest inside the car (not in the boot).

The lowest rate for seven days' car hire starts at around €170. If you're travelling with children and lots of luggage, it's probably cheaper to drive and easier to drive your own. Otherwise, what works best for you depends on time of year, what fly/drive or rail/drive deals you can find, and whether or not you like long drives.

Getting around

Public transport is thin on the ground in the Dordogne and Lot, so unless you mean to walk or cycle, you'll need a car. Every newsstand sells maps of the region – the Michelin or Blay 1:250000 series are both good and frequently updated; walkers will need IGN Série Bleue 1:25000 maps, which you can also buy before arrival (loisirs.ign.fr).

Rail

France's national railway, SNCF, has a very useful online service (voyages-sncf.com,) for checking schedules and booking tickets. The website doubles as a tour operator, offering discounts on hotels, ski packages, flights and rental cars, and they'll post tickets outside France. Their toll number (T3635, €0.34/min) applies throughout France. A variety of **InterRail** (raileurope.co.uk or raileurope.com outside Europe) passes are available for all ages but they're really only good value if you mean to do several days of long-distance travelling outside the Dordogne and Lot.

France's sleek TGVs (*trains à grande vitesse*) nip along at 280 kph or more and are very useful for getting close to the area. You need to book in advance, and the longer in advance, the cheaper the fares (TGV Prems).

The regular regional trains, **TER** (T0891-700900, €0.23/minute) are better for everyday travel: they are cheaper, carry bicycles without charge and you don't have to book in advance; you can even avoid queues by buying a ticket with your credit card from a machine in the station. These tickets are valid for two months, but you must date-stamp (*composter*) them in the station before boarding or you'll be subject to a fine. Travel from Monday afternoons to Friday mornings (*période bleue*) is cheaper than weekends and holidays (*période blanche*). There are discounts for over 60s, under 26s, and under 12s. Sometimes, on minor routes, buses are used instead of trains.

Périgord Blanc et Pourpre The main line through the area is Bordeaux-Périgueux-Limoges. From Périgueux, some trains for Bordeaux stop at Mussidan; for Limoges, at Thiviers. There are only a couple of trains a day on the old route from Périgueux to Agen; these stop at Les Eyzies, Le Bugue, Le Buisson, Siorac-en-Périgord, Belvès, Villefranche-de-Périgord and Monsempron-Libos. There are half a dozen trains a day from Bordeaux to Bergerac, on the line to Sarlat.

Périgord Vert The only rail service is a line from Périgueux that passes through Thiviers and La Coquille on its way to Limoges.

Périgord Noir From Sarlat there are four trains a day for Bordeaux; on three of them you can change at Le Buisson for Périgueux. To head for Paris and the north, or south to Gourdon and Cahors, you'll have to take the bus to the station at Souillac.

Northern Lot Souillac is on the main SNCF Paris-Cahors-Toulouse line, though not all trains stop there, and it usually has four trains a day to Martel and St-Denis-les-Martel, where it connects with another line running from Brive to Figeac. On this line, most trains stop at Rocamadour and Gramat.

Lot Valley There are mainline trains from Cahors to Paris, Montauban and Toulouse (some for Paris stop at Gourdon and Souillac, though the SNCF is currently scheming to close these stations), and also services to Gramat and Rodez.

Road

Bicycle

Although the French have great respect for cyclists, it's always best to avoid the busier routes: check out suggestions of routes and maps on bikely.com and bikemap.net.

Bus/coach

Most lines are limited to only a few runs a day, and they primarily serve as school buses. Some do run more frequently, such as from Périgueux to Bergerac, or the SNCF buses from Cahors up the Lot Valley to Monsempron-Libos (which has train links to Périgueux) and eastwards to Figeac. It's best to check with the nearest tourist office.

Périgord Blanc et Pourpre CFTA (cftaco.fr) runs services from Périgueux to Bergerac, Périgueux to Sarlat via Montignac, Périgueux to Montignac via Rouffignac and St-Léon, and Montignac to Terrasson.

Périgord Vert The main services are operated by CFTA, running from Périgueux to Angoulême through Brantôme and Mareuil, and lines Ribérac-Mareuil, Périgueux-Hautefort, Périgueux-Excideuil and Périgueux-Ribérac. From Nontron, you can only get to Angoulême, via Varaignes and Javerlhac.

Périgord Noir The service is rarely convenient because of limited routes and sparse schedules, especially on non-school days. There are a few each day from Sarlat to Souillac, via Carsac and Carlux. There is usually one bus a day from Sarlat to Montignac and Périgueux, which connects to another line from Montignac to Brive. Schedules are online at cg24.fr (under 'Routes et transports').

Northern Lot Coach service is extremely limited throughout this sparsely populated region. You'll see schedules in the tourist offices for a lot of lines running through St-Céré, Souillac, Martel and Gramat, but they're all really just school buses, running one or two trips a day.

Lot Valley SNCF buses run from Cahors station up the Lot to Figeac and down to Monsempron-Libos station (Fumel); these are usually timed to meet the Paris-Toulouse trains. There are usually five buses a day from Cahors to Figeac, via St-Cirq-Lapopie and Capdenac; slightly more to Monsempron-Libos, passing through Douelle, Luzech, Prayssac and Puy-l'Evêque.

Car

Motoring in the Dordogne and Lot presents no great difficulties. Most roads are well signposted, but good maps and/or Sat Nav are essential. Driving in the city centres, with their one-way systems, can be frustrating; if you get lost follow the handy *Toutes Directions* signs, which usually follow a ring of streets around the city with many useful signs along the way.

Petrol and diesel (*gazole*) are currently €1.20 for unleaded, and just over €1 a litre for diesel. It's always cheapest at supermarkets, many of which now have 24-hour machines that take credit cards. Parking garages cost €3-5 an hour.

Unless otherwise signposted, the speed limit on *autoroutes* is 130 kph. On D (departmental) roads it's 90 kph, and in towns (once you've passed the white sign announcing the town's name) it's 50 kph. Speeding fines start at €68 and can go as high as €4500 if you fail a breathalyser test.

Although it's been declining of late, the French accident rate is still higher than in the UK or North America. If you are involved in an accident, you'll be asked to fill out a form called a *constat amiable*. If your French isn't up to it, wait for help rather than unwittingly incriminating yourself. If you need the police, T17.

Car hire It's almost always cheaper to hire a car before you arrive, and essential to do so in summer. Compare the many car rental websites (try autosabroad.com, auto-europe.co.uk, and comparecarrent.com) with the packages offered when you book flight or train tickets. Most firms require that you be at least 21 years old and have a credit card, with the name of the driver matching the name on the card. There are supplemental charges for listing another driver or travelling with a child seat. Check the insurance and damage waiver before setting out, and always carry all the papers with you.

Directory

Customs & immigration

UK and EU visitors need a valid passport to enter France. The standard tourist visa for non-EU visitors is 90 days for the whole EU zone.

Disabled travellers

Because they are so rural, the Dordogne and Lot are a bit behind in providing access in hotels and sites; in places such as caves and châteaux it's just not feasible, and it's recommended that you travel with an able-bodied companion. When booking hotel rooms, ask for a *une chambre adaptée*.

Emergencies

SAMU (medical emergencies) T15, Police T17, Fire service T18, European emergency line T112.

Etiquette

The French are very polite. Greet everyone in shops, restaurants and hotels, with "*Bonjour, Madame/Mademoiselle/Monsieur*" and say "*Au revoir*" when you leave. They also love to make *les bises* (cheek air kisses), even when first introduced, if at least one member of the party is female (man to man, a handshake will do).

Families

The Dordogne and Lot are a great destination for family holidays; people here are fond of children, there's plenty to see and the slow pace of life offers a break from the stresses of family life. Most restaurants offer a *menu enfant* (usually *steak frites*). High chairs are rarer, but hotels usually have family rooms and cots.

Health

Comprehensive travel and medical insurance is recommended. EU citizens should apply for a free European Health Insurance Card or EHIC (ehic.org), which entitles you to emergency medical treatment on the same terms as French nationals. Note that you will have to pay all charges and prescriptions up front and be reimbursed once you return home. If you develop a minor ailment while on holiday a visit to any pharmacy will allow you to discuss your concerns with highly qualified staff, who can give medical advice and recommend treatment. Outside normal opening hours, the address of the nearest duty pharmacy (*pharmacie de garde*) is displayed in the pharmacy window. The out-of-hours number for a local doctor (*médecin généraliste*) may also be listed.

In a serious emergency, go to the accident and emergency department (*urgences*) at the nearest Centre Hospitalier (numbers listed in the Essentials section at the beginning of each chapter) or call an ambulance (SAMU) by dialling T15.

Insurance

Comprehensive travel and medical insurance is strongly recommended, as the European Health Insurance Card (EHIC) does not cover medical repatriation, ongoing medical treatment or treatment considered to be non-urgent. Check for exclusions if you mean to engage in risky sports. Keep all insurance documents to hand; a good way to keep track of your policies is to email the details to yourself. Make sure you have adequate insurance when hiring a car and always ask how much excess you are liable for if the vehicle is returned with any damage. It is generally worth paying a little more for collision damage waiver. If driving your own vehicle to France, contact your insurers before you travel to ensure you are adequately covered, and keep the documents in your vehicle in case you need to prove it.

Money

The French currency is the Euro (€). There are ATM machines in every town, and nearly all hotels, restaurants and shops accept credit cards, although many North American cards lack a chip necessary for them to work in toll machines or in 24-hour filling stations. Check with your bank before you leave, and also ask about how to save money on cash withdrawal charges. It's very difficult these days to find a French bank to change currency: try airport exchanges or main post offices.

Police

There are two types of police in France. The **Police Municipale** mainly handle traffic issues in cities; the **Gendarmes** take care of everything else. In France you can legally be stopped for ID checks for no reason (usually for belonging to a minority or looking scruffy). If your passport or any other valuables are lost and stolen, visit the **gendarmerie** for the necessary paperwork.

Post

La Poste is reliable, but recently many rural offices have been closed down, or replaced by counters in shops. Most newsagents and *tabacs* sell stamps (*timbres*) for postcards and letters to Europe (€0.70) but hardly ever for North America (€0.85). Post offices are closed Saturday afternoons and Sunday, and usually for lunch, too.

Safety

Crime of any kind is rare in the Dordogne and Lot. Just be as sensible as you are at home: don't leave tempting items visible in your car, insure your camera, and don't carry all your money and cards in one place.

Telephone

The French have dispensed with area codes, and all numbers dialled within the country now have 10 digits. If a number begins with 06 it's a mobile phone. When dialling from abroad the country code is 33; leave out the first 0. For directory assistance, dial 118 218.

Time difference

France uses Central European Time, one hour ahead of GMT.

Tipping

French bar and restaurant bills nearly always include a 15% service charge, so tipping a little extra is discretionary. Taxi drivers appreciate it if you round up the fare, or add an extra couple of euros for help with your bags. Give the guide a euro or two at the end of a guided tour.

Tourist information

Dordogne Tourist Board, T05 53 35 50 24, dordogne-perigord-tourisme.fr.
Lot Tourist Board, 107 quai Cavaignac, T05 65 35 07 09, tourisme-lot.com.

Voltage

The current in France is 220 volts, 50 Hz; use standard European two-pin round plugs.

Language

You'll find that people speak at least basic school English in hotels, restaurants and major tourist sites, so don't worry too much if your French is very rusty. Older people in the countryside may well not speak a word of English though, and you may have difficulty understanding their southern accents, which are quite a bit different from the Parisian taught in school. If tours are only in French, there will nearly always be a handout or audio guide in English.

Basics

hello *bonjour*
good evening *bonsoir*
goodbye *au revoir/salut* (polite/informal)
please *s'il vous plaît*
thank you *merci*
I'm sorry, excuse me *pardon, excusez-moi*
yes *oui*
no *non*
how are you?
comment allez-vous?/ça va? (polite/informal)
fine, thank you *bien, merci*
one moment *un instant*
how? *comment*?
how much? *c'est combien*?
when? *quand*?
where is …? *où est …*?
why? *pourquoi*?
what? *quoi*?
what's that? *qu'est-ce que c'est*?
I don't understand *je ne comprends pas*
I don't know *je ne sais pas*
I don't speak French *je ne parle pas français*
how do you say … (in French)?
comment on dit … (en français)?
do you speak English? *est-ce que vous parlez anglais*? / *Parlez-vous anglais*?
help! *au secours*!
wait! *attendez*!
stop! *arrêtez*!

Numbers

one *un*
two *deux*
two *deux*
three *trois*
four *quatre*
five *cinq*
six *six*
seven *sept*
eight *huit*
nine *neuf*
10 *dix*
11 *onze*
12 *douze*
13 *treize*
14 *quatorze*
15 *quinze*
16 *seize*
17 *dix-sept*
18 *dix-huit*
19 *dix-neuf*
20 *vingt*
21 *vingt-et-un*
22 *vingt-deux*

30 *trente*
40 *quarante*
50 *cinquante*
60 *soixante*
70 *soixante-dix*
80 *quatre-vingts*
90 *quatre-vingt-dix*
100 *cent*
200 *deux cents*
1000 *mille*

Shopping

this one/that one *celui-ci/celui-là*
less *moins*
more *plus*
expensive *cher*
cheap *pas cher/bon marché*
how much is it?
c'est combien? / combien est-ce que ça coûte?
can I have …? (literally 'I would like') *je voudrais…*

Travelling

one ticket for... *un billet pour...*
single *un aller-simple*
return *un aller-retour*
airport *l'aéroport*
bus stop *l'arrêt de bus*
train *le train*
car *la voiture*
taxi *le taxi*
is it far? *c'est loin?*

Hotels

a single/double room
une chambre à une personne/deux personnes
a double bed *un lit double/un grand lit*
bathroom *la salle de bain*
shower *la douche*
is there a (good) view?
est-ce qu'il y a une (belle) vue?
can I see the room?
est-ce que je peux voir la chambre?
when is breakfast?
le petit dejeuner est à quelle heure?
can I have the key?
est-ce que je peux avoir la clef?/La clef, s'il vous plaît

Time

morning *le matin*
afternoon *l'après-midi*
evening *le soir*
night *la nuit*
a day *un jour*
a week *une semaine*
a month *un mois*
soon *bientôt*
later *plus tard*

what time is it? *quelle heure est-il?*
today/tomorrow/yesterday
aujourd'hui/demain/hier

Days

Monday *lundi*
Tuesday *mardi*
Wednesday *mercredi*
Thursday *jeudi*
Friday *vendredi*
Saturday *samedi*
Sunday *dimanche*

Months

January *janvier*
February *février*
March *mars*
April *avril*
May *mai*
June *juin*
July *juillet*
August *août*
September *septembre*
October *octobre*
November *novembre*
December *décembre*

Index

B

C

D

E

F

G

H

I

J

K

L

Index

S

T

U

V

W

Z

Credits

Footprint credits

Project Editor: Jo Williams
Text Editor: Beverley Jollands
Picture editors: Kassia Gawronski, Rob Lunn, Emma Bryers
Layout & production: Emma Bryers
Maps: Gail Townsley
Proofreader: Catherine Charles
Series design: Mytton Williams

Managing Director: Andy Riddle
Commercial Director: Patrick Dawson
Publisher: Alan Murphy
Publishing managers: Felicity Laughton, Jo Williams
Picture researchers: Kassia Gawronski, Rob Lunn
Marketing: Liz Harper, Hannah Bonnell
Sales: Jeremy Parr
Advertising: Renu Sibal
Finance & administration: Elizabeth Taylor

Print

Manufactured in India by Nutech
Pulp from sustainable forests

Footprint Feedback

We try as hard as we can to make each Footprint guide as up to date as possible but, of course, things always change. If you want to let us know about your experiences – good, bad or ugly – then don't delay, go to footprinttravelguides.com and send in your comments.

Every effort has been made to ensure that the facts in this guidebook are accurate. However, travellers should still obtain advice from consulates, airlines etc about travel and visa requirements before travelling. The authors and publishers cannot accept responsibility for any loss, injury or inconvenience however caused.

Publishing information

FootprintFrance Dordogne & Lot
1st edition

May 2010

ISBN 978-1-906098-92-6
CIP DATA: A catalogue record for this book is available from the British Library

Published by Footprint
6 Riverside Court
Lower Bristol Road
Bath BA2 3DZ, UK
T +44 (0)1225 469141
F +44 (0)1225 469461
footprinttravelguides.com

Distributed in North America by
Globe Pequot Press

The colour maps are not intended to have any political significance.